ABI 6524   WW
10/13/2000
$28.00

DUBOSE HEYWARD

For Bob Wachsman
with all good wishes—
DuBose Heyward—

DUBOSE HEYWARD

*A Charleston Gentleman
and the World of Porgy and Bess*

JAMES M. HUTCHISSON

UNIVERSITY PRESS OF MISSISSIPPI / JACKSON

Publication of this book was made possible in part by The Lexington Foundation.

www.upress.state.ms.us

Copyright © 2000 by University Press of Mississippi
All rights reserved
Manufactured in the United States of America

08   07   06   05   04   03   02   01   00   4   3   2   1
∞

Library of Congress Cataloging-in-Publication Data

Hutchisson, James M.
    DuBose Heyward : a Charleston gentleman and the world of Porgy and Bess /
    James M. Hutchisson.
        p.   cm.
    Includes bibliographical references and index.
    ISBN 1-57806-250-0 (cloth : alk. paper)
        1. Heyward, DuBose, 1885–1940.   2. Heyward, DuBose,
    1885–1940—Characters—Afro-Americans.   3. Afro-Americans—South
    Carolina—Social life and customs—Historiography.   4. Authors, American—20th
    century—Biography.   5. Gullahs—South Carolina—Historiography.   6. Folk-
    lorists—South Carolina—Biography.   7. Heyward, DuBose, 1885–1940. Porgy.
    8. Charleston (S.C.)—In literature.   9. Charleston (S.C.)—Biography.   10. Afro-
    Americans in literature.   I. Title.

PS3515.E98 Z68 2000
818′.5209—dc21
[B]   99-048551

British Library Cataloging-in-Publication Data available

For Rachel

Contents

Acknowledgments

It is a great pleasure to acknowledge the assistance of colleagues and friends who have shared insights and information with me, offered encouragement, and critiqued parts of my work in progress. James L. W. West III suggested Heyward as a topic. Harlan Greene, who must be the undisputed authority on Charleston in the 1920s, freely shared his knowledge with me, especially regarding John Bennett and the Poetry Society. Over numerous, protracted lunches Martha Severens listened to my ideas and suggested resources. John Jebb read parts of an early draft and made many recommendations. David Shields's skepticism toward the received wisdom about Charleston's role in modern southern literature got me started, and the impact of many stimulating conversations with him helped me finish.

My editor at Mississippi, Seetha A-Srinivasan, took a special interest in this project from its inception. Her guidance has been greatly appreciated. Others who offered advice or suggestions were Betsey Carter, Judith Giblin James, Robert L. McLaughlin, Sally E. Parry, and James Williams, who directed me to Ann Douglas's groundbreaking study, *Terrible Honesty: Mongrel Manhattan in the 1920s,* which informs much of the cultural context of this book. In like manner, Michael O'Brien's revisionist writings on Charleston and modern southern culture helped guide me to my focus. Charles S. Watson's recently published *The History of Southern Drama* does justice to Heyward and his wife, Dorothy, as playwrights, and I am happy to acknowledge the influence of his thinking here, too.

A biographer is aided considerably by people with firsthand information. I thank John Bennett Jr., Bill Banks, Selma Dotterer, Abe Dumas, Ella Gerber, William Heyward Grimball Jr., Phoebe Haas, Betty Hamilton, Kitty Matthew, Arnold T. Schwab, Ann and Linn Whitelaw, and Harriet Williams. At St. Philip's Episcopal Church, Sally Steers and Mary Bissell were helpful. Any errors of omission or commission, of course, are mine alone.

Among institutions, my greatest support continues to come from the unfailingly generous Citadel Development Foundation, which, in addition to other awards, made possible a year's sabbatical leave in 1996–97. Once again, Dean Roger C. Poole provided funding when I needed it the most, and Robert A. White, former English department head, helped me get it. Albert J. Cardinali, trustee of the Dorothy and DuBose Memorial Foundation in New York, answered questions and provided support for this work. I thank him for allowing me to quote from unpublished Heyward papers. All such writings are reprinted by permission of the fund and are copyrighted by the owner.

Special thanks are reserved for the staff of the South Carolina Historical Society, where I did the bulk of my research in 1995 and 1996. I am grateful to Carey Allen, Steven Hoffeius, Kathryn Meehan, Alex Moore, Peter Rerig, Susan Wyssen, and especially Peter Wilkerson, who gave me access to a large number of Heyward papers that had not yet been cataloged. Similarly, at the Caroliniana Library of the University of South Carolina, Tom Johnson showed me the unprocessed Frank Durham papers, especially a diary, hitherto unknown, that Heyward kept during his Caribbean voyage. Nena Couch, at the Jerome Lawrence and Robert E. Lee Theatre Research Institute of Ohio State University, was helpful in obtaining photographs. While I was researching at libraries at the University of North Carolina in Chapel Hill and at Duke University, the staff members there were most accommodating. When I could not leave Charleston, interlibrary loan wizard Debbe Causey came to my aid, making documents from far-flung places magically appear on my desktop.

I thank Allison Butler Jackson for assistance in the early stages of my research and Anne Stascavage and Ellen D. Goldlust-Gingrich for shepherding the manuscript through its later stages.

For granting me permission to quote from unpublished papers in their collections, I thank the following libraries: Harry Ransom Humanities Research Center, University of Texas, Austin (George B. Waller Papers); Houghton Library, Harvard University (Thomas Wolfe Papers); Library of Congress, Music Division (Gershwin Collection, MacDowell Collection); Library of Congress Manuscripts Division (Doubleday Collection); University of Mississippi (Herschel Brickell Papers); Newberry Library (Sherwood Anderson Papers); Hillman Library, University of Pittsburgh (Hervey Allen Collection); University of South Carolina (Frank Durham Papers); Southern Historical Collection, University of North Carolina, Chapel Hill (Paul Green

Papers); Alderman Library, University of Virginia (James Southall Wilson Papers); Yale Collection of American Literature, Beinecke Library, Yale University (James Weldon Johnson Papers, Theatre Guild Collection, Barrett Clark Papers, Gertrude Stein Papers).

The following institutions answered queries and/or sent me material through the mail: Agnes Scott College; American Academy of Arts and Letters; Berg Collection, New York Public Library; University of California, Davis; University of California, Los Angeles; Columbia University; Duke University; Emory University; Fisk University; University of Georgia; University of Mississippi; New York State Historical Association; Princeton University; Radcliffe College; Schomburg Center for Research in Black Culture; Southern Illinois University; State Historical Society of Wisconsin; University of Wisconsin-Madison; Vanderbilt University; Vassar College; and Wellesley College.

My greatest debt is to my wife, Rachel. She has made the most difference.

J. H.
Charleston, June 1999

Introduction

DuBose Heyward is primarily remembered today as the author of the slim novel *Porgy* (1925), on which George Gershwin based *Porgy and Bess* (1935), the American folk opera about life in a Negro tenement in Charleston, South Carolina. Most people do not know that with his playwright-wife, Heyward also wrote a nonmusical stage version of *Porgy*. When it debuted in 1927, the play revolutionized the American theater with its innovative use of black folk materials, like the spirituals and other work songs of southern blacks. Heyward's involvement in the southern literary scene of the 1920s and 1930s is also not widely known. He helped found the Poetry Society of South Carolina in Charleston in 1920; like similar literary groups in Richmond, New Orleans, and Nashville, the Charlestonians exercised a small but significant influence on the revival of southern literature during that region's cultural renaissance.

Moving from poetry to fiction writing with *Porgy*, Heyward became an important analyst of southern Negro life. *Porgy* was the first major southern novel to present blacks realistically, rather than in the stereotyped roles of happy darkies or loyal body servants. Heyward evolved into a major social critic with *Mamba's Daughters* (1929), a two-tiered novel of black and white society in Charleston, and with *Brass Ankle* (1930), a daring play about miscegenation. In the mosaic of the early southern renaissance, before the mature work of the Fugitives, Thomas Wolfe, and William Faulkner, Heyward was the most visible presence. Moreover, Heyward's fiction of social commitment aligns him with such reform novelists of the 1930s as Erskine Caldwell, T. S. Stribling, and H. H. Kroll.

As a man of letters, Heyward lectured widely, moved in luminous literary circles, sojourned briefly in Hollywood and New York as a screenwriter, and organized major gatherings of southern writers in 1932 and 1933. He continued to be among the most innovative of southern writers. With the plays *Porgy* and *Brass Ankle* he initiated a renaissance in southern drama that would later crest with the work of Tennessee Williams. During the era that produced *Gone with the Wind* and other cloak-and-sword epics memorializing the lost cause, Heyward wrote *Peter Ashley* (1932), a historical novel that blends romanticism with realism and social criticism. In 1936 he took up the southern artist as a fictional subject and produced *Lost Morning;* only later would that subject become one of interest to southern writers such as Wolfe. And what of *Porgy and Bess?* Heyward's role here has also been forgotten or presented inaccurately. In addition to writing the libretto, Heyward composed the lyrics to many of the opera's arias, among them "Summertime" and "A Woman Is a Sometime Thing."

Heyward's life story is most interesting for its intersection with two related issues: Charleston as a literary center and the representation of black life in southern fiction. The confluence of these two cultural tributaries eventually resulted in *Porgy and Bess,* which, with *Gone with the Wind,* must be reckoned as one of the great icons of the American South.

The nascent southern renaissance in the early 1920s was energized by groups of aspiring poets, novelists, and critics who gathered in southern cities: the Fugitive poets in Nashville, the cosmopolite crowd associated with the *Double Dealer* in New Orleans, the writers and editors of the *Reviewer* in Richmond, and later, and the essayists and culture watchers who formed the *Journal of Social Forces* in Chapel Hill.

But what of Charleston? In most literary histories of the period, Charleston, like Heyward, appears marginal. It is true that Charleston produced no major poets, as Nashville did in John Crowe Ransom and Allen Tate, and no enduring exemplars of modernism, as New Orleans did in William Faulkner and Sherwood Anderson—neither one native to that city, but both energetic presences there in the 1920s. Charleston also did not evince the rebellious spirit of the Richmond or Chapel Hill groups. Yet Charleston had its luminous moment, too, when Heyward and the Poetry Society captured the literary spotlight in the early 1920s as leaders in the new southern literature. A good many writers (John Bennett, Hervey Allen, Josephine Pinckney, and Beatrice Witte Ravenel among them) and practitioners of the related visual arts (Alice R. H. Smith, Alfred Hutty, and Elizabeth O'Neill Verner) gained national recognition. Heyward was the group's brightest star.

Nonetheless, Charleston has been all but ignored by those examining the evolution of modern southern literature, perhaps because the standards by which southern writing has been canonized seem to exclude Charleston. The view of southern literature famously espoused by Tate has held sway. In Tate's view, detachment, alienation, and living through change were what made a southern writer. Moreover, in the intense self-scrutiny to which liberal-minded southerners like Howard W. Odum, W. J. Cash, and others subjected their region in the 1930s, Charleston must have seemed beside the point. The popular image of Charleston, then as now, was of a community as shallow and unreflecting as a tidal marsh, drowsing in the lap of the past, uninterested in change—a place like Rhett Butler's Charleston in *Gone with the Wind*, where only grace and charm matter, not the problems of a complex, changing world. This image is inaccurate. In the 1920s and 1930s Charleston was changing, and the city was aware that it was changing.

As for alienation, while Heyward never rebelled against his community in the way, for example, that Wolfe and others did, he did leave Charleston, realizing that his potential for artistic growth lay in being able to examine his environment critically, from without rather than from within. Heyward was also able to detach himself sufficiently from the orthodoxies of Charleston's institutions of race and class to critique them in a measured but forceful manner. *Mamba's Daughters* and *Peter Ashley*, in particular, are all about change. Indeed, the quasi-autobiographical male characters in those books meditate on the relative merits of rebelling versus belonging, as Heyward himself did.

Like Heyward, and like most Charlestonians, these characters end up choosing to belong. But that choice should not marginalize Charleston in the canon of southern literature. If such writing, again to paraphrase Tate, concerns the force of tradition, then one must realize that the tradition handed the Charlestonians was quite different than that handed to the Agrarians. As Michael O'Brien and other intellectual historians of the South have noted, the Deep South was given a broken tradition that needed to be radically reassessed and reformed. Charleston was given a weakened but still intact tradition; Charlestonians such as Heyward were thus placed in the bind of advocating change while simultaneously preserving tradition. This problem led Charleston to play a unique role in the southern renaissance. In Heyward's writing, it also makes for a complex, fascinating dynamic.

Moreover, as the neo-Agrarian standards by which southern literature has been canonized begin to change, Charleston's literary contributions attract fresh interest. The city was virtually alone in its interest in marginalized voices. A number of Heyward's peers were women: Ravenel, Pinckney, Smith, Verner. And the focus of these and other artists and writers like Hutty and Bennett—and, of course, Heyward—was the representation of Negro life (something of a cultural irony, given Charleston's identity as a white community). These concerns were far distant from the goals of the Nashville group, for example, and are made more interesting by the uniqueness of the black people who lived in Charleston. The Gullahs were distinct from other southern blacks in their strong racial memory and homogeneous community ethic. Their customs and social values emphasized an ethnicity more pronounced than that of Negroes in Mississippi or in other parts of the Deep South. Thus, the artistic conjunction of women and blacks makes Charleston's literary endeavors notable. And the two strongest influences on Heyward were his mother, Jane Screven Heyward, and his wife, Dorothy Kuhns Heyward, who had their own interests in the Gullahs as subjects for art. Each woman affected the development of Heyward's aesthetic values and social attitudes.

The representations of the Gullahs by Heyward and others in Charleston ran parallel to some major modernist concerns, notably the widespread national interest in cultural primitivism. Part of the ethos of white modernism derived from African American folktale and folk song. In the post–World War I decade, as Americans repudiated English and European cultural traditions and became fascinated with their own artistic resources, they discovered that their deepest cultural roots lay in the unacknowledged but long-exploited African American folk traditions of story and song. Both became essential factors in America's dawning global hegemony in the fast-growing field of popular culture.

American fascination with cultural primitivism, of course, manifested itself in many other regions—one thinks of Mary Austin's and Georgia O'Keeffe's work in the Southwest and even the vogue of T. E. Lawrence's writings about Arabia. The interest in music, however, the key cultural index of African American culture, crested in New York, where white urban Americans frequented the more than 125 Harlem nightclubs, led by the Cotton Club and Connie's Inn, to "go slumming"—that is, to participate, if only as voyeurs, in what was palpably the most exciting, because "primitive" or "exotic," subculture in America. Perhaps the most notable example of white absorptions of black art was the dance craze that swept the nation, the

Charleston. It first appeared in New York in a Negro musical, *Runnin' Wild*, in 1922, and was quickly embraced by whites. Like other white artists, Heyward absorbed black art forms, blended them with those of his own culture, and came to recognize the shared cultural heritage of black and white.

Study of Heyward's life thus provides an opportunity to examine Charleston's role in the cultural history of the 1920s. What cultural forces in Charleston shaped Heyward's interest in black culture and eventually led to the creation of *Porgy and Bess?* That work, with its simple but powerful story of passion and violence, was a completely new form in American art and an excellent example of how Charleston's ethnic-rich culture was exported to the world. As an example of multicultural art, *Porgy and Bess* may be unparalleled. Todd Duncan, who played the first Porgy, once recalled his audition for Gershwin and noted the cultural ironies: "Imagine a Negro," Duncan said, "auditioning for a Jew, singing an old Italian aria!" To that might be added the fact that the words Duncan sang in the show were written by a white man from the South.

Other cultural questions present themselves. How do Heyward's writings about blacks compare with other white and black representations of black characters during the southern renaissance? What of race relations in Charleston (the coastal south) versus Richmond (the Upper South) or New Orleans or Mississippi (the Deep South): how do Heyward's views of the Negro help in understanding this cultural matrix? Where does Heyward's poetry lie in the spectrum of early modern verse? And what of his artistic experimentation? He worked in almost every major genre: poetry, short fiction, novels, plays, film, and opera.

These questions become more interesting because of Heyward's personal history, one peculiarly unsuited to writing about African Americans without patronizing them. Heyward was descended from the choicest Charleston stock: Heywards had helped found the colony in 1670; his father's great-great-grandfather was a signer of the Declaration of Independence; and several of his ancestors had been instrumental in quelling slave rebellions, in particular the well-known Denmark Vesey conspiracy of 1822. But by the time Heyward was born, in 1885, the once-powerful and wealthy city had slid into genteel poverty, the economic aftermath of the Civil War. Heyward grew up in a family that was, in the saying of the day, "too poor to paint and too proud to whitewash." He observed an often sterile and insular white society that contrasted glaringly with the celebratory and community-oriented world of the Gullahs, particularly the black women who helped raise him (in fact, Heyward's first language may well have been Gullah). Since poverty reigned on both sides of the color line in Charleston, Heyward was positioned to observe the delicate interplay between whites and blacks. Both communities were, in different senses, disenfranchised. And both later became the subjects of Heyward's work.

Heyward's life has never received a full-length treatment. In 1954, Frank Durham, who knew Heyward during the last years of the author's life, published *DuBose Heyward: The Man Who Wrote Porgy.* This book is an invaluable starting point for study of Heyward, and I have drawn liberally on Durham's spadework in establishing the biographical record. However, as a product of its time, Durham's book mostly evaded the crucial issues of race, gender, and cultural politics—those issues that form the centerpiece of this examination.

Moreover, during the nearly fifty years since Durham conducted his research, a large number of manuscript collections have been made public, and they contain important primary documents. One crucial set of papers came to light after the death of the Heywards' only child, Jenifer, in 1985—letters that Heyward wrote during the staging of the play *Porgy* in New York in 1927 as well as letters written during his and Dorothy's two tours abroad earlier that year and in 1929. Also among these papers is an unpublished autobiography by Dorothy Heyward, which contains much new information especially concerning Heyward's role in the composition of *Porgy and Bess.* Yet another collection of primary documents turned up after the death of Frank Durham, among them a diary Heyward kept during an important trip he made to the Caribbean in the spring of 1937 in search of material for a new opera he proposed to do with George Gershwin.

Although there is much discussion in this book of *Porgy and Bess*—its origins, composition, and later incarnations—I have not tried to give a comprehensive history of the opera. That task has been more than ably handled by Hollis Alpert in his definitive study, *The Life and Times of Porgy and Bess* (1990). Like Durham, Alpert also discusses Heyward's career, but his focus, of course, is on the opera itself and in particular on its later history.

My emphasis is contextual and cultural: I seek to place Heyward and his works within the milieus that helped create them and to examine Heyward in relation to other writers, northern and southern, and how they represented race. The locution of Heyward's times for referring to African Americans has been adopted for the majority of this book. In places where using such terminology does not seem appropriate or necessary for historical authenticity, however, the current convention has been followed.

DuBose Heyward's life is the story of a man who moved from social conservatism to a liberal, although nonrevolutionary, advocacy of black rights—a man who developed a social conscience through writing. Neither completely an apologist for the Old South nor a propagandist for the New South, Heyward is a fascinating subject. His life and work are a window on Charleston and modern southern culture, both black and white.

DUBOSE HEYWARD

Chapter One

Story and History

Class and Color in Charleston

J ANE SCREVEN DUBOSE was always mindful of Providence, for she had lived through tragedy at a very young age. Like many dispossessed southern families after the Civil War, the DuBoses had lost their fortune and fallen deeply into debt. Jane's father had once owned acres of farmland in St. John's Berkeley, near the South Carolina midlands, tended by hundreds of slaves, but the war had destroyed his crops and taken away his source of labor. Debt mounted, creditors stepped in, and the family's assets were liquidated. Jane's father died soon thereafter, leaving her and her mother, older brother, and sister with little to bank on. They came to Charleston in the early 1870s, fleeing an unpleasant past.

Charleston was a pragmatic choice: a more diverse and cosmopolitan area, it offered better options for employment and, Mrs. DuBose hoped, marriage for Jane and her sister. But the family suffered another loss when Jane's sister died shortly after their arrival. Charleston had suffered its own tragedies, too, and in this sense, the move was symbolic. No other southern city has had such a history of boom and bust. Charleston was a city of catastrophe—of contagion, natural disaster, and invasion—yet it always recovered. When the DuBose family arrived there, Charleston was reeling from the economic blows dealt by the Civil War. Like Jane DuBose, Charleston was fragile, and it was poor. The city and its history would become a key factor in the making of Jane's new identity, just as its traditions and social values would fix the identity of her son, DuBose Heyward, for the greater part of his young adulthood.

In the late nineteenth century, Charleston was a fallen world, and its fall had been precipitous. Prosperity had reigned supreme in the city since its founding in 1670. Charlestonians very quickly developed a reputation for high living—and for control of the slave trade, because slavery made the high life possible. Boatloads of slaves arrived regularly, first from Bermuda and later from the West Indies. Some were bound for work in the fertile rice fields—Charleston's first lucrative crop—and some were used as domestic servants. The black population grew quickly—alarmingly so, to most Charlestonians. By the early 1700s, blacks far outnumbered whites in the city, giving Charleston the largest black population among the North American colonies. Rumors soon swelled of alleged barbarous plots by the slaves to murder their white masters, creating white fears of blacks that would haunt Charlestonians for nearly ten generations.

The large supply of slave labor also fueled the rice plantations, which flourished after the Revolutionary War. Later, when cotton began to be harvested, and it looked as though the region's natural resources would never be depleted, more slaves were imported. Entire tribal communities were plucked from Angola, on the African coast. These slaves would be known in Charleston as "Gullahs," after their place of origin, and they would display a unique tribal identity. Their strong ethnic homogeneity would distinguish them from other slaves in the south. Gullah was also the name of their language, a tribal dialect that too was unique.

The white masters of these slaves comprised a Charleston oligarchy of planters, merchants, and lawyers who oversaw the city's commercial enterprises and prospered from their success. The members of this elite spent their leisure hours perfecting the pursuit of pleasure and creating a white genteel culture that made Charleston unique among southern cities. Charlestonians seemed to do things differently from everyone else. Their houses sat sideways on the street so that their ends faced the water and caught the ocean breeze. Other architectural styles seemed similarly Caribbean, not southern. Businessmen returned home at midday for a noontime siesta, and dinner was served in the middle of the afternoon, at three o'clock. Gullah vegetable vendors roamed the streets, hawking their wares by singing out in a strange, melodious patois.

Charleston pursued the arts with a passion: theaters, concerts, dances, and horse races were commonplace. Civility and hospitality were basic cultural tenets, as was attendance at nightly balls and other entertainments. Social traditions were created, many of which are still upheld today. The St. Cecelia Society provided quiet evenings of music; Harmony Hall was available for plays and other entertainments; the Library Society, the first private library in America, offered edification through books. These pleasures created a community known for its refinements—the urbane ease of its gentlemen and the delicate beauty of its ladies. Hector St. John de Crevecoeur, who visited the city just before the revolution, found its inhabitants "the gayest in America."

But the Civil War wounded Charleston. Cutting off the city's supply of slave labor, the conflict effectively ended Charleston's reign as the South's commercial capital. The city then turned inward, dwelling on its present tragedy and past glory. Gloom blanketed the city like ash. Its prostration was complete.

Charleston was also overbalanced by a series of natural disasters that seemed biblical in range and proportion. The important rice culture and market from which much of the city's early wealth had derived had been wiped out by a hurricane. While cotton farming still took place upstate, the coastal, or sea island, cotton had been greatly damaged by the boll weevil. Yet oddly, plans for economic revival were often rebuffed. Charlestonians stubbornly clung to the prewar image of themselves as unique and in some ways superior to the up-country and the rest of the South.

Most important, principles of taste and appearance reigned supreme. Certain things were not done; a code was upheld, even if impractical. Thus, after the war, there was a brief attempt to capitalize on the mining of phosphate, a fertilizer, but a plan to lay railroad lines from the outlying areas into the city, so that trains could bring shipments to the docks, was vetoed because the tracks would have been unsightly. So while other southern ports like New Orleans, Mobile, and Savannah flourished, Charleston slumbered. The result struck many as a paradise lost. A northern visitor to Charleston around this time described it as "a city of ruins, of vacant houses, of widowed women, of rotting wharves, . . . weed filled gardens [and] acres of pitiful and voiceful barrenness." Many of the once-handsome eighteenth-century residences had degenerated into barrooms and bordellos. Sanitation and the prevention of disease, always a concern because the area's low elevation prevented efficient drainage, now became an even more pressing problem.

Most interesting, a sort of shadow aristocracy developed, creating an unusual relationship between former black slaves and their former white masters. The personal fortunes of Charleston's elite white families were gone, and they were left to trade only on their illustrious names. But the level of income was not the only thing that changed. In some neighborhoods the white/black ratio was almost even. Although eventually Negroes would establish enclaves of their own, at the turn of the century privation preserved Charleston's prewar integration, creating an enforced intimacy in living conditions and a peculiar interplay between the races. As one observer wrote at the time, "the magnificent and the mean jostle each other very closely in all quarters of the city; tumble-down rookeries are side by side with superb houses."

The young Jane DuBose resembled her adopted city, for her early life there was tenuous and unsteady. Raised to affirm the southern ideals of feminine beauty and delicacy, Janie, as she was called, was unused to hardship. Her childhood of loss made her superstitious and fearful that tragedy lay lurking around every corner. The tragic splendor of Charleston seemed to her an outward symbol of this philosophy.

Janie yearned for a man to take care of her—what she regarded as the first desideratum of southern womanhood. She soon met her deliverer. Edwin Watkins Heyward had a family history similar to hers. He was the son of planters whose roots stretched deep into the South Carolina soil and back as far as the founding of the colony. The most famous of DuBose Heyward's paternal ancestors, his great-great-grandfather, Thomas, signed the Declaration of Independence. As an outward display of his wealth, Thomas's father, Daniel, built a stately home on Church Street, afterwards famous as a place where General George Washington once spent the night. After the Civil War, the Heywards had lost their fortune, and their sons were reduced to eking out a living as best they could.

Ned Heyward had no strong prospects for work when he and Janie were married in November 1884. But he was courtly toward her, and he had not lost the original aristocratic luster that identified him as a Heyward. Janie, in turn, became enamored of a name with roots in Charleston. Appropriately, Ned and Janie were married in a lavish ceremony at the most venerable

Episcopal church in the city. The show of wealth belied an existence of privation.

Janie tried to suppress her worst fears of poverty and loss. She clung to her new husband for the security that she could not summon on her own. When Ned finally found a job as a wage laborer at a rice mill, he worked almost constantly, volunteering for extra duty whenever he could. Selflessly devoted to Janie, Ned bought her small gifts they could not afford and new furniture that was a gross indulgence. "Ned did *every* thing for me," Janie later wrote in her journal, "he even used to cut my finger nails." "What does Boy live for but to make you happy?" Ned would ask her. Appearances again masked reality. Their early married life was peripatetic and tenuous. They started out living in a small house with friends, then moved from cottage to cottage as leases expired or money dried up. Janie's mother lived with them, stretching the family's already thin financial resources.

Their first child was born just about nine months after their marriage, on 31 August 1885. Janie named the boy Edwin DuBose and decided that he be called by his middle name, after her Huguenot ancestors. But virtually everywhere Janie looked, her fears about the future seemed confirmed in a series of ominous portents. Her firstborn was a sickly child, and Janie charted DuBose's illnesses in her journal, interspersing poems she had written among the medical entries and other descriptions of their daily life. The poems all concern loss: many memorialize children who had died, as typhus, scarlet fever, and diphtheria were everywhere. Other poems are prayers for the safekeeping of the men in her life, her husband and son, whom she feared might be in harm's way. At the time, Charleston was considered a sickly place. Many illnesses were caused by contaminants in the city's drinking water, which was often unsanitary. Then there was the constant fear of hurricanes and earthquakes, which made Janie even more uneasy.

Another of her fears was confirmed on the evening of DuBose's first birthday in 1886. An earthquake of devastating proportions rocked the old city, uprooting homes and businesses and sending telegraph poles and wires crashing into great tangled masses on the streets. People rushed outside to find the air thick with dust and smoke. When the quake had ended, some two thousand buildings had been damaged, and hundreds of people were homeless. By great good chance Janie had taken DuBose down the coast to Grahamville (near Beaufort), where the effects were not quite as severe. Ned had remained in Charleston to work. He had just returned from the mill when the quake struck, at 9:15 P.M. As he felt the first tremor, he sprang through the door to the outside, just barely dodging parts of the ceiling as they began to fall. As Janie described the incident in her journal, "By the time he got out of the piazza, every wall was down, the chair in which he had been seated was crushed to pieces; and all the furniture, together with many of the ornaments, was scratched and broken." To Janie, their lives were thus spared by Providence, but the incident only exacerbated her fears.

Recouping what losses they could, the family moved again. In 1887, another child was born, a girl, named Jeannie DuBose. By great coincidence, she was delivered at 9:15 in the morning, the same time of day when DuBose was born and the same evening hour when the earthquake had struck—perhaps an affirmation to the superstitious Janie of the validity of signs. Some of Janie's anxiety subsided as she found happiness in raising her children, but her fears revisited her in 1888, when DuBose was nearing the age of three.

At about noon one spring day in 1888, Janie's brother, Edwin, appeared at the house to tell her that Ned had been badly hurt on the job. Janie, with an apparent sixth sense, looked at her brother and screamed, "No. . . . He is *not* hurt; he is dead! He is dead. I will never, never see him again; Oh God help me." Janie never asked how the accident happened. Ned apparently became caught in some machinery, and his death was probably not instantaneous. Depression assaulted her again. When Ned's body was laid in the family parlor for viewing, Janie kept her children in another room, determined that they not have "an unpleasant remembrance" of anything connected with their father.

The memory of loss fueled Janie's fears that the horror of Ned's death might reassert itself in some new frightening way. And DuBose's near-constant illnesses caused her life to be "bound up" in the boy. One Easter afternoon, she took the children to decorate Ned's grave and afterwards confided to her journal, "I pray there will not be another there next Easter!" Later, she remarked, "Who can tell what may happen in a year?"

Janie's first savior was Ned Heyward. Her second was the Gullah Negro. As the years wore on, Janie tamed her fears through the therapy of writing. First there were consolation poems, then she delved into the history of Charleston with energetic research into local customs, architecture, and lore. As an arm-chair historian, Janie became well known in the area, and her writings started to appear in some regional magazines and newspapers. In the early 1900s, however, Janie discovered the Gullahs as a neglected subject for art. She entered their world with a zealous curiosity, these people around whom she had grown up but never thought about in a meaningful way. Having lived a life focused on history, with its overdetermination of tradition and place, Janie broke out of that environment and entered an exotic subculture in which history was replaced by story: mythmaking, tale telling, and singing. She at once saw the exuberant vitality of this world and contrasted it with her own. In a moment of cultural clairvoyance, Janie foresaw a brighter future for herself if she could absorb something of the inner strength of this alien race.

Nearly all of Charleston's Negroes at that time were Gullahs. Their unique racial characteristics made them distinct from other southern Negroes. Their geographical isolation—they were confined primarily to the barrier islands in South Carolina and Georgia—created a strong ethnic homogeneity. Their ancestors in slavery had been a single self-contained African community that was imported wholesale by South Carolina slavers and kept intact on the assumption that doing so would decrease the slaves' desire to revolt. As an ethnic group, the Gullahs' ties to their African heritage were more concretely intact than those of other Negroes. Their African ancestors were readily identifiable through a steady line of descent; thus, their racial integrity well prepared them for entry into a multiethnic, multilingual world—a difficulty other southern Negroes had experienced. Most interesting, the Gullahs' religious belief system was dualistic, combining some elements of traditional Christianity with paganistic elements, another continuation of their African culture. Their belief in a spirit world of ethereal components and in one's ability to "conjure" that world through voodoo ran counter to the Protestantism that the white masters of their slave ancestors had evangelized. The Gullahs had thus resisted, by force of preserving cultural memory, acculturation into the ways of the Americas, especially the antebellum South. These unique racial characteristics made them an intriguing subject for art.

Having gained access to a world that few white people knew intimately, Janie set about chronicling it with gusto. First she studied the Gullah dialect carefully, recording its style and slang, its idioms and metaphors. She then began writing down the tales told her by the Gullah servants whom she knew. Vernacular poems and stories followed: three books of privately published verses beginning in 1905 and then in the early 1920s "plantation stories" with Gullah narrators, similar to Joel Chandler Harris's Uncle Remus tales. Capitalizing on the eagerness of northern audiences to learn more about the southern culture they had glimpsed during the Civil War, Janie sold her work to a famous recitalist of the day, Georgia Ray Macmillan, whose performances at ladies' afternoon teas and socials featured "the stories and songs of the Charleston darkey by Jane Screven Heyward." By the early 1920s, just as her son was beginning to explore his own creative tendencies, Janie was giving performances herself, up and down the eastern seaboard. By her death in 1939 she was known as one of the most famous "dialect recitalists" of the twentieth-century South.

The recurring theme in Janie's stories was the peculiar sisterhood between black and white women. She felt such a bond with her Gullah servants. In this way, she drew strength from a racial Other, seeing a degree of faith and inner vitality that she herself wished she possessed. Although many of her stories were comic, they revealed much about the relationship between black and white cultures. In "The Rolling Eye," for example, the white mistress "fears" the wildfire rage of the Gullah servant toward her young thieving nephew. Janie evokes a wonderful comic interplay between white and black—the servant is alternately depressed and enraged as her mistress tries in vain to recuperate from a bad case of nerves. And both women are kept afoot and unsettled by the rapscallion boy. In contrast, "Ole Miss" is a generational story of the abiding friendship between the white mistress and her maid as the two grow old and literally die together—a faithfulness "never parted either by Fate or [by] circumstance."

The Negroes in Janie's sketches largely conformed to the stereotype of African Americans in southern literature at the time. These faithful servants appeared in countless apologias for the prewar South. However, like white writers who wrote about southern blacks before her, Janie also recognized the kinship, both emotional and cultural, between whites and blacks, especially the Gullahs, whose cultural tenets were so concrete. The central concerns of white southern art—memory, place, community, and narrative—are also the primary concepts of Gullah culture.

Janie also saw how the commodities of Gullah life were lacking in white

Charleston society. Whereas Gullahs were expressive, Charlestonians were largely reticent. The Gullahs celebrated community ties; Charlestonians were preoccupied instead with civility and sociability. Janie appropriated these qualities of the Charleston Gullahs and in certain ways remade herself. She became a strong-willed, independent-minded woman of great inner strength. Most important, in writing about the Gullah world, Janie practiced a kind of cultural ventriloquism that was new in southern writing. She foresaw a better future for herself through vicarious participation in African American life.

This was the culture her son would later immortalize in Porgy, Bess, Black Maria, Serena, and the other denizens of Catfish Row. To Janie may be credited not just the novelty of a white Charlestonian gaining intimate access to a foreign subculture but also the spark of curiosity that she passed on to her son. Of the many confidences mother and son exchanged, both overt and intuitive, Janie's knowledge of the Gullah world must be the most important, for it eventually liberated Heyward from the bonds of place and name, just as it did his mother. As Heyward later said when he described the making of *Porgy*, he was curious about the nature of "this life which was going on within our own, yet was apart from it." It possessed a certain "indefinable quality" that remained with whites "only in a more or less vestigial state, and at times seemed to have departed altogether. . . . From admiration of the manifestations of this secret law my feeling grew to one of envy."

Janie exposed Heyward to Gullah culture early in his life. Heyward's first job was for an insurance company canvasing the black slums to collect "burial money." In part this practice was a prudent economic initiative by the Gullahs, but it was also a superstitious safeguard against harm. "Give the boy a quarter!" the residents would shout, and the young Heyward would pocket the change for his employers. Heyward also knew of the Negro field laborer. For three successive summers between 1900 and 1903, just up to his eighteenth birthday, Heyward worked on the plantation of one of his DuBose aunts, where he supervised the black field hands.

Then, in the fall of 1905, he took an unusual job in Charleston's warehouse district, on the docks. Heyward was employed as a cotton checker for a steamship line headquartered alongside the Cooper River. The Bay Street district at the time was an unsightly and "heathenish" area. Tenements, bordellos, and capacious warehouses lined the streets, many of the buildings sagging and tilting, as if the combined wear of many years' use had at last taken its toll. At night, besotted sailors lurched unsteadily from saloon to saloon, arm in arm with prostitutes. Sin proliferated, and the prophecies of courageous Baptist ministers who ventured into the area to reform the wayward were confirmed by steady waves of robberies, beatings, and whiskey-inspired knife fights. Heyward observed this exotic otherworld with a mixture of curiosity, fear, and keen excitement. The Negro inhabitants were unlike any whom Heyward had known. He later described the environment in *Mamba's Daughters* as so "detached from actuality" that it "seemed to invade the territory of dreams. Negroes crossing a dock head single file, with cotton bales on their trucks—a frieze of rhythmic bodies against a blue-green sea horizon" (17). Here was a third subspecies of the Gullah Negro—except for the field hands he had supervised on his aunt's plantation, Heyward had known only household servants, a much different sort of Negro, the "mauma" who tended the children of the white family for whom she worked. This is the sentimentalized figure of local-color sketches of the day, the woman who, in the words of one of Heyward's contemporaries, "crooned [him] to sleep on [her] dark breast," the one to whom he "had gone . . . with his childish joys and sorrows as freely as to his mother." Such descriptions also tended unrealistically to confer on such women a sense of power as "the one to be reckoned with."

Such suggestions of authority were merely a cultural conceit: as independent as the mauma seemed to be, she still took her orders from the household's white mistress. And the mauma's sphere of influence was restricted to the white world in which she worked, so her autonomy was limited. By contrast, the African American that Heyward saw in the shadows of Bay Street lived in a world set apart from the prevalent white culture. Through Heyward's naive eyes, these people were almost savages. He was entranced by them, amazed at their physical strength and vitality. Here also was evidence of social stratification among the city's black population. "Respectable" black families lived side by side with "brutes" and vagrants. Just as the small but recognizable mulatto brown elite held themselves apart from the common laborer and servant classes, so too did this black subculture exist independently of the more "gentle" African Americans whom Heyward had known. And here was an untouched, self-contained environment, out of the reach of white influence—a world that seemed suffused with a sense of liberation that he thought lacking in his own society. The experience affected him deeply.

Part of Heyward's fascination with the brute humanity that he observed on the docks was driven by envy. Heyward was in awe of the Negroes' physical strength; their immense power seemed mythic to him. In contrast, Heyward was stigmatized by his physical frailty and persistent illness, which lowered his self-confidence and his self-esteem. He was strongly affected by the gospel of manliness that so dominated popular culture at the time. The doctrine had been preached from the highest quarters—by the Rough Rider president himself, Theodore Roosevelt, who had overcome a sickly youth to become a model physical specimen. The energy and ambition that Roosevelt symbolized pervaded American life: the fitness movement was beginning, homeopathy and other nontraditional methods of healing were becoming widespread, and in the popular consciousness, virility was regarded as a necessity for "success." But Heyward was nearly an invalid for much of his youth.

When he was eighteen he contracted polio, a devastating condition at that time in the South, for none of the physicians there had yet witnessed it. It was thus some time before Heyward was diagnosed, through the serendipitous intercession of a northern cousin who paid for his treatment at a Philadelphia hospital. The disease left its mark on him permanently with weakened shoulder and arm muscles, a thin, fragile torso, and tendency to fall prey to other illnesses. The atrophying of Heyward's muscles also sometimes gave him a cadaverous look: as an adult, his clothes always seemed to hang loosely about his frame. Moreover, he later developed painful arthritis in his hands. At its worst, the condition made his fingers bunch downward into a shape resembling a crab's claw. Writing was often physically painful for him.

After recovering from the polio, Heyward was struck down by a typhoid epidemic, second in severity only to consumption. He was invalided for eighteen months and sent to take in the salubrious mountain area near Hendersonville, North Carolina, an area where wealthy Charlestonians typically kept summer homes. Then in 1906, by bizarre bad luck, Heyward was hit with pleurisy and had to undergo another lengthy rest and cure. That time, he left the humid Charleston air for the deserts of Arizona, where he spent nearly two years recuperating on a combined sanitarium and work farm. A later short story, "A Man's Work," satirically describes the intent toward "uplift" that such a camp exhibited. But Heyward could be nothing but melancholy. He rued his physical frailty and felt excluded from the manly life. This event represented the beginning of a pattern in Heyward's young adulthood in which he was presented with social roles that he could not embrace and denied roles that he desired: he wanted to be a writer more than anything else.

Years later, Heyward drew on these experiences in several stories that have Western settings or take place in sanitariums. The stories concern masculinity as well as the contrastive elements of health and illness, a theme he would later use in his Negro fiction. The tales imitate the style and subject matter of much magazine fiction of the day, especially that pitched to a male audience. The titles include "Be a Man," "A Man's Job," "Making a Man of Rayburn," and "The Brute." The tales extol the culture of robust virility, the outdoor life, and hard work. "The Winning Loser" and "The Steel Trap" have outdoor settings—the latter's is a lumber camp. In "The Mayfield Miracle," set in a sanitarium, the narrator witnesses a final attempt at heroism by a once-strong man who has been confined to a wheelchair. Underlying the tales, however, undertones of irony and wistfulness alternate, suggesting that Heyward felt mingled contempt and envy at the masculine culture that excluded him.

When he finally recovered from these illnesses, Heyward was eager to start a life. The problem was that he did not have the education necessary to go the normal routes and study law or medicine. He had dropped out of high school to work full time—mostly to ensure that the family stayed solvent, but also because he was indifferent to his studies. He was more imaginative than scholarly, he disliked the monotony of learning by rote, and he was dreamy and absentminded. Banking seemed an option for a time but did not pan out. He finally chose the only alternative left to him, business. Thus in 1908 he opened a general-service insurance agency with a childhood friend, Harry O'Neill. O'Neill was an unflappable optimist, a booster, a go-getter. Heyward, more cautious and reserved, proved to have sound business instincts as well as a natural charm that brought much business the firm's way. The company flourished.

Among southern communities, Charleston was (and still tends to be) among the most class-conscious. Because of its long aristocratic history, Charleston places a much heavier burden of upholding tradition on its gentry than elsewhere in the Deep South. Heyward, a young gentleman descended from the purest South Carolina stock, was compelled to observe a code—to dress well; observe the seasonal customs of parties and cotillions; associate with like-minded people; engage in the leisure pursuits of the upper class, such as fishing, gaming, and sailing; and, when the appropriate moment arrived, enter a gentlemanly profession.

Her vicarious immersion into the Gullah world notwithstanding, Janie was still mindful of appearances. Like the character Kate Wentworth in *Mamba's Daughters,* Janie was determined "to hold a place for her children in the class to which they had been born" (122). She was not so indifferent to her culture as to break the prevailing social code. As the narrator of *Mamba's Daughters* states, "you were born a Wentworth and you refrained from doing certain things . . . that was all there was to it" (122). So Heyward obliged his mother and dutifully set out on a "proper" career that accorded with his social station.

Heyward now settled into his expected societal role and saw his life's work in the traditional Charleston contexts of commerce, civic activism, and social duty. "I was the world's most devoted society man," he later recalled. He entered fully into this life, shouldering the heavy burden of social obligations—"almost nightly balls and membership in all the clubs." Heyward was never completely comfortable in this role, but he managed it with grace and aplomb. He had an innately chivalric manner. His publisher, Stanley Rinehart, once recalled that at a cocktail party he gave in Heyward's honor in New York, the author left the room in midsentence to escort a young lady downstairs and out to the street, where he helped her into a taxi.

Heyward also expanded his horizons a bit and made up for his partially lost youth. With a family friend, Heyward traveled to Europe in the summer of 1914, his first trip outside the United States. Economic instability there seemed to be growing since Germany had declared war on France. As a businessman, Heyward wanted to see living conditions firsthand. He toured Scotland briefly, then went to Paris, where he just barely glimpsed "something of the gay life . . . before the war declaration changed the face of things." Coming out of the theater one evening, Heyward saw "an excited mob" heading toward him, "shouting and singing." He subsequently learned that a rabid military enthusiast had been shot just before the mobilization of troops. The mob was "a crowd of Socialists bent on vengeance."

The following morning, Heyward saw long lines of excited Parisians in front of banks that had closed their doors and were refusing to pay deposi-tors. At the Gare du l'Est, the travelers witnessed the sweethearts and moth-ers of soldiers bidding them goodbye; then, just a few hours later, they saw another "surging mob" converge on a hotel that was rumored to be owned by a German. The crowd threw rocks and cobblestones at the building "until they had worked themselves into a frenzy," seizing tables from sidewalk cafes and smashing their way through the plate-glass front of the hostelry. Heyward watched as the mob moved down the boulevard, systematically demolishing the "beautiful fittings" of "beautifully illuminated cafes" if their signs indicated they were owned by Germans.

Heyward thrilled to these scenes of primal anger and passion—quite in contrast to his prosaic existence as a Charleston businessman. So fascinated was he by these displays of mob anger that he and his companion "trailed around with them" the whole evening. Heyward left Paris with the German army just seventy miles away and arrived in New York a few days later, after a rough passage. The intensity of the adventure seems to have been enough for Heyward for a while. Immediately after he and his companion debarked, they rushed to Broadway to find a newsstand and the latest Charleston paper: "we sat right down on the curb and devoured everything in it."

Heyward's concluding comments suggest his innocent provincialism and jingoistic Americanness. But conversely, Heyward had an experience that most of his fellow Charlestonians would only read about. He had seen war at its most glamorous and was drawn in by its falsely romantic allure. He had witnessed firsthand a range of emotions brought on by disorder and tragedy. He had also had a small taste of an "exotic," alien culture quite different from his own.

Back home, Heyward continued his forays into Charleston's Negro com-munity. As an insurance agent, he sometimes speculated in real estate, and one of his first projects was renovating a row of Negro tenements. The prop-erties were all sold in good time, at a considerable profit for Heyward's com-pany. When war fever hit Charleston in the spring of 1917, Heyward undertook another unusual "career" as a "Four Minute Man," selling war bonds. These volunteers were local businessmen and civic leaders who gave brief (four-minute) speeches at war rallies, urging their fellow citizens to buy Liberty Bonds to support the servicemen at the front. Assignments were made to speak in different districts, and Heyward was given the outlying rural areas populated by blacks. (John Bennett, an acquaintance from the local yacht club who would soon become an important figure in Heyward's life, worked the black city neighborhoods.) Heyward was enormously successful at this work.

More than simply doing his part to help the war effort, Heyward seems genuinely to have immersed himself in the cause and lived out his role as an orator. He later recalled for his wife, Dorothy, an engagement where he became so wrought up in delivering his speech that his audience was practically incited to riot, so zealously had they absorbed the impact of Heyward's message. Such a story is difficult to believe, given Heyward's mild-mannered personality—it sounds almost as though he were living out a fictitious role, perhaps preparing to fictionalize a community to which he wanted to gain access. Heyward visited Negro war-work sites, the Victory Club for Colored Soldiers and Sailors, and the headquarters of the War Camp Community Service. He also heard for the first time the "National Anthem of the American Negro," by J. Rosamund Johnson and James Weldon Johnson, two African American artists whom he would later befriend. (Heyward pasted a copy of the song into his scrapbook and later used it in *Mamba's Daughters*.)

Heyward's writing talent was largely mimetic. He moved easily among different modes of writing—poems, novels, plays, even screen treatments. Heyward's speeches reveal an impressive absorption of the locutions and rhythms of patriotic rhetoric. The zeal evident in these speeches also suggests a keen awareness of his black audience. At times Heyward could launch into a perfect reproduction of pulpit oratory: "Suppose we all waited for the other fellow to do the buying, and the issue was not subscribed. . . . 'But' many of you say, and quite sincerely, 'Can I afford to buy a bond?' Fellow Americans, you cannot possibly afford—NOT TO. . . . You will personally and individually cast your vote of confidence in the glorious cause upon which this Country has embarked, and in the men who are staking their lives to back it up." The speech combines the calculated pauses and emphases of classical oratory with the verbal stratagems of a medicine-show pitchman. Heyward clearly enjoyed giving these performances.

Heyward's intense involvement in this project demonstrates his ability to absorb and adapt to a variety of rhetorical situations. The work was also a means by which he compensated for his inability to serve abroad. Most important, it gave him yet another exposure to black Charlestonians and perhaps even an opportunity to divine their emotional and psychological makeup.

The experience also seems to have given him an outlet for his creative energy, for from a very early age he had shown an interest in the arts. Janie had read to Heyward and his sister nightly when they were children. The "heartrending narratives" of Dickens appealed to him greatly, but he reportedly loved most the stories of such romanticists as James Fenimore Cooper, Sir Walter Scott, and William Gilmore Simms. The memory of Scott's narratives in particular made the older Heyward value and delight in regional dialect and the sound of the poetic word. Janie later encouraged his interests in drawing. He became fond of sketching the scenes around him in Charleston, especially the harbor and its sailboats—the start of a lifelong fascination with the sea. In 1903, while recuperating from polio, he took lessons in painting. He continued this interest in 1917, when he returned to the North Carolina mountains after his pleurisy attack. At that time, he studied drawing with Louis Rowell, a local artist. Heyward's imagination was more pictorial than verbal, as one can see in his early fiction, where narrative exposition is usually conveyed through authorial description rather than through dialogue. This quality also explains Heyward's attraction to the theater. He was involved with Charleston dramatic groups off and on during the 1910s, sometimes in play production, sometimes as an actor.

Heyward also tried his hand at playwriting. In April 1913 a local acting troupe presented a light comedy that he had authored, *An Artistic Triumph*. The otherwise forgettable play, which combines stock elements of a Restoration comedy and a late Victorian melodrama, nonetheless shows Heyward indulging his artistic yearnings and attempting to resolve a serious conflict in his life: that between the worlds of commerce and of art or between the life of an intellectual and the life of a society man.

The play is set (of course) in Paris, in the studio of a struggling American artist named Bert. He has promised his girlfriend, Dolly, that if after two years he has not been successful, she may leave him and he will not press her into marriage. Bert plans to have friends assist him in setting up a wealthy art patron. A fake English "lord" will advise this patron that Bert is a brilliant young unknown. The patron will then buy Bert's work en masse, Bert will be successful, and he will get the girl. The plot turns on a series of mistaken identities, and in the end, Bert's plan is revealed. But the wealthy collector buys Bert's art anyway, love prevails, and everyone is happy.

The failure of the patron to be duped by Bert's scheme suggests Heyward's realization that art should not function merely as a tool for social aggrandizement. Rather, society and art, functioning together, can create a genuine appreciation of beauty and, by extension, cultural edification for the people. This principle later became the governing aesthetic of the Poetry Society, which Heyward helped to found. But Heyward is satiric as well as serious minded in the play. He gently pokes fun at the elite Charleston establishment into which he was born by having the patron, Mr. Waltimer, profess to be a great collector not of art but of "something far more expensive . . . my unique and comprehensive collections of ancestors, and my acquired grove of family trees. I paid $999.00 . . . for conclusive proof that I was a descendant of a signer of the Declaration of Independence, and a small fortune for a trace of Royal blood."

As Heyward's doubts about his destiny as businessman and social climber grew, he repeatedly returned to this theme. He satirized high society in a number of early stories, such as "Dorothy Grumpet, Graduate Lady," in which he points out the uselessness of a $10,000 finishing-school education, or "The Ultimate Test," in which a dissolute aristocrat is derided for living off his inheritance instead of doing useful work.

The play also suggests the high seriousness with which Heyward began to regard the artistic life. The play has an overwrought reverence that elevates art to the pantheon of the gods. One character vents his "bitter resentment" at how commercialism has "converted the exhibit we used to know as the home of all that was uplifting and best in art, into a common mart where are offered wares of men who attain notoriety in proportion to their ability to disgrace the deity of whom they claim to be votaries." Similarly, in "The Mayfield Miracle," an unpublished story, Heyward argues that the love of the beautiful is the most important requirement for a fulfilling life. He was clearly yearning to be a writer. The problem was how to pursue this goal without shirking his traditional obligations in work and society. Like his fictional alter ego in *Mamba's Daughters*, Saint Wentworth, Heyward rued the fact that "art found it difficult to hold its own in competition with society in Charleston" (138). In the novel, Saint feels like "a spirit that is trying to inhabit two separate planes of existence" (161). In *An Artistic Triumph*, the protagonist mixes economic and aesthetic motives in his formula for artistic "success," but the experiment is a failure.

Heyward's early drift toward the theater also suggests his view of art as a community construct. Janie helped form this part of his aesthetic orientation. During Heyward's late teenage years, Janie ran a guest house on one of the barrier islands that lay beyond Charleston Harbor. Here she created a convivial place by urging her guests to entertain each other by composing impromptu poems or presenting oral "interpretations" of verses and tales. To Janie, one of the requirements of art was that it stimulate communal activity, an element of Heyward's own aesthetic. Her son enjoyed participating in group-oriented activities such as recitals, plays, and games. En route to Glasgow, for example, he helped organize a shipboard concert to benefit a charity, and later at the MacDowell Colony, where he and Dorothy did much of their writing, he frequently participated in impromptu performances.

Janie's emphasis on community-oriented displays of story and song, of collaborative creativity, was another of her borrowings from Gullah culture, in which tales and music were group events aimed at strengthening the network of associations within the culture. Her son's vignettes of Gullah life in *Porgy* abound in community scenes—the craps game, the saucer burial, the picnic on Kittiwah Island, even the huddling in the courtyard during the hurricane.

Furthering his artistic ambitions, in late 1917 Heyward took an early stab at writing for moving pictures. The attempt reveals his entrepreneurial spirit as well as his search for a way to combine art and commerce, since the movies were just then beginning to be recognized as a potentially profitable venture. Heyward wrote a screenplay set in Charleston and tried to entice producers to buy it by committing the Chamber of Commerce to help finance the project by offering city services and the use of houses and gardens for free. Heyward told the motion picture company that he could use his "large connection here" to secure permission to film private residences.

The enticements did not work, but the screenplay is interesting because it shows Heyward using Charleston material for the first time. The plot, set in the nineteenth century, is melodrama with a race-oriented twist. An aristocratic family buys a Negro woman and her light-skinned baby girl at auction. Years later, as the girl grows up, the son of the family falls in love with her, and the girl is eventually accepted by the family as one of their own. But the son's jilted sweetheart spreads the word that the girl is a Negro, and the family is almost driven from the town in disgrace. At the last minute, a passing sailor tells the son that the girl is actually white, the long-lost daughter of a wealthy family, stolen on a voyage to America.

Heyward recycled some of the plot in his later historical novel, *Peter Ashley* (a slave auction and a horse race figure prominently in the book, as they do in the screenplay). And the tragic mulatto theme also factors into *Brass Ankle*. In the early story, he was experimenting with race as material for fiction, rather boldly so for a southerner in 1917, and his treatment of the black "passing" theme suggests an acquaintance not just with the work of such white authors as Mark Twain (*Pudd'nhead Wilson* [1891]) and William Dean Howells (*An Imperative Duty* [1893]), but possibly also such African American writers as Charles Chesnutt (*The House behind the Cedars* [1900]), James Weldon Johnson (*The Autobiography of an Ex-Colored Man* [1912]), and Nella Larsen (*Quicksand* [1928]).

Heyward's early life was influenced by his mother and his city. Janie's "discovery" of Charleston's black community and the reengineering of her identity through vicarious participation in the life of the Gullahs affected Heyward deeply. He saw the contrast between white and black cultures, but as a young man the demands on him to live his life according to history—as a Charlestonian and a Heyward—were too great for him to ignore, as desperately as he wanted to break out of those roles. He was dissatisfied with the life of commerce and indulged his artistic yearnings by painting, drawing, and acting in local theater. He had also tried a variety of writing modes— stories, plays, and movie treatments. But his writing efforts, however earnest, lacked focus and direction. Heyward needed a mentor, someone to encourage him, guide him, and critique his work. He also needed to be in an environment that would stimulate and nourish his imagination. He had not thought of Charleston in those terms before, but he was soon to think otherwise.

Chapter Two

The Poetry Society
and the Charleston
Renaissance

I
N THE FALL OF 1918, Heyward renewed his acquaintance with John Bennett, a friend with whom he had worked as a Four Minute Man selling war bonds to the city's black population. Bennett, a native of Chillicothe, Ohio, had married into a prominent Charleston family and settled in the city in 1898. The fifty-three-year-old Bennett had just published *Master Skylark* (1897), a popular children's tale set in Elizabethan England that remains a best-seller today. On learning that Heyward had literary ambitions, Bennett took a new interest in his friend, and over the next several years mentored Heyward by critiquing his works in progress, suggesting books to read, advising him on the kinds of fiction that appealed to contemporary readers, and, most important, inspiring Heyward, galvanizing the younger man's determination to be an author.

Bennett and Heyward would eventually establish the Poetry Society of South Carolina and help develop a nascent artistic movement in the city into the Charleston renaissance, a harbinger of the great southern renaissance of the 1920s. Charleston was at the head of this southern arts revival but played a role different from that of other literary groups in such cities as Richmond and Nashville. For the most part Heyward and his fellow Charlestonians rejected modernist innovations in language and form. Conversely, however, the Charlestonians were in the vanguard of the new southern literature since many in their circle were women, and their chief artistic enterprise was the representation of Negro life. Moreover, Heyward, as spokesperson for the group, evangelized for the cause of southern poetry in accordance with the critical temper of the period and its promotion of poetic schools through little magazines and aesthetic manifestos. By 1922 Charleston was recognized nationally as the most influential center of southern poetry, and it was widely assumed that the most enduring southern literature would emerge from Charleston.

Although Bennett was Heyward's senior by twenty years, Heyward was drawn to the other man because his early life history resembled his own. Both men had been lackluster students and had had early interests in drawing. Bennett trained at an art school in Cincinnati for one year in 1882 but then had to return to Chillicothe when his father's business failed. Like Heyward, Bennett was thus denied a life in the arts and was instead thrust into the role of family provider. "Scratching gravel for subsistence," Bennett took a job as a cub reporter for the local paper. He eventually moved up into positions with more prominent newspapers, but, like Heyward, working unhappily as an insurance salesman, Bennett also felt constrained in his job and longed to live a different life. In 1891 Bennett decided to write children's stories, and his first work was published in *St. Nicholas* magazine. Mary Mapes Dodge, the editor there, asked for more of Bennett's work, and thus began a successful writing career.

Soon after settling in Charleston, however, Bennett's interest in children's literature receded, and in its place arose a new fascination, which he pursued with such diligence that it might even be said to have bordered on a compulsion: the culture of the low-country Gullahs. Bennett devoted virtually the rest of his life to this interest. He collected photographs of the people; he studied their music, particularly the spirituals that were so integral an element of their religious faith; he researched their African origins; and he investigated the intriguing elements of their culture, including superstition, voodoo, medicine and herbs, and the interpretation of dreams and omens.

Bennett—an outlander—was the only person in Charleston actively researching such material at this time. Jane Heyward and one or two other minor authors, such as Ambrose Gonzales (another South Carolinian) would soon follow, but southerners would not pursue this rich material fully until much later. In contrast, northerners had been collecting Negro folklore since before the Civil War. Abolitionists had compiled the first collection of spirituals and secular songs in 1867, and critical articles also were being written on such material. Bennett was forever planning numerous fiction and non-fiction books on these topics, but he seems to have worked rather slowly. Nonetheless, he produced three books in which Gullah folktales figure prominently: *The Treasure of Peyre Gaillard* (1906), *Madame Margot: A Grotesque Legend of Old Charleston* (1921), and *The Doctor to the Dead: Grotesque Legends and Folk Tales of Old Charleston* (1946).

Like Janie and her fascination with Gullah culture, Bennett's interests in the Negro race piqued Heyward's curiosity. Bennett's Gullah writings probably also showed Heyward the possibilities for point of view: the stories are related via the perspective of a white man, outside the Gullah culture. This persona is driven by an anthropological curiosity and a sentimental desire to preserve the folk and social history of an "exotic" subculture that was vanishing with the coming of modernism. Bennett's writings therefore differ from similar collections of black folktales, like Joel Chandler Harris's, for example, wherein the intent is to instruct via humor and to embellish a character type for artistic purposes. The combination of scholarly seriousness and sentimentalism in Bennett's books is unique among white-authored tales of black culture. One can see the influence of this unusual impulse in Heyward's *Porgy* and later works.

Through Bennett, Heyward met Hervey Allen, a Pittsburgh native about Heyward's age. Just discharged from the army, where he had been wounded in France, Allen taught English at a local military academy. A large, muscular man, Allen contrasted sharply with the skinny and rather frail Heyward, yet the two became close friends. Heyward had a vicarious interest in Allen's "manly" exploits, and Allen had also published a collection of Kiplingesque army verses entitled *Ballads of the Border* (1916). Allen thus embodied the image of the hypermasculine author then epitomized by Kipling, Richard Harding Davis, and others, a type of artist that Heyward would have given much to be like. Each man's intense desire to write, "to find some safe vent for their emotions," as Bennett put it, drew them to each other. Bennett thus found himself with two students eager for guidance, which he was happy to provide.

Thus evolved an informal discussion meeting each Wednesday evening at Bennett's house. Bennett would critique the younger men's works in progress. He was a plain-speaking critic: his remarks soon became known as "fanging" and the meetings as "fang-fests." Heyward profited more than

Allen did from the exercises. Lacking self-confidence, Heyward needed more of Bennett's help. He responded to Bennett with gratitude, determination, and enthusiasm. "I cannot say that I am sorry to learn that the Swamp Angel [an early story] needed fanging," Heyward told Bennett in July 1920. "I realize that I am at that stage of the game where only the sort of constructive criticism that I get from you can help me. The time was when I rather withered under adverse comment. Now I welcome it, and know that I must either admit its rightness, or offer good and sufficient reason for adhering to my opinion."

The origins of this discussion group paralleled those of many literary movements in America that began in a spirit of "clubbishness"—the Delphians of Baltimore, the Boston-based Saturday Club and Transcendental Club, or the Bread and Cheese Club presided over by James Fenimore Cooper, for example. Like their predecessors, the Charleston circle valued sociability and "conversability" over edification or didacticism. The group's members were most concerned with polite letters—diversion, entertainment, and, most important, affirmation of place and of regional orthodoxies. Only later would Heyward come to question these assumed shared values and move beyond the local or provincial.

As mentor for Heyward, Bennett did some things well, others not so well. Bennett was a good grammarian and a good speller, skills that Heyward lacked. A self-taught writer, Bennett directed Heyward to examples of good prose, which Heyward used as models. Bennett was also a role model for Heyward—a father figure. Heyward looked to Bennett for inspiration and for approval of his fledgling efforts. Bennett had not been exposed to a wide range of literature, however, and he was not a particularly good writer. His reading tastes were conservative, and he was quick to deride experimentation, the bedrock of literary modernism. When his daughter once showed him one of her efforts at free verse, Bennett dismissed the whole movement with "acid opinions"; likewise, he lashed out at the "smut" in James Joyce's *Ulysses* and other modernist works. Bennett urged Heyward to write something both popular and thoughtful, but his notions of such material were of "honest, man-talk, popular stuff, with genuine romance, real life, authentic feeling, true sentiment and your quiet wit and humane analysis of men and motives"—what sounds like a hodgepodge of catchphrases from popular culture and correspondence-school writing primers. In addition, Bennett's own writing (excepting his children's books) was often verbose and overwrought and sometimes lacked focus and a sense of narrative pacing. Bennett admitted his shortcomings as a writer. He often noted the "strenuous labor" he had to undergo to write well and conceded that he knew more of "printing, publishing, and . . . editorial whims" than of composition. But in Charleston, as in most of the South, writers of great merit were not in great supply. And Bennett was, after all, published. Thus, by the summer of 1920, Heyward was referring to Bennett as "the Master" and asking him, half-seriously, to "lay a blessing" on Heyward's head as he worked at being a writer.

It is unlikely that, had Heyward had a mentor with more avant-garde tastes, his fiction would have been more modernistic. Raised in so genteel a culture, Heyward's natural tendencies were toward "polite" literature. Bennett doubtless helped plant the idea in Heyward's imagination that led to his writing fiction about the Gullahs. Yet ironically, the effects of Bennett's dilettantism and conservatism may also have made Heyward's inchoate interests in the Gullahs slow to develop.

The Wednesday evening meetings eventually evolved into the Poetry Society of South Carolina, founded in October 1920. This society encouraged the efforts of other artistic groups in Charleston, thus generating a cultural revival there. The Charleston movement, like similar movements in New Orleans, Richmond, and Nashville, helped initiate the great southern literary renaissance, which would reach full flower later in the decade.

Like these other groups, the Charlestonians banded together in response to the famous lambasting of southern culture by H. L. Mencken. In 1917, Mencken published an excoriating critique of the South entitled "The Sahara of the Bozart." The title referred to the dearth of culture south of the Mason-Dixon line. To Mencken, the South was "a vast plain of mediocrity, stupidity, lethargy, . . . torpor and doltishness" (143). "It is, indeed, amazing," he wrote, "to contemplate so vast a vacuity" (136). Mencken derided southern poetry as "doggerel in . . . a farm newspaper"; the southern novel was "treacly and insignificant"; and southern drama was nonexistent (136). The rebellious pundit cataloged every cultural failing imaginable: "In all that gargantuan paradise of the fourth-rate there is not a single picture gallery worth going into, or a single orchestra capable of playing the nine symphonies of Beethoven, or a single opera-house, or a single theater devoted to decent plays [or] a single prose writer who can actually write" (137). The hyperbole notwithstanding, Mencken was correct. Whether from the exhaustion and privation created by the Civil War (as Heyward thought), or from the loss of so many of its youth in battle, the South had produced very little writing of value since the 1850s. The time was ripe for a renewal of interest in the arts, and Mencken had thrown down the gauntlet. Southerners were quick to respond.

In Richmond, a literary revival was already underway. Emily Clark and Hunter Stagg had founded the *Reviewer,* a journal that published the writings of promising young southerners and urged a critical examination of southern tradition. Even more so than Charleston, Richmond—as capital of the late Confederacy—was closely linked to the Lost Cause. Beginning with the work of Ellen Glasgow and James Branch Cabell, however, Richmond's writers underwent a dramatic literary transformation. They moved from depicting a South of "moonlight and magnolias," as Glasgow put it, to one of "blood and irony." Like the Charleston circle, the Richmond group boasted a large number of women, and a flowering of feminist novels had appeared there—three in 1913 alone: Glasgow's *Virginia,* Mary Johnston's *Hagar,* and Henry Sydnor Harrison's *V. V. Eyes.* These works exposed the southern male's chivalrous pose as sham (later treated by Amelie Rives in *The Quick or the Dead?* as well) and prefigured much later southern fiction by such women as Flannery O'Connor, Carson McCullers, and Eudora Welty.

None of the Charleston group, however, was as artistically sophisticated or as rebellious as these figures. The writing published in Richmond, moreover, had an international seasoning absent from the work of Heyward, Bennett, and others. The *Reviewer* published a mix of established writers like Glasgow, Johnston, John Galsworthy, and Robert Nathan with new voices like Frances Newman, Julia Peterkin, Allen Tate, and Paul Green. The magazine repudiated the aesthetic values and social attitudes of the late-Victorian South, and its editorial direction was more or less guided by Mencken, who took a personal interest in the *Reviewer*'s fortunes, unlike in Charleston, where Mencken was, at least initially, seen as the enemy.

A different way to view Charleston's artistic development in the 1920s is to compare it to that of New Orleans. Both cities evolved into literary centers through the confluence of similar cultural currents, but the two cities did so at different times. Before the Civil War, New Orleans, like Charleston, was central to river commerce, a gateway of the shipping industry. Both cities flourished economically, but only Charleston developed into a prewar literary center with the evolution of the Simms-Timrod-Hayne group that gathered at Russell's Bookstore. English literary expression in New Orleans did not emerge fully until after Reconstruction. A nostalgic backward glance marks the writing of this period by such authors as George Washington Cable, Lafcadio Hearn, Grace King, and, to a degree, Kate Chopin. In contrast, Charleston was mostly silent during this postwar period.

In the 1920s, the literary voices of both cities emerged full and clear. Each city experienced new economic vitality, each possessed a corps of educated citizens within a diverse population, and each contained a rich mix of artistic pursuits like writing, musicianship, painting, and sculpture. And like New Orleans, with its self-conscious awareness of its cultural and racial mix (Spanish and French cultural presences that mingled with Negro slavery), an "exotic" subculture evolved that was a fruitful subject for art.

The material culture of 1920s New Orleans was also similar to that of Charleston. Growing from a small walled enclave into one of the wealthiest cities in North America gave New Orleans, like Charleston, a legacy of other-worldliness—in its dilapidated carriage houses and Greek Revival mansions. This sense of a haunted past drew many artists from other regions (adopted Creoles)—William Faulkner, John Dos Passos, William Spratling, Roark Bradford—unlike in Charleston, where most of the artists were native sons and daughters. In addition, the New Orleans group was more or less presided over by one central figure, Sherwood Anderson (just as John Crowe Ransom presided over the Nashville group). And these writers were, unlike the Charlestonians, full converts to the modernist aesthetic in literature and avid readers of such authors as Joyce and Virginia Woolf. In 1920s Charleston, in contrast, writers and painters—including Heyward at the start of his career—represented in their art a nostalgia for a time long gone, what New Orleans writers had left behind at the end of the nineteenth century.

The chief organ of the New Orleans group, the *Double Dealer,* also differed from the main forum of the Charlestonians, the Poetry Society *Year Book.* Both were established around the same time in response to Mencken's "Sahara of the Bozart" essay, but only the *Double Dealer* achieved sustained national recognition, and it did so even though it folded in 1926. The *Double Dealer* published Faulkner's early *New Orleans Sketches* as well as work by

Anderson, Ernest Hemingway, and Hart Crane. All these figures, of course, went on to attain a fame never reached by Heyward, Pinckney, or Bennett. And ultimately New Orleans was to demonstrate more staying power in the artistic imagination, as it went on to produce or adopt such writers as Tennessee Williams, Walker Percy, and John Kennedy Toole.

Other centers flourished in the South. In Nashville, a group of aspiring poets, the Fugitives, shared Mencken's view that the stream of a southern literary tradition was stopped up at the source and no longer potable. As the Fugitives stated in the first issue of their magazine, they "fled from nothing faster than the high-caste Brahmins of the Old South." A like-minded group in Chapel Hill, consisting of Paul Green, Addison Hibbard, Howard W. Odum, and Gerald W. Johnson, also supported Mencken's indictment in their essays and suggested ways to feed the South the cultural nutrients it needed to develop into a robust literary community.

These groups in large part agreed with Mencken's assessment of the South as a benighted place that needed to reexamine itself, to tear down whatever traditions remained and start afresh, with a new critical vision and spirit. These figures also presented themselves as rebels, shaking up the South's complacent self-satisfaction through their articles and editorials. The Charlestonians were different. They did not accept Mencken's criticisms wholesale, and they did not uncritically subscribe to his view of a "dead" southern literary tradition. In the foreword to the first *Year Book* of the Poetry Society, published in 1921, Hervey Allen (with input from Heyward and Bennett) wrote that Mencken was a "literary General Sherman" who had attacked the South viciously and unfairly. But the Charleston group conceded the truth of some of Mencken's points and thus accepted his indictment as a challenge. In their essays and *Year Book* prefaces between 1921 and 1925, the Charlestonians alternately sympathized and disagreed with certain northern views of southern literature. In some ways the Charlestonians perfectly fitted Mencken's conception of the sort of people who could enlighten a benighted South. Yet in other ways they were attempting the difficult task of repudiating past traditions while still remaining "traditional." Thus, Charleston's bifurcated role in the early southern renaissance is unique.

Born of an aristocratic family, Heyward was the ideal representative from Mencken's "civilized minority"—that remnant of the old southern elite that

Mencken hoped would assert itself and wage war on cultural ignorance. Bennett and Allen too shared Mencken's idea of new southern writers as bringers of light, arbiters of taste who would intellectually elevate the lower orders. Education became the primary goal of the Poetry Society. Unlike similar groups, such as the Fugitives, the Charlestonians did not necessarily seek to produce poets; instead, the group brought to Charleston the best writers of the day, the better to enlighten the citizenry about art. As Heyward wrote in the foreword to the first yearbook, the Society sought to "stimulate an interest in the reading, writing, and critical appreciation of poetry in the community."

The way that the organizers ran the first meeting suggests that they thought of themselves as educators and "civilizers." They "elected" a slate of officers a priori, people they felt had the natural ability to carry out this function. The person who became president was not even present at the meeting. The other offices fell to Bennett (vice president) and Josephine Pinckney (recording secretary and treasurer). Heyward became the corresponding secretary, an important role that did much to advance his career. Heyward also set the society's tone and conducted most of its important business.

Discerning first that the organization should emphasize its social character and thus carry out its mission as a bringer of light, Heyward set membership dues at the rather high figure of five dollars yearly. The organization thus appeared socially desirable and drew its members from the upper echelons of the community. An initial list of prospective members was compiled by consulting the city's social register; when that list looked too aristocratic, it was leavened with some names from the telephone directory. Heyward also suggested that membership be limited to 250 people. By the end of the first year, there was a waiting list.

Then, drawing on his entrepreneurial instincts, Heyward took charge of publicity—again responding to Mencken's challenge by calling for a new southern poetry. Heyward enjoined the community to "keep abreast of the revolutionary movement of the times and to keep alive the spirit of appreciation in poetry both old and new." In addition to bringing distinguished writers and critics to the city, the Poetry Society fostered creativity by sponsoring poetry-writing contests. This venture, like the lecture series, was quite successful—probably because of the munificence of the awards. The Blindman

Prize, which carried a $250 award, brought seventeen pounds of mail, including contributions from Africa, India, and the Philippines. But lest the society be suspected by outsiders as having commercial motives, Heyward, again with a businessman's pragmatism, emphasized that the cash awards existed merely to provide "adequate return for the labor involved in producing a poem of . . . quality."

Eventually, the Poetry Society did give a nod to those Charlestonians who wanted to learn to write poetry. Some meetings were held in which draft poems were read aloud and critiqued by the members. But as Heyward predicted, this phenomenon began to create ill will, and he stepped in with a compromise solution: a subgroup would be formed, and manuscripts could be submitted anonymously and in advance to a reading committee, which would then critique the works at fortnightly meetings. Heyward, Allen, and everyone else participated in the discussion, but by common consent, the last word was reserved for Bennett, whom the group congenially dubbed "Mr. Hypercritic." Finally, the organization produced a yearbook that printed the prizewinning poems and reported on the year's activities. The yearbook, which Heyward edited until 1924, also brought news of other poetry circles, announced the following year's agenda, and publicized society business.

Heyward saw that Charleston was an unexploited source of artistic material. The city was a clear exception to at least one of Mencken's blanket generalizations about the South. He had claimed that the region lacked a suitable environment for literature: "How can dignified and serious poets," he asked, "flourish on a soil where neighborhood jinglers are hailed as geniuses, and ninth-rate doggerel is solemnly compared to the work of the great masters? No great work of art was ever produced in a town in which half the citizens turned out in nightshirts and sidearms to terrorize the other half" (143). Typical of Mencken's generalized vision of the South as a place inhabited solely by poor whites, shamans, and demagogues, this statement ignored the potential of a city like Charleston to produce art. Before the war Charleston was the cultural capital of the Old South; Heyward believed that with such precedent, an artistic revival was possible. After all, Charleston had produced William Gilmore Simms and Henry Timrod, *Russell's Magazine* and the *Southern Review*. Charleston had been home to several legitimate theaters since the early eighteenth century. Moreover, Charlestonians had always been a receptive, discriminating audience of readers. They had long supported a private lending library, for example, and other cultural endeavors.

The history and physical character of the city was also compelling. On visiting Charleston, Harriet Monroe, editor of *Poetry* magazine, saw the possibilities immediately, noting that "no art has yet expressed adequately" the "wealth of historic tradition and association in Charleston." In the history of the city, Monroe thought, there lay "a pathetic comedy of servantless impecuniosity," or perhaps "a tragedy of some free spirit beating its wings against ancient barriers." So too Amy Lowell, then the reigning grand dame of contemporary poetry, was fascinated with the poetic potential of Heyward's city: "The town is beautiful with the past, and glorious with the present; its wealth of folklore has been very little touched upon in poetry. What a mine for some one, what an atmosphere!"

Seen in this light, Charleston—more than Nashville, Chapel Hill, Richmond, or New Orleans—could arguably be said to have been the best candidate to lead the new southern literature. What did Charleston contribute to the southern renaissance and how did these contributions affect Heyward's work? Many of the writers, painters, etchers, and musicians in Charleston broke with tradition and spoke with a voice that critically probed the southern consciousness. Many were women, and their artistic mission was representing southern black life, making them unique among the early artists of the southern revival.

A groundswell of artistic activity had already begun in Charleston when the Poetry Society emerged. Alice Ravenel Huger Smith, for example, a watercolorist who painted romanticized scenes of the low-country plantations, brought considerable fame to Charleston in the 1920s. Smith depicted the Gullah culture of the low country but did so in a mostly sentimentalized way. A true provincial, Smith had no formal art training and claimed never to have desired to leave Charleston. By contrast, Elizabeth O'Neill Verner, an etcher and printmaker, employed realistic art methods. Verner had traveled widely, studying at the Pennsylvania Academy of Fine Arts and journeying to Europe and Japan, where she promoted her work. The work of these two artists was complementary. Verner's black-and-white cityscapes were more literal than Smith's work. In addition, Verner drew her material from the city's rich Gullah culture, which she depicted without sentimentality. Verner's portraits of Gullah women engaged in the artisanship of their race—weaving sweet-grass baskets or braiding wreaths of wildflowers—convey strength of character and will. As Heyward would do in *Porgy*, Verner also obliquely commented on the relationship between Charleston's whites and blacks. She showed the Gullah women at work against the backdrop of Charleston landmarks, like a venerable Episcopal church, which symbolized the authority of white society. The theme of Verner's, Smith's, and later Heyward's work was community: they emphasized the ethnic homogeneity of the Gullahs in relation to the more class-conscious white society.

The pictorial arts flourished in Charleston. Under the influence of two visitors, Gabrielle Clements and Ellen Day Hale, the Charleston Etchers Club was formed, another group comprising mainly women. Charleston welcomed its most important resident artist in February 1920, when Alfred Hutty arrived. Born in Michigan in 1877, Hutty had been trained in stained-glass work in St. Louis and then gone on to Woodstock, New York, an important artists' colony. At his death in 1959, Hutty was one of the foremost etchers in America. Hutty discovered Charleston on his way to Florida, searching for a warm climate in which to winter. He fell in love with the "old culture" of the city almost immediately after arriving and wired his wife to come quickly—he had "found heaven." Hutty offered classes at the newly established Gibbes Art Gallery school, later became involved with the Etchers Club, and then turned to drypoint printmaking. Like Verner, he found a fascinating subject in the Gullah people. He too did not caricature or sentimentalize the people he portrayed, but like Heyward later, he was a sympathetic interpreter of Gullah life.

Charleston's artists commingled freely, and certain quarters of the small city began to resemble an artist's colony. Hutty, for example, became involved with a theater group, the Footlight Players. Bennett joined the Etchers Club, and Smith held a literary salon in her home. In similar fashion, Laura Bragg, the director of the Charleston Museum, gathered artists, writers, and students at her summer home. Heyward attended several of these weekends, and they affected him deeply. He later credited Bragg with broadening his appreciation of art. Bragg resembled Janie Heyward. Both women were energetic and strong willed, atypical for that time and place. Like Bennett, Smith, and Verner, Bragg and Janie were also devoted to the work of cultural preservation, an impulse that would soon drive Heyward's writing.

Of course, such salons as Bragg's and Smith's had been born and had died countless times over in southern cities since the Confederacy, but for so small and isolated a city, Charleston's cultural efforts were unusually successful. The work of these figures drew other artists to Charleston in the 1920s. Some of them, like Edward Hopper and Childe Hassam, worked there en route to other locales; others, like Anna Heyward Taylor and James Fowler Cooper, came to South Carolina to study local subjects after traveling elsewhere.

Fledgling writers were also in residence, among them Josephine Pinckney, a descendant of Eliza Lucas Pinckney, the colonial author who epitomized the self-reliant woman. Mentored by Smith and Bragg, Pinckney began her career as a poet, then after a long period training herself to write prose, produced five novels (most of them concerning Charleston) of meticulous craftsmanship and polish. The most famous of these was *Three O'Clock Dinner*, a best-seller of 1945.

Beatrice Witte Ravenel, another poet, was also descended from an aristocratic Charleston family. While studying at the Harvard Annex in Cambridge, Ravenel's poems and stories were noticed by Thomas Wentworth Higginson, who heralded her as a new literary talent. Ravenel married in 1900 and devoted the next seventeen years of her life to homemaking. But in 1918 Ravenel's "long silence was broken," as Heyward put it, with the first of a series of verse collections, *Arrow of Lightning*, notable for their depth. Ravenel's subjects were marginalized communities—octoroons, the Yemassee Indians, the mothers of missing soldiers. Yet another Charleston author was Herbert Ravenel Sass, best known for a Civil War novel, *Look Back to Glory*, published in 1933. Sass, however, was primarily a naturalist and had a special interest in the Native Americans indigenous to the region. He published several collections of stories that focused on the history and geography of the Carolinas and the relationship between its native inhabitants and the natural world.

In the early 1920s, therefore, Charleston was not at all a cultural backwater. A concerted artistic movement was gaining momentum, and a true renaissance atmosphere was evolving. Notable in its large number of women artists and its concern with the representation of black life, Charleston was in the vanguard of the arts at the time. It drew others to the city, and the many forms of art practiced there stimulated Heyward's creativity.

The artistic earnestness of the 1920s, a time when the "new" poetry, the "new" theater, and later the "new" Negro prevailed, is well demonstrated by the Poetry Society and Heyward's enterprises of cultural evangelism. A festival atmosphere prevailed at the Poetry Society's first meeting in January 1921. Bennett's opening speech predicted that Charleston would lead a renewal of the arts in the South. He then read a selection of poems by Pound, Frost, and Whitman, with such new southern voices as Heyward, Henry Bellaman, and Beatrice Ravenel. So cheered were the society's organizers by the evening's success that the next day Bennett circulated a pen-and-ink drawing from a magazine that depicted a French country fair. Underneath it, in neat italic printing, Bennett added a mock "proclamation" describing the recent meeting: Heyward and others were named in Frenchified fashion, along with such faux attractions as "Prince Guillaume Lala D'Allons" and "his famous troupe of fiery unrestrained alexandrines in bewildering poetic feats."

Heyward was excited about the new society and the widespread revival of interest in poetry in America. He enthusiastically set about his duties as secretary of the society, learning much about the profession of letters in the process. By contacting guest speakers, for example, Heyward maintained a profitable correspondence with many notable poets of the day.

Carl Sandburg, the popular balladeer and later biographer of Abraham Lincoln, headlined the February 1921 meeting, giving a reading and singing some of his own compositions for the guitar. Monroe spoke on "the new poetry" at the March meeting. Then, perhaps to balance these "radical" factions, Heyward brought in Jessie Rittenhouse, founder of the Poetry Society of America, to speak on "Modern English and American Conservative Poets" at the April meeting. At subsequent gatherings, Charlestonians heard a succession of distinguished literati: Robert Frost, John Crowe Ransom, Donald Davidson, Vachel Lindsay, Louis Untermeyer, Stephen Vincent Benet, Alfred Kreymbourg, and Henry Seidel Canby.

One poet who befriended the Charleston group was Amy Lowell, a woman often in search of protégés. The well-connected, cigar-smoking writer from Boston belonged to the same poetic dynasty as nineteenth-century versifier James Russell Lowell, and her brother was the current president of Harvard University. In a literary coup d'état, Lowell had recently usurped the leadership of the Imagist poetry movement from Ezra Pound and had earned a reputation in literary circles as a force to be reckoned with. She had met Allen earlier, and he quickly became one of her "students." After her lecture in Charleston in 1922, Lowell maintained a friendly interest in the careers of Heyward, Josephine Pinckney, and Beatrice Ravenel until her untimely death in 1925. Although not an avant-garde poet, Lowell experimented with free verse and polyphonic prose. The Charleston writers' admiration for her work suggests their measured interest in a kind of literary innovation that did not sacrifice traditional poetic techniques. Lowell also produced verse that, like that of the Charleston group, was heavily visual and sensual in nature.

Heyward's contacts with such established writers paid off. His name became associated with southern literature, and he began to publish poetry in prominent places. Among his best early poems are a series of verses with simple mountain folk as their subjects (later collected in his second book, *Skylines and Horizons* [1924]). These highly compressed poems evoke the hardship, loneliness, and isolation of such a life. Told from the point of view of a sympathetic outsider whose own fears are juxtaposed with the beauty and spontaneity he sees in the countryside, the poems were admired by no less an authority than Frost, who later came south to meet Heyward. In 1921, *Contemporary Verse* published what is probably Heyward's best early poem, "Gamesters All." By 1921, Heyward had a string of poetic successes to his credit. Monroe took "The Mountain Graveyard" for *Poetry,* and Ellery Sedgwick of the *Atlantic* accepted another, "A Yoke of Steers." "The Autumn" appeared in *Everybody's.*

This poem, Heyward's first treatment of the Negro, tells of a black man who is surprised by a white sheriff bursting in on an illegal craps game, then shot dead as he tries to flee. The speaker envies the black man's courage: "God! What a man!" the narrator comments, noting his "massive shoulders hunched, . . . / With head bent low, and splendid length of limb." The speaker is saddened by the thin illusion of "justice" in the actions of the sheriff, who dismisses the shooting as a "fair game" in which the black man was given a head start running away. Typical of Heyward's position, the poem does not rail against racial inequality, but it does implicitly condemn such a callous disregard for human rights. More important, it sympathizes with the humble craps shooter rather than with the white representative of the law, as a white southerner might be expected to do at this time. "Gamesters All" also suggests Heyward's feel for black speech rhythms and his interest in incorporating jazz and blues into poetry, as he would later do in such poems as "Jasbo Brown" and in *Porgy and Bess*. "Gamesters All" won the *Contemporary Verse* prize and was selected by another important editor-critic, African American William Stanley Braithewaite, for his annual verse anthology.

These early poems, for the most part conventional, contain glimmers of unconventional thinking about the South, glimmers that would brighten and widen into a more heterodox vision as Heyward's writings matured. In many ways, these works follow Mencken's prescriptions for a new southern litera-ture. They emphasize southern themes and subjects and are frankly sectional in focus. They critically reexamine established southern attitudes. And they are nonsentimental and realistic in their depiction of common folk, both white and black. In these poems one can see the inchoate ideas and attitudes developed in *Porgy*.

Although the Poetry Society took the majority of his free time, Heyward continued to write poetry. In 1921, he and Allen decided to collaborate on a volume of verse; the poems were to concern the landscape and history of the low country. In the early spring, Heyward left Charleston for his mountain cabin, Orienta, to write. From there, in May, he wrote to Bennett about his progress. It was "heavy sledding keeping studied stuff . . . from becoming self-conscious," he said, but he had "some live lines" that he thought were good. Heyward felt that the moment for a volume of regional poems was at hand. He exhorted Allen, "if we don't get over with this chance, we might as well trot to the junk yard. There will never be another chance like it." Re-garding his poem, "The Pirates," about the capture in Charleston of Stede Bonnet, Heyward found it difficult to sustain a lengthy narrative effort: "it is hard to keep it from reading like the old 'English History in Rhyme' that made a cynical poetry hater of me in my youth," he told Allen. The two men exchanged poems and critiques by mail and then submitted them to the scrutiny of "Hypercritic" Bennett. When Bennett told Heyward that two poems were "some of the best stuff" he "had ever put over," his pupil was elated. But Heyward was also prone to easy discouragement, and without a good word from Bennett he would quickly become disconsolate.

In fact, Heyward complained to Bragg that summer that both his life and his writing were at "loose ends," but this situation was remedied when Allen was invited to the MacDowell Colony, an artists' retreat in rural New Hampshire. The colony was run by the widow of American composer Edward MacDowell, who had bought the hilly and secluded sixty acres in 1896. Here, practitioners of the visual, literary, and musical arts could work in serene isolation, then gather at night for talk and diversion. Heyward, burdened by his office work and his mother's near invalidism, was attracted to the prospect of "hours and days of uninterrupted work." He thrilled to the idea of "stimulating intercourse" with first-rate authors and soon inveigled his own invitation.

Going to the colony was a pivotal moment in Heyward's life. The contrast between its rarefied intellectual atmosphere and his life as an insurance agent in Charleston struck him immediately. Although he was developing artistically and his Poetry Society work was circulating his name in the literary world, Heyward was still toiling in the hulks. Thus, after a few days at the colony, Heyward was greedily soaking up the artistic atmosphere like a man who had just come out of exile. He had been doggedly seeking this world of art for many years. Heyward shared a studio with Allen about three-quarters of a mile from the main house, Colony Hall. In the mornings they would run through the wet grass to breakfast there, shaking off the mud from their shoes as they went. Then it was back to the studio for a morning's labors. Lunch was brought to them in a picnic basket; after eating, they usually napped, worked until the late afternoon, and then took dinner at Colony Hall.

In the evenings the colonists gathered for talk, music, and other recreations. During these gatherings Heyward met his famous fellow lodgers. None of them resembled even the most liberal or artistically inclined Charlestonian Heyward knew. These people were, by contrast, rebels and bohemians. They opened Heyward's eyes to a new view of the calling of art. Among them was Max Bodenheim, for example, a poet and novelist whose dissolute lifestyle and flair for self-destructive behavior led Kreymbourg to call him "the yellow-haired child of melancholia." Equally notorious for scandalizing the conventional world was the beautiful poet Elinor Wylie. She so charmed Heyward that the young southerner became infatuated with her. (Word circulated back in Charleston that Heyward had been seduced by a "poetic vamp" who advocated "free love.") Heyward never chose to live the kinds of lives these artists did, but his fascination with such people probably accounts in part for his own mild "rebellion" later on, marrying a young actress-playwright, leaving Charleston, and becoming a novelist, for the most part, of the American Negro.

The MacDowell Colony also acquainted Heyward with people whose work would eventually push him away from poetry writing and toward fiction writing, folklore, and the popular arts. On hand that summer was Allan Nevins, a composer and music critic whose early experiments in wedding popular musical idioms to established forms anticipated Gershwin's work. Another colonist, Padriac Colum ("a poet of the real old bard type"), collected and translated Celtic mythology. Heyward also met Gilbert Seldes, then in the process of composing *The Seven Lively Arts* (1924), the first serious study of popular entertainment in America, and Constance Rourke, who, like Seldes, gave a prominent place to black folk music in her pioneering study, *American Humor* (1931).

Heyward's most important relationship was with Edwin Arlington Robinson, who had praised Heyward's mountain poems. Robinson, author of "Miniver Cheevy" and "Richard Cory," held a bitter and nihilistic view of humanity, quite unlike Heyward, but Robinsonian touches appear in Heyward's verse—the vocabulary and rhythm of ordinary speech, the portrayal of the mood of a season, the emphasis on individualism and self-reliance, and the empathetic depiction of human suffering and defeat.

The colony confirmed Heyward's belief that art was best produced as part of a group effort, the yield of a concerted effort by a community. Such was the basis of his fervor for the Poetry Society and its allied groups in Charleston and his involvement in the 1930s with conferences of southern writers. Moreover, the colony furthered Heyward's new view of writing as a profession rather than the old southern conception of literature as an avocation, another view embodied in Bennett. When Bennett came to the colony as Heyward's guest a year later, his presence showed Heyward the differences between the Peterborough artists and the Charleston group. Whereas Heyward was entranced by the colony's diverse environment, Bennett was soured by it. He wrote his wife of the "psycho-neurotic" Wylie and the sordidness of her "affairs." Of Robinson, Bennett wrote, "one sees negation in his very face, and his noncommittal affirmation of any positive belief in his very manner." Bennett's statements reflect the prevailing aesthetic of the Poetry Society, a taste for conservative, even "uplifting" verse, which contrasted with much modernist literature. Heyward subscribed to this view as well, but unlike Bennett he was receptive to the variety of arts that flourished at the colony.

The critical temper of the postwar era expressed itself in "little magazines"— *Pagany, Contact, Contempo,* and Monroe's *Poetry,* perhaps the most visible of the group. Many of these publications offered forums for the new poetry. All of them seemed at one time or another to print manifestos of aesthetic principles, declarations about what American poetry should and should not be. As a spokesperson for the new southern poetry, Heyward was invited by Monroe to coedit, with Allen, a special April 1922 issue of *Poetry.* The introductory essay, "Poetry South," is among the earliest documents of the southern renaissance. Heyward and Allen surveyed current southern poetry and made some predictions about its future. Artistic conservatism underlay virtually every idea in the article. Asserting the primacy of regionalism, Heyward and Allen derided "city-verse" as needlessly experimental. By extension, they thought the "sameness" and drabness of American cities compelled poets to find experimental or "alien" forms of expression. Heyward and Allen emphasized the southern past as the best possible material for southern poets, but they also suggested more unconventional topics. "The burning racial problem," for example, offered "a tremendous theme and a possible chance of legitimate propaganda for the present."

Nonetheless, in urging southern poets to use such material, Heyward and Allen everywhere emphasized caution: "The southern muse must be careful how she handles the tar-baby." Using the jazz idiom in southern verse (as Heyward had done in "Gamesters All") was compelling, but the force of tradition and the pull of "taste" still controlled him: "strong social and racial prejudices" might prevent the use of jazz, he asserted. Heyward also raised technical questions: how could one integrate the "choppy effects of syncopated rhythms" into the "intimate mood of memory and contemplation" that the South had to express? Yet Heyward was clearly intrigued by the potential of African American material: "the weird, the bizarre and the grotesque in Negro life and story, and the tone of the 'spiritual' will have to be reckoned with." These comments reveal a tension that undergirds much of Heyward's work. On the one hand, he desired to be in the vanguard of the literary arts, but on the other hand, he felt compelled as a Charlestonian to uphold the concept of "taste" in literature. "We will accept with modern spirit the new forms in verse," Heyward and Allen wrote, "but accept them as being valuable for their loosening effect upon the old rather than being all satisfactory in themselves." Such equivocation may explain why none of the Fugitives—not even Ransom, who had published one book of poetry—was represented in the selections.

Heyward returned to the MacDowell Colony in the summer of 1922. There he attended to the publication details of *Carolina Chansons* (as his and Allen's book was entitled) and eagerly awaited its November appearance. He continued to write verse, and through the happy conjunction of books and romance, he met his future wife, Dorothy Hartzell Kuhns. She was a fascinating woman, much advanced for her time. Her rise in the world of letters reveals much of the grim determination needed by women in the early twentieth century to succeed in male-dominated professions.

Dorothy had arrived at the colony fresh from George Pierce Baker's Workshop 47, the famous playwriting course at Harvard College that numbered among its graduates Thomas Wolfe (a classmate of Dorothy's) and Eugene O'Neill. She and Heyward were drawn to each other for many reasons, one of which was their physical frailty. Dorothy was thin, weak, and highly susceptible to illnesses, which would sometimes lay her out for weeks on end. Both were also used to caring for their sick families: Dorothy's father, mother, and grandfather were at different times invalided and had to be waited on by her. Both also had an innocence and childlike wonderment about them. Waifish and fragile-looking, they were so similar that they were often mistaken for brother and sister. In 1930, a journalist described them as "Hansel and Gretel lost in a wood, perhaps of their own making." In part their innocence accounts for their fascination with the Gullahs, about whom both would write in fiction and plays. Heyward and Dorothy were irresistibly drawn in by the customs and mythology of these African Americans, who were so foreign to the writers' experiences.

Dorothy had grown up in a large family in rural Ohio. She had a self-reliant streak in her that Heyward admired; it doubtless made him think of his mother and of Bragg. When Dorothy's father and mother died, she was shuttled off to live with one or the other of her six aunts (she tells of these experiences in her play, "The Cinderelative")—none in sympathy with her ambition to be a playwright. The suitor of one of these aunts, detecting a strong intelligence and ambition in Dorothy, enrolled her in the National Cathedral School in Washington, D.C. There, she lived with another aunt and uncle, the William Baylys. Mr. Bayly was in the diplomatic corps, and one of Dorothy's memories of living in the capital was going to visit Mrs. McKinley at the White House. These and other experiences gave Dorothy a cosmopolitanism that DuBose did not possess. But like her future husband, Dorothy was determined to be a writer—specifically, a playwright. She pursued her goal doggedly, and her ambitions grew.

"My memory does not go back far enough to a time when I did not intend to be a playwright," she wrote in an unpublished memoir. Although saddled with family responsibilities and the expectation of her small, provincial town that she would "simply stay home and be a good little housewife," she made her escape, enrolling in a playwriting course taught by Minor Latham at Columbia University's extension school. From there she took the advice of a friend, who said that if Dorothy wanted to be a playwright, she should learn the theater from the inside. Dorothy therefore landed a role as a chorus girl in an "embarrassing" Broadway musical. To the accompaniment of a song called "Button, Button," the chorus girls leaped on stage "in their scanties," carrying their dresses "in little suitcases," then ran down the aisle and sat "on the lap of some businessman" and asked them to help "button up" their dresses. Dorothy felt degraded. "I now shudder to think what my four uncles would have thought of their niece doing this, though they were all in favor of such a good show if they were to see it themselves," Dorothy later wryly observed. To her relief, she got bounced from the show.

In the summer of 1922 Dorothy arrived at the MacDowell Colony as a "fellow" from Baker's Workshop 47. She later recalled meeting Heyward: "As I took his hand I was conscious of its extreme thinness. I later learned that polio had left the upper part of his body affected; his hands were okay to write and lift, but not too heavy objects. Well-padded coats concealed the damage to his arms and chest." Heyward soon forgot his desires for "poetic vamps" and began pursuing Dorothy. This development displeased Allen, who thought that Dorothy would distract Heyward from writing. Out for a walk in Peterborough one evening with another colonist, Allen "shook his big head at the clouds" and said, "No more 'Mountain Graveyards' for Du-Bose," and was most solemn. On the contrary, however, Dorothy assisted Heyward in his work and stimulated his imagination in substantial new ways.

When Heyward returned to Charleston from Peterborough that fall, he again felt a letdown. But at least now he had Dorothy to confide in by letter. Their correspondence reveals a restlessness and an incipient antagonism toward the orthodoxies of life as a southern gentleman. Heyward began writing Dorothy as soon as he boarded the steamer. Still immersed in the life of the colony, he told Dorothy that, thankfully, there wasn't "a single Charleston shopkeeper on board," so he would not have to play the role of southern citizen that he had come to dislike. He later spoke of the insurance business as "the other side of my life" and complained of the difficulty of writing "an intelligent letter" at the office. "The Colony was grand. . . . [I]t is very hard to be thrown from that dream world into sharp realities, to compete with these human business machines." He also missed the atmosphere of freedom there: "there is nothing more hateful [than] the definite drag of an inflexible routine," he complained. Heyward recognized that as the culture of commercialism (land, oil, timber, tobacco) usurped the old agrarian ideals of his region, the New South was becoming awash in a riptide of boosterism that might undermine the emergence of the arts. Like Mencken and his apostles in Richmond and Chapel Hill, Heyward was beginning to react against the provinciality and ethnocentrism of southern cities.

Put back to work, he described himself as "broken to harness." And he was ashamed to find that he was treating people rudely because he was so unhappy with his life. Nonetheless, Heyward knew he had to earn a living, and the specter of success still haunted him: "I am trying autosuggestion every night now for business confidence and success and I hope it will make a hard-headed Shylock out of me," he cynically noted. On another occasion, he mischievously enclosed a poem torn from the pages of a popular magazine, "If Winter Comes," telling Dorothy facetiously, "in my amusements you see, I am the typical American." Heyward's patience with social obligations had also just about reached an end. In a revealing passage in *Mamba's Daughters*, Saint Wentworth, like Heyward, sees the superficiality of such an existence and realizes that his spirit has been hamstrung by the bonds of tradition and family: "What did clothes matter?—dances, girls, surfaces— what was the use of it all? . . . [T]he clothes, lying mutely before him, pulled against his mood and brought him back to . . . . the wreckage of the past" (122–23).

Heyward began to see that a break with the life of business and a plunge into the life of art was inevitable. To Dorothy, he portrayed his future optimistically ("Some day I shall not only know movie stars, but even actors—watch me"), and he saw Dorothy as an essential part of it: "I tell you all of this—I consult you about it, because it is very momentous. If I leave here, it is final. . . . What I would take with me in the way of income would be small. . . . In spite of the fact that you and I seem to be rather like characters in an Ibsen drama being jerked about by fate—and probably being led toward a most depressing curtain, I can't help hoping that things might break right one of these days and we might still like each other well enough to want to be together." Heyward felt like the true artiste—isolated, indifferent to all material concerns.

His ambitions swelled even as his bank account dwindled. Near Christmas, he lost his savings in a bad investment, but, he told Dorothy, "lest we grow despondent over mundane things, let us remember that the great desire of my life is to write real poetry, and it seems that in proportion to my stripping of worldly wealth I gain in artistic growth and recognition." Feeling some of the burdens of Poetry Society work, he resigned the secretaryship and felt "tons lighter." He could now do the "downright hard thinking" about his future that he had been contemplating since returning from the colony that summer.

Carolina Chansons: Legends of the Low Country was a great success. In the eight poems that Heyward contributed to the thirty-one in the volume, he aligns himself with poetic traditionalism rather than with the Imagists, futurists, and other vanguard movements. The philosophy undergirding the poems, the faithful depiction of the region, accords with the prevailing thinking of other Charleston artists. The manner of the poems resembles the rather sedate Georgian mode of such poets as Swinburne and Meredith, who typically depicted country lanes and cottages, apple and cherry orchards, rose-scented walks, and village inns. Such poems, usually inspired by nature, tended to emphasize a moral point and suggest an intensely intimate relation of the poet to the setting.

One detects this relationship in such poems as "Dusk," for example, the subject of which is Charleston itself. The poem resembles Smith's watercolors: in each there is a sense that the low-country landscape is represented exclusively in terms of the painter's or writer's feelings for the environment.

In "Dusk," Heyward emphasizes this relation with repeated personal pronouns contrasting poet and setting, "him" and "her":

> Hers is the stifled voice
> Hers are the eyes and the stir
> Of hidden music shaping all my songs,
> And these my songs, my all, belong to her.

Similarly, in "Silences," Heyward celebrates tradition in city's church bells and links the visitor's imagination with the true images of the Charleston's past. In all the poems Heyward's presence as a lover of legend is in evidence. Others draw on local lore and experiment with narrative. "The Last Crew," for example, concerns the efforts of a "fish-boat" submarine crew to sink the Union ship *Housatonic* during the Civil War.

In their preface, Heyward and Allen claim that the book's primary contributions to poetry lay in presenting these memories "in their natural matrix." The emotions generated by the poems can only occur in this regional context. But their claim that the verses are the southern counterparts of Frost's or Robinson's "New England" poems, that their regional settings, like those writers', "border on the void into the universal," is dubious. The poems lack the transcendent power of Frost's or Robinson's work. By excluding elements from their verse that might be inimical to the moods they were seeking, Heyward and Allen achieved those moods too easily and thus produced largely sentimental verse.

Nonetheless, Heyward and Allen assert (as in the earlier "Poetry South") that the cultural work of the Charleston group was a revolt against earlier forms of southern art. The Carolina poems are devoid of "condescending pity" and "nauseous sentimentality"—the character of most earlier southern poetry, according to Heyward. Moreover, the poems also break with the past in their straightforward presentation and insistence on historical authenticity. But for Heyward, regionalism—southernness—was literally a subject for poetry. For Frost and other poets who took their inspiration from a particular region, the principle was less a topic than an underlying attitude and a starting point for the exploration of universal human truths.

The more evocative—even reaching toward universal—poems are the two that Heyward wrote about Negroes. His thinking about blacks as a subject for art was maturing. In "Poetry South," he had asserted that using black folklore in verse was an attractive prospect but that poets had to be careful in handling the dialect, lest the "syncopated rhythms" of jazz disrupt the "intimate mood of memory and contemplation" that characterized southern poetry. Heyward would later find fruitful, innovative ways to incorporate the jazz idiom in his work, especially *Porgy and Bess.* In October 1923 he published a more sociological statement about the Negro in the *Reviewer,* a piece called "And Once Again—The Negro." Heyward thought the black man lived happily in an insular, self-contained world that was threatened by the do-gooder intentions of "civilizing" white Christians (a point to which he returned in his last book, *Star Spangled Virgin*). Such people did not understand that the black world had its own code, just as complete as that of the white world. Heyward mourned the loss of the Gullah world—hence the emphasis in these early poems and in *Porgy* on preservation—and looked on it "with wistful envy." He initially saw black primitivism as a last bulwark against progress and Puritan restraint. Although in later works his admiration for African Americans grew, and he eventually became more optimistic about the race's development, at this time he foresaw a "supreme tragedy" in their imminent "salvation."

In "Once Again" Heyward remarked of the fictional depiction of the black man, "I cannot see him as a joke. More certainly I cannot see him as a menace." That point of view informs "Gamesters All" and "Philosopher," the other Negro poem in *Carolina Chansons.* In "Philosopher" the speaker warns potential white reformers that imposing the white code on blacks is to stifle "the music" in their "shuffling feet" and, likewise, to plan out a "future" for blacks under a white system of ethics and behavior that is not necessary. Heyward would gradually revise this view as well: in *Porgy* he would accept the inevitability of the Negro's new position in the world and in so doing discover the ways in which black art could enrich a global, democratic artistic community. Later, in *Mamba's Daughters,* Heyward would recognize even more fully the changing times and prophesy that African Americans' art could propel them higher in the world than he had earlier thought possible.

Carolina Chansons pleased most reviewers, northern and southern, as evidence that a southern literary renaissance was underway. Enthusiastic notices came from Monroe in *Poetry,* Henry Bellaman in *Voices,* Beatrice Ravenel in the (Columbia, South Carolina) *State,* Henry Seidel Canby in the *New York Evening Post,* and Gerald Johnson in the *Greensboro Daily News.*

Johnson averred that the book could be given to anyone—"an educated northerner or . . . an Englishman" as evidence of the promise of southern writing—"Or [even] to H. L. Mencken." William Stanley Braithewaite sent Heyward a blurb to use in advertising, but—indicative of the less-than-progressive attitude of some of his fellow southerners—when Heyward innocently forwarded the comment to the editor of a regional paper, the latter declined to print it. It was "not advisable," the editor wrote Heyward, to print the comments of "a cullid gentleman, whatever his standing might be among the Cabots and the codfish" of New England.

The book's success increased Heyward's self-confidence, and he began to see himself as a spokesperson for a southern literary revival. By 1922, the Poetry Society was a recognized national leader in modern southern verse, exerting an influence that could be felt throughout the region. In January 1923 Heyward delivered the keynote address at the Poetry Society of America conference in New York, "determined to make a favorable impression for the south." The speech occasioned a flattering editorial in the *New York Times* that spoke of the "great awakening in southern letters." Heyward then decided to apply some of his entrepreneurial skills to advance the cause of southern poetry, querying his publisher, Macmillan, about compiling a southern literature anthology. Heyward unabashedly told his editor there that he was the only person for the job: "no one else in America has at his command the information regarding, and the friendship of the new southern poets that I have." Macmillan, however, declined.

As Heyward became more aware of his "status" as a writer, he yearned for wider recognition, beyond the South. The dichotomy between northern and southern literature could be seen in the differences between the Poetry Society and the MacDowell colonists. Heyward wanted to unite these twin halves of his artistic self, and in the spring of 1923 he thought he had happened on a way of doing it. The colony was in financial trouble, and Heyward began working on a plan for a colony of his own. He proposed to donate five acres of his North Carolina property on which to build ten cottages. Heyward's colony would be "in [the] hands of artists from [the] first," a purer environment of artists living and working as a community and thus a more intense "experience" than at the MacDowell Colony. Heyward wanted Peterborough regulars to "come down and meet southerners," so he could have his own Parnassus in the South. As it turned out, the Peterborough retreat was kept open. Nonetheless, Heyward's scheme suggests just how highly he valued the colony and how much he depended on it for his intellectual nourishment.

He continued to note the distance between Charleston and the colony in more than geographic terms when a series of crises beset the Poetry Society. They showed Heyward that if he continued to live in Charleston, his creative energies might be diverted from art and wasted in refereeing political disputes and ego-bruising squabbles within the society. The battles also show the limitations of the Poetry Society and suggest reasons for its diminishing importance to Heyward.

The first contretemps involved Fugitive poet Ransom when his "atheistic" poem, "Armageddon," won the Blindman Prize. Bennett thought the poem "no less than blasphemy" and told Heyward, "a small theological cyclone is brewing against printing it" in the yearbook. Heyward was less concerned about the poem's theology than about its potential to rend the fabric of community that he had established within the society: "after all," he wrote to Allen, "the society is a society, and we have been trying to make it so by giving a voice and a job to all who have shown interest." Mustering all his reserves of gentlemanly grace, Heyward offered a compromise solution: print the Blindman poem in a separate pamphlet, along with the honorable mention poem, a word about the judges, and a special note about the prize. "In this way we could present a number of copies to each of these people, which would be impossible with a year book. . . . The members need not read the poem, and we could send the pamphlet to a select number of our friends etc. and get it discreetly placed under proper eyes in the North. Or rather improper eyes—God bless them." The plan was approved, but Heyward took the episode hard: "I am very glad we are well out of the 'Armageddon' mess," he told Allen.

A second incident, less serious, concerned Janie, whom society members thought was benefiting unfairly by her son's position as a spokesperson for the group: her career giving dialect recitals of Gullah folktales was thriving. This time, Bennett was less restrained. He told Heyward flatly that he "must omit the item about [his] Mother's work" from the yearbook foreword. Bennett portrayed the society malcontents as people who could, if riled, throw up formidable obstacles to Heyward's career, but Heyward simply laughed at the matter, as he looked well beyond Charleston for his career. Heyward privately told his confidant, Allen, that he was "quite proud to be elevated to the dignity of having enem[ies]."

In early August, Bennett wrote Heyward of still more trouble. Jean Toomer, the Georgia-born poet who was soon to become a major figure in the Harlem Renaissance, had been a nonresident society member for some time, and Bennett had just learned that Toomer was African American. Bennett again predicted a potential catastrophe for the society. Toomer's *Cane,* a collage of stories, poems, and vignettes that addressed his conflicted southern heritage, would be published in the fall, and society members would learn that Toomer was not white. "Now, what is to be done?" Bennett asked Heyward. "Strike out the book-notice and expunge the name from the list of members?" Or, not renew Toomer's membership by stating that he "obtained such on false pretenses?" Perhaps Toomer "joined the society with the deliberate intention of starting trouble for us." Heyward evidently convinced Bennett of the egregiousness, or at least gentlemanly impoliteness, of expelling a paid member because of his skin color. Toomer's name remained on the roster; *Cane* was published without any discredit to the society. This incident, combined with the other imbroglios of that summer, distressed Heyward and pushed him farther from the group.

Specifically, it pushed him farther from Bennett. Signs of stress, impatience, and nervous agitation began to show in Bennett's letters to Heyward. Bennett was overwrought about getting the yearbook printed in a manner consonant with the grave importance that he attached to it. He justifiably began to feel that such work had been left to him, with no assistance from Heyward or Allen, who had, to his mind, abandoned Charleston for the sake of their careers. By the end of the summer, annoyance had accelerated to bathos; Bennett portrayed himself as a martyr to the cause of southern art. Speaking of the yearbook, he wrote Heyward, "I did . . . what appeared to me the best way to secure the end I was directed to secure. If it was not the best, I hold myself shriven, and exonerated. I did my damndest and gave a summer to it I had planned to spend with my broken family. Good-by, old man. I am not certain of seeing you again."

Although Bennett had inspired Heyward and guided him through his apprenticeship, the old man, like the old city to which Heyward had been bred, was becoming less relevant to Heyward's literary ambitions. Heyward soon realized that Bennett was not a very skilled writer. Later that year Heyward was to tell Allen, in a flash of bald honesty, that Bennett had suffered his "usual attack of cholera morbus over the year book; symptoms: great nervousness, violence, and a most disastrous running of beautifully done reams of copy. He made a seven page article of Activities of the Past Year, which he has signed, and which he swears cannot be cut a word. He had five pages of his own poetry in it: and under comment, his hat is off to about a hundred irrelevancies." Heyward saw that Bennett, with his training in printing, typography, and design, was more suited to working on the appearance of the yearbook than its contents. In early June, Bennett had written with pride to Heyward that he had drawn "a fine black-and-white decorated mediaeval initial" for the foreword and had directed him to begin the essay with the letter *P*—"for that's the letter I have done."

Heyward was realizing a truth that comes to many fledgling artists: eventually one may outgrow one's teacher. Bennett had stimulated Heyward's thinking and set him off on his journey of artistic self-discovery. Now Heyward was charting a different course, veering away from the calm waters of literary traditionalism that so characterized his sea-drinking city. Other worlds and other ways of thinking lay in the horizon. Heyward admired Bennett and truly loved Charleston, but they also embodied values that he could no longer uncritically embrace.

Chapter Three

Porgy

The Negro in the New South

LTHOUGH THE SOUTHERN RENAISSANCE is associated with the work of Faulkner, Wolfe, and the Fugitive-Agrarian poets, the actual movement began much earlier—in the late 1910s and early 1920s—with two much different types of writing: social realism, as practiced by Frances Newman, Elizabeth Madox Roberts, T. S. Stribling, and others, and Negro literature. Heyward's *Porgy*, published in 1925, belongs to both these classes of fiction. Such African Americans as James Weldon Johnson, in *Autobiography of an Ex-Colored Man* (1912), and Jean Toomer, in *Cane* (1922), explored the Negro world when the South was taking its first halting steps toward racial justice. Heyward's *Porgy* was the only major work by a white writer to delve deeply into the southern black experience. It set in motion a series of social inquiries and fictional explorations that would eventually make the dynamics of race relations and the racial burden of history the most significant theme of modern southern literature.

Heyward's Negroes differ from those of later southern fiction, however. The Gullah inhabitants of Charleston face the dilemma of being new inhabitants of a new social order, created sui generis from the welter of Reconstruction politics. They are also, like their white Charleston neighbors at the time, bound by class and are upholders of their own set of cultural traditions. As a novelist Heyward speaks as a sympathetic but ultimately perplexed white man seeking answers to the "Negro problem." However, Heyward was also moving toward more liberal positions—writing social criticism, distancing himself from Charleston, lecturing as an outlet for testing new ideas, and marrying the decidedly outspoken Dorothy Kuhns.

Heyward had continued to pine for Dorothy throughout the summer of 1923. In late August she visited Heyward at the MacDowell Colony when her summer job as a camp counselor in Maine ended. Heyward proposed to her almost immediately. In so doing, Heyward bucked convention. A liberal-minded woman, Dorothy had some difficulty gaining acceptance by Heyward's friends. Mrs. MacDowell, for example, equated Dorothy's weak constitution with a weak mind and spirit—a gross misreading of Dorothy's character—and told Heyward that his life would be spent tending to the sickly Dorothy, whom Mrs. MacDowell thought would be wheelchair bound in just a few years.

Heyward decided to marry in a Manhattan chapel rather than arrange a ceremony in Charleston commensurate with his name and social position. This move must have irked his acquaintances there and probably disappointed Janie, too. Dorothy recalled that when she arrived in Charleston, the community was sociable to her, but she did not feel welcome for many years. She sensed the community's silent disapproval of her—a "career woman," someone involved with the theater (a profession of suspect legitimacy) and a nonsoutherner. Marrying Dorothy was therefore a strong indicator of Heyward's resolve to create a new identity.

It was a heady moment for Dorothy, too. Her workshop play, *Nancy Ann*, won Harvard's Belmont Prize, edging out Thomas Wolfe's *Welcome to My City*, a play about a small town's opposition to Negro rights. With the five hundred dollar award came a guaranteed Broadway production. Dorothy thus had to rush back to Cambridge to collect the award; not wanting to be separated at so momentous a time in their lives, she and Heyward flouted convention and rode the same night train to Boston.

These were busy days. Macmillan had just accepted a second volume of Heyward's poetry, *Skylines and Horizons;* Dorothy was commuting between Charleston and New York while her play was in rehearsal; and Heyward embarked on a southeastern lecture tour in December 1923 and January 1924. The tour was a natural progression from his appearances at Poetry Society meetings, and it was an easy way to make good money. He wrote a basic lecture, "Contemporary Southern Poetry," and gave it, with only minor variations, at some fifty engagements that year. Heyward's ideas at this point had not developed much beyond what he had said in "Poetry South." In the lectures, he declared that an "epoch-making" revival of the arts was under way in the South. The new southern poetry was innovative in departing from "the 'thee' and 'thou' cant of 50 years ago" by stressing sincerity and simplicity in its treatment of themes. Heyward did not like the current experimentation in "city poetry," and again he cautioned against using jazz as a poetic idiom: for the southerner to attempt to portray the black man "in the broken rhythm of syncopation would be only travesty," Heyward thought. He concluded his lecture with readings from the work of William Alexander Percy, Robert Frost, and others as well as a scattering of his own poems.

Audiences were drawn to Heyward in part because of the unassuming figure he presented: he seemed not a poet at all but merely a member of the solid citizenry, someone whose statements about the importance of art had the ring of common sense and strong knowledge about them. Gerald W. Johnson, then on the staff of the *Greensboro Daily News* and soon to become one of the South's keenest culture watchers, described Heyward as "indistinguishable from an insurance agent, except by the fact that he wears a dress coat carelessly, and not as if it carried the weight of the sins of the world." Johnson continued, "this species of protective coloring is a matter of some importance, because his mission is the introduction of poetry as the avocation of a man, and not merely a pretty accomplishment for calf-lovers and gal-children." Johnson noted that what the philistines needed was not a "missionary" but a "prophet who will come upon them filled with wrath"—in other words, another Mencken. Johnson thought that Heyward had the makings of "a modern Ezekiel" when his poetry turned to such subjects as "a mountain woman, or a Negro murdered casually," but when Heyward presented his views on art, Johnson heard only "soft words" that did little "to convince the south that poetry is a lethal weapon."

Johnson's remarks reveal the differences between the early Heyward, just awakening to the possibilities for social criticism in the South, and more liberal-minded writers, like the Chapel Hill circle to which Johnson belonged. A little later, Johnson wrote Heyward directly to ask him if what he was doing with his evangelistic message of poetry merely as beauty and spiritual uplift was but offering jewels, silks, and furs to "a pauperized section." Heyward rebutted with another question: wasn't Johnson asking too much of a poetry group by requiring it "to *civilize* (to use a term of Mencken's) an entire section of the country?" Eventually, Heyward and Johnson would be united in their goal of promoting a southern cultural revival. Their sharp differences early on made possible a beneficial exchange of ideas, which led to Heyward's "conversion."

Heyward may not have shaken the rafters with prophecies and lamentations, but his congenial evangelizing for southern poetry was successful. Newspapers throughout the region heralded his appearance as the advent of the "Missionary Poet" and devoted many column inches to a description of Heyward's goals for southern writing. Chief among these ideas was that poetry should be a participatory, democratic activity rather than an isolated, elitist, and aesthetically ambitious undertaking—a great contrast to the ethos of modernism. The lectures also increased Heyward's contacts; his connection to Johnson, for example, led him into correspondence with Howard W. Odum, editor of the newly established *Journal of Social Forces,* a major forum in the South for Mencken's doctrine. The lectures also fulfilled Heyward's desires to act, since the lecture arena was a kind of surrogate theater and his readings dramatic interpretations of scenes and ideas. Most important, the lectures gave him a feeling of independence, of a world outside Charleston where he could earn a living as an author.

In the spring of 1924, Heyward made the most daring move of all. He decided to give up his business and devote full time to writing. He had an idea for a novel—southern in theme but different in significant ways from typical southern fiction. Dorothy helped push Heyward in this direction, but for some time he had been contemplating the question of the Negro's status in the modern world. Moreover, Heyward equated the prospect of artistic liberation and a plumbing of his social conscience with the unfettered spirit he had glimpsed among the Gullahs—what Janie had earlier seen and shown her young son. In his *Reviewer* essay on the Negroes, Heyward had written of his envy at this spirit. "In an ideal civilization," he mused, "a man should expend but half of his power to secure the necessities of physical existence, and devote the remainder of his time to the realization and enjoyment of life." Heyward now felt that the time was right to break with the old order. Heyward was truly taking a gamble, because he had little money and no guarantee of success.

"Not a breath of this to a soul," he wrote to Hervey Allen, "but my bonds are loosening. . . . I think Dorothy and I can make a go. In the words of the Negro spiritual, 'My soul so happy til I can't sit down.' " When John Bennett heard the news, he was "fair knocked . . . speechless," concerned that with Allen gone and now Heyward also leaving, the Poetry Society would founder. "Am I left holding the bag?" he asked Allen. "La renaissance est fini," Allen sardonically replied. There was also the question of "allegiance." Many Charlestonians feared that Heyward had "flung Charleston overboard" for good, and Heyward had to reassure them that he would not stray "from my region." "I know too little about anywhere else," he wrote to one friend.

Heyward was not being disingenuous, but when he announced that he was writing "a novel of contemporary Charleston," his acquaintances probably envisioned a drawing-room comedy or tale of southern manners, perhaps on the order of *An Artistic Triumph*. This type of fiction, however, was far from Heyward's mind. Instead, he envisioned a folk novel about the Charleston Gullahs—a world quite separate from the "civilized" white community. This alien and exotic subculture would be shown to have its own beliefs, social values, and economic structure. It would be also presented in a straightforward manner. Heyward saw African Americans as simply human beings—different in their behavior and thinking from whites—but not like the ignorant lackeys of earlier, sentimental southern writing, like that by Thomas Nelson Page and other apologists for the Old South. As Heyward later said, "I grew to see the primitive Negro as neither a professional comedian, nor an object for sentimental charity, but a racially self-conscious human being, living out his destiny beside us, and guided by a code." In the homogenous culture of Catfish Row, Heyward presents a people whose lives are mainly untouched by the realities of the world beyond the harbor. They accept their destiny, although they are not defeatists. They find happiness in community, vibrant and intense. They view the white world as remote and close ranks on those few occasions when it "threatens" their self-contained world.

The idea for this novel had occurred to Heyward at least five years earlier when he noted a newspaper article about a local black man named Samuel Smalls, "a cripple . . . familiar to King Street, with his goat and cart." "Goat-cart Sammy," as he was known, had been charged with allegedly shooting one Maggie Barnes. Smalls had been "up on a similar charge some months ago," according to the report, and received a suspended sentence. The beggar had "attempted to escape in his wagon, and had been run down and captured by the police." This incident took place many blocks north of where Heyward eventually located Catfish Row, a crowded Negro tenement called "Cabbage Row" in the heart of the city. (Heyward also took details from similar structures along the waterfront.) Heyward clipped the article and later fashioned a story around it. Curiosity about the Negro race drove him: "What, I wondered, was the unique characteristic . . . that endowed them with the power to stir me suddenly and inexplicably to tears or laughter; when the chaste beauty of the old city created by my own people awakened a distinctly different and more intellectual sort of delight? What was the mysterious force that for generations had resisted the pressure of our civilization and underlaid the apparently haphazard existence of the Negro with a fundamental unity?"

Heyward thrilled to the excitement of peeking in on this alien life: "What was the quality in a spiritual sung in the secrecy of some back room that brought the chance listener up short against the outer wall with a contraction of the solar plexus, and lachrymal glands that he was powerless to control?" As he wrote the novel, he imaginatively immersed himself so deeply in this other life that he at one point wrote to Allen of being "obsessed with the material": Heyward had driven so hard at writing during the previous two days "that last night my head almost blew off, and I have had to lay off it today." For a time Heyward worried that he could not pull off this feat. He described the book to Bennett as "so experimental" that he was merely "feeling it out." But eventually Heyward felt that he had "closed [his] hands about something alive. . . . The Spirit of God has been perched on the studio gable for a month, and where the stuff came from else, I can't imagine. . . . I am pretty drunk over it now." He called the novel *Porgo*, after the crippled black beggar who was its protagonist.

After a summer's work Heyward completed a draft, which he showed to Bennett. Allen had worried that Heyward would fall "into the error of writing from the undiluted, unchanged point of view of the defensive Southerner." But when Bennett read the manuscript, he was "instantly struck" by its novelty—"by the absolutely unexampled newness of its outlook upon the southern Negro as subject." "There had never been anything like it," Bennett later recalled, comparing its heavily visual aspect to a genre painting by Teniers. Charleston buzzed with gossip about Heyward's book, and Bennett privately wondered what the city's "select" would do when they realized that "their own beloved Poet" had produced a "radical . . . novel on Negro Life."

Bennett also secured a publisher for Heyward. John Farrar, a senior editor at George H. Doran, gave a Poetry Society lecture in December, which Heyward could not attend. At lunch the next day Bennett described Heyward's novel to Farrar as an innovative portrayal of African American life by a southerner. Farrar took the manuscript with him to read. Heyward knew nothing of this event; he knew only that unless he found a publisher, he would run out of money and have to resume selling insurance. Allen had even started taking up a collection—an "author's fund"—so that Heyward could keep writing. But in a scene worthy of the richest southern melodrama, Farrar read the manuscript, loved it, and offered Heyward a contract. Heyward was more than a little astonished: "I do guess it will really be a go with them," he told Allen. "God knows how I happened to do it. I don't."

As might be expected, success changed Heyward. It altered his relationship with Charleston and with the Poetry Society. With *Porgy* accepted for fall publication, Heyward began considering topics for new books, and they all were unorthodox in their own ways. One concerned Charleston's involvement in the politics leading up to the Civil War—what would eventually be published in 1932 as *Peter Ashley*—but he was more interested in "contemporary tragedies": "I have a seed in my insides somewhere that wants me to come through in a contemporary story of white and black," he told Allen. It might "drive me from my door step here, but it will not go altogether unnoticed elsewhere." This novel would be published four years later as *Mamba's Daughters*, one of Heyward's most admirable works. But Heyward needed time for reflection and development before this story could take shape.

He was not to have it. Still worried about money, he arranged an extended lecture tour through May, hoping thereby to "clean up enough to keep the wolf on the next door-step for a while" and to try out some new ideas on southern writing. In these fresh lectures, Heyward said that the South now tended toward "group development," Charleston being the prime example of such a trend. Heyward also remarked on the Fugitives, pointing out that their "group plan" differed from the Charlestonians' in that the former group strived for "wider recognition" as a body than as individual poets—another sign, perhaps, that Heyward was separating himself from the

Poetry Society. He added more talks to his growing repertoire: "New England Contemporary Poets," "Art in Relation to Life," "Tendencies in the
Modern Novel," and "The Negro as Subject for Art in Literature." His scope
and purposes had widened. He now surveyed the field of letters nationally
and publicized *Porgy;* the Poetry Society was less prominent in his remarks.
Dozens of speaking engagements as far north as New York and as far west as
Ohio kept Heyward on the move, but racing around the country at fire-truck
speed was not his idea of authorship: "I am not a poet who enjoys the sound
of his own voice," he told Allen. "[I]s it worth while doing all this . . . stuff
for publicity? Do other important people do it?"

When Heyward got some breathing room, he took stock of his plans and
commitments as well as caught up on correspondence with people he had
not seen much of lately, like Bennett. Heyward casually wrote Bennett that
they needed to "talk over" Poetry Society plans. Bennett shot back testily
that he had been "trying to talk Poetry Society plans with you for some
months without success." And to Heyward's blithe suggestion that Bennett
"find some sacrificial lamb" to be the next president, the latter retorted that
Heyward should find one himself. Bennett then added, "you may think that
I do not mean it. Please understand that I mean every word of it. I am sick
unto death of carrying other peoples' affairs. . . . You say I take my responsibilities too seriously. I have at last come, to whatever position I occupy and
to whatever small reputation I have managed to secure, by taking my responsibilities seriously all my life, and I am afraid at sixty years it is too late to
teach an old dog new tricks." Thus began Heyward's eventual break with
Bennett.

That year, Heyward closed his accounts for good by resigning from office
in the Poetry Society. As for his old mentor, Heyward did not understand
the earnestness with which Bennett regarded the Poetry Society. Bennett
had shepherded it through difficult times since Heyward's and Allen's depar-
tures: he paid speakers and yearbook costs himself, presided at meetings,
and played ombudsman and soothed hot tempers during numerous disputes.
Heyward had recognized the thanklessness of such jobs, which is why he
fled them. The previous summer he had told Bennett that to get people to
help him, he would have to "go forth in the night time with a can of ether, a
black jack, and a pair of good hand-cuffs." Now Bennett had been left alone
to do such difficult tasks.

Bennett must also have been angry at Heyward for not sufficiently appreciating his efforts on behalf of *Porgy*. Not only had Bennett sold the novel to Farrar, but during February (while Heyward was again away lecturing) Bennett had painstakingly reviewed the manuscript "from head to tail," putting in punctuation and correcting Heyward's spelling. Bennett had also helped publicize the novel in Charleston. Heyward responded by telling Bennett that he simply could not "earn a living out of literature" in Charleston and that the time had come "to face an inevitable situation": "we have a society there that will be willing to go on a permanent basis as a literature society which will bring three or four lecturers a year, and stage the usual receptions." He admitted that it was "heart-breaking to feel the driving power that we put behind the constructive [part now] flagging, but we might as well realize that that part of it did not amount to a tinker's damn except to a few devoted souls." Heyward correctly saw the Poetry Society as an amateur effort that had accomplished its goal of stimulating the arts in Charleston. Past his apprenticeship, Heyward now saw (like Allen and later Josephine Pinckney) that he needed to go elsewhere. Heyward was a relatively young man whose trajectory would be meteoric. Bennett, in contrast, was an older man who was losing a lifeline to some of the most significant work of his career. Nonetheless, Heyward felt somewhat more guilty about the society's disintegration than he let on to Bennett. He wistfully wrote to Laura Bragg, "What will become of the poor old Poetry Society? 'Mudder less Chillen have a hahd time when mudder is dead.' Apparently."

Bennett had been a father figure to Heyward and had given him a goal and a sense of direction. Unfortunately, Bennett was also easily agitated and was oversensitive, making him insecure and sometimes obsessive about friendships—personality traits that annoyed Heyward. While vetting Heyward's manuscript of *Porgy*, Bennett wrote to his daughter that in looking back on his life he was "bitterly indignant at the injustice of the world . . . and the strange unkindness of those whom I had thought my friends." Bennett's letters to Heyward after the latter had left Charleston sound calculated to induce guilt, like the rhetoric of a disappointed parent or a jilted lover. This pressure from Bennett and the somewhat claustrophobic atmosphere of the old city surely contributed to Heyward's decision to loosen his ties to Charleston, as did Heyward's recognition of the contrast between the Poetry Society and the MacDowell Colony as well as other arts communities.

Most off-putting to Heyward was the hermetic life of abnegation that Bennett lived. It is ironic that Bennett's energetic immersion in the ways of the Gullahs had produced a different effect in him than the same immersion had produced in Heyward and his mother. Rather than being drawn into a vital world of intense feeling and community values, Bennett regressed into a narrow space marked by pedantry and self-absorption, like a scholar whose life's work is suddenly nullified by someone else's research. Heyward and his mother survived the sometimes stultifying environment of Charleston because they imaginatively transmuted their existences into the Gullah world of redemption and faith. They crossed over; Bennett did not.

What of the Poetry Society? What was its effect on Heyward's artistic education? A way to find out is to compare it to its more famous literary cousin, the Fugitive group. Both circles sought to identify elements that were traditionally theirs as southerners, and both sought to preserve them. Both groups wrote as a corrective to contemporary cultural fragmentation. Both groups protested the abandonment of a social ideal in which, as John Crowe Ransom wrote, humans and nature "seem to live on terms of mutual respect and amity." And both groups said they were in revolt against the old—a lyric South of the former century satisfied with things as they were, a South concerned only with beauty and emotional ecstasy almost to the exclusion of anything like reality. The difference between the Charlestonians and the Fugitives lay in their views of the function of poetry in the wider world.

The Fugitives proposed to create a community in which the high arts would not be limited to a cultivated intellectual minority group but available to all. Yet the group produced intellectualized, highly specialized writing for what was at least initially a very small audience of like-minded individuals. Heyward and the Poetry Society, conversely, were expansive in their methods and aims. Their aesthetic orientation could be described as Pre-Raphaelite or late Ruskinian. Their goal was not to dissociate themselves from the community by cloistering themselves in a tower of art. By contrast, they thought that it was essential to remain connected to the culture that produced them and that only by participating in that environment could one develop a sensitive awareness of the past and create a feeling of stability in the flux of a changing world.

Moreover, the Poetry Society was driven by civic activism to enfranchise a wide community of readers. They used the word *society* in its widest possible sense. Pinckney, writing in 1930 about the group's origins, noted that its founders conceived of the organization as having "a double function; it was to be a forum and a studio," and since poetry had always had its way to make with the general public, the society sought to bring to the platform poets and critics with important things to say. The yearbook presented to the public a record of the year's poetic achievements. The group had a strong sense of poetic imperialism as well, to carry the good word about art to the hinterlands. Heyward spoke to poetry groups around the country; on an excursion abroad, Bennett spoke on poetry to the Rotary Club of Manila and to the Young Men's Club of Nagoya, Japan. Finally, unlike the Fugitives, the Charlestonians did not intend to produce poets. "Poets are made by other processes, and poetry will out regardless of societies," Pinckney wrote.

The Charleston group also included a large number of women, and, unlike the Nashville group, which worked in ivory-tower isolation, it was oriented toward communality, collaboration, and education. Heyward collaborated, in part or in whole, with Bennett and Allen on the yearbook contents, with Allen on *Carolina Chansons,* and with Dorothy and many others on plays, fiction, film, even children's literature, and, of course, *Porgy and Bess.* The theater, in particular, presented art as a public, communal experience. Also unlike the Fugitives, the Charlestonians were interested in salvaging the best parts of an intact tradition, one against which they had little desire to rebel for the mere sake of rebelling, and forge something vital from equal parts of old and new. The Fugitives believed that southernness should manifest itself as "an underlying attitude of mind and heart." Heyward and his fellow Charlestonians, conversely, employed southern landscapes, people, and history only as poetic subject matter. Further, the Fugitives used a poetic vocabulary that conveyed subtle connotative distinctions. They were adept at nuance and indirection, interested in the concrete properties of words for presenting intellectual abstractions. Heyward's diction, in contrast, was effusive, purposefully abstract. Like his predecessors Lanier and Poe, he tended toward abstract beauty rather than truth. In sum, the Charleston group sought to make art accessible to the community that inspired it—the precise target of Mencken's blast. The flourishing of the Poetry Society in its early years sent a signal to the South that a literary renaissance was possible. As Bennett said, "Our great work has been . . . breaking the ice for an extended movement to appreciation [of poetry] throughout the south . . . and establishing the practice of verse-making as a sturdy pursuit."

The Charlestonians' verse is inferior to that of the Fugitives; it lacks the universality of the latter's best work. Yet while the poetry Heyward produced never rivaled the mature work of Ransom, Tate, and others, Heyward's self-appointed mission as educator and bringer of light laid the groundwork for the South to develop a flourishing literary environment. And most important, *Porgy* did signal a break with the past in its depiction of African Americans. This interest of Heyward's was a subject that hardly occurred to the Nashville group.

In August 1925 in the *New York Herald-Tribune*, Heyward received a review that he probably regarded as prescient. It praised not his verse but rather his piece for the *Reviewer*, "And Once Again—The Negro." The *Tribune* writer noted that the best poetry seemed to be coming from Tennessee, and that Charleston, once the most visible poetic center, was now lagging. It is unlikely that this dismissive statement bothered Heyward very much. As excerpts from *Porgy* appeared in the *Bookman* that fall, Heyward's imagination had clearly shifted from the private passions of lyric poetry to a different kind of feeling—the intensity of story, as it was employed by the Gullahs. Like his mother before him, Heyward had crossed over from the world of history, the overdetermined, narrow world of Charleston—of place and name—into the world of story, wherein such elements were replaced by a deeper, more genuine awareness of community and self.

Published in September 1925, *Porgy* was a national best-seller, hailed as a giant step forward in the depiction of American Negro life. Heyward's story of a crippled black beggar and the woman he comes to love and to lose during one summer of passion and violence is moving in its simplicity. Porgy falls in love with Bess, the abandoned lover of Crown, a wanted murderer. Porgy and Bess find true contentment in their life together, until Crown returns to reclaim his woman. Porgy kills Crown and is protected from the police by Maria, a fellow resident of Catfish Row, but Porgy later foolishly runs from the police when he sees a buzzard, which he interprets as an evil omen. Porgy is then arrested and jailed for ten days, and while he is in custody Bess is lured away by a nefarious acquaintance of Crown's named Sportin' Life, who plays on Bess's weakness for "happy dust," or cocaine.

She goes off with him to Savannah. When Porgy is released by the police, he finds that he has lost Bess. As the novel closes, he sits in "an irony of sunlight," a figure of tragic pathos, defeated.

Porgy was lavishly praised by critics in both the North and the South. James Southall Wilson, writing in the *Virginia Quarterly Review,* said, "No more beautiful or authentic novel has been published in America for a decade." For the first time in America, Wilson wrote, a white writer had created "a real negro, not a black-faced white man." Porgy "thinks as a negro, feels as a negro, lives as a negro. White men enter his life only as his life touches theirs; not as their lives touch his." In previous fiction, Wilson wrote, the Negro existed "as part of the white man's life" and was shown "in his relations with the dominant race to point a moral or prove a purpose." Heyward, "with all the sympathy of a poet," created "a real man as he lives within his own race." Most telling, Wilson noted that in *Porgy* Heyward "gave freedom to the negro's soul in the region of art," where the white man had also held "dominion over him."

Similarly, the *New York Times* noted that the novel was a "sympathetic and convincing interpretation of Negro life by a member of an 'outside' race": "The white world but vaguely impinges upon [the black characters'] absorptions, their sorrows, their tragedies." In his column, "It Seems to Me," Heywood Broun wrote that he was fully prepared for "another of those condescending books about fine old black mammies and the like," but instead found a serious and unpatronizing treatment. Heyward, he wrote, found "Negro life more colorful and spirited and vital than that of the white community," and if the two races don't mix, he added, "it may well be the Nordic who lags." Emily Clark, Jay B. Hubbell, Herschel Brickell, Frances Newman, Addison Hibbard, and many others echoed these judgments. And, although Mencken did not review the book, it certainly conformed to his oft-stated belief that folk literature and the depiction of Negro life was a way the South could rescue itself from artistic oblivion.

In Charleston the novel was a qualified success: Charlestonians were proud of their native son for bringing national fame to the city. If the novel happened to tweak some residents' sensibilities, they politely ignored such issues in public and talked about only the less controversial elements of the book. Heyward heard the range of his neighbors' reactions from Bennett: one was "delighted"; another began it "with apprehension and doubt"; still others thought "the paper was wasted on which it was writ!" But the consensus was that *Porgy* was "a book of most uncommon quality and power." Those troubled by the novel expected the characters to be white, not black. Dorothy recalled that everyone thought Heyward, as a gentleman of Charleston, would write about white Charlestonians, and if he did depict African Americans, they would be one-dimensional, their "dearest concern . . . the welfare of their white folks." "Coming out of Ohio," Dorothy recalled, "I saw nothing strange in DuBose's deep interest in understanding and respect for the Negro. Looking back, however, he seemed something of a phenomenon."

Heyward was looked on with suspicion in certain quarters of the old society to which he had been bred. Some thought Heyward had chosen to write about African Americans simply to get attention. Yates Snowden, a professor at the University of South Carolina and a friend of Heyward's, thought the novel was brilliant but was "wild" for Heyward write about people from the upstate, "Pinopolis folk . . . WHITE," with his "fine vein of irony and tenderness." Bennett, too: if Heyward came back to Charleston occasionally, he might "find it quaintly interesting": he might then find his way clear "to do a book about our amusing Caucasians."

Porgy represented what in an essay published earlier that year Heyward called a "new note in southern literature," a catalyst that he hoped would revitalize southern writing and propel it into the modern age. The innovation, he said, circumspectly forecasting his intentions in *Porgy*, was presenting a "psychologically true . . . picture of contemporary southern Negro life." Heyward claimed that such a picture would at least have "the virtues of honesty and simplicity" and would leave "an authentic record of the period that produced it." Heyward was thus striving for a degree of verisimilitude in depictions of black life that, prior to *Porgy*, had been largely absent from southern literature.

It is instructive to consider *Porgy* in the context of the development of southern literature, particularly in the mosaic of the early southern renaissance. The movement had begun in 1921–22 with the little magazines and the critical spirit they embodied in Richmond, New Orleans, Nashville, and Charleston. By 1925, when *Porgy* appeared, Heyward probably seemed to most observers of the emerging southern literary scene to be the most promising figure. Ransom was only just beginning to publish poetry, and among fiction writers the only southerner gaining significant notice was Elizabeth

Madox Roberts, whose *The Time of Man* was published to great acclaim in 1924. James Branch Cabell and Ellen Glasgow, leaders of the advance guard in Richmond, were aging. New Orleans and Chapel Hill had not yet produced major authors, although Paul Green's play *In Abraham's Bosom* would appear in 1926. Thus, Charleston and Heyward seemed the leaders of the southern literary awakening. Three characteristics of the movement in its early phase stand out: much of the fiction was social realism; women artists were a significant presence; and the Negro was a subject.

Negroes of the southern renaissance differed dramatically from their fictional predecessors. In colonial literature Negroes were presented as noble savages, like Native Americans, equipped with the requisite Christian virtues. In antebellum literature Negroes emerged as humble peasants or loyal body servants. (Even abolitionist literature perpetuated the Negro stereotypes of prewar southern writing—characters not truly human, although capable of salvation.) The southern poets Sidney Lanier and Irwin Russell in the 1870s had written passable dialect verse with black speakers, but even Russell's laudable 1878 poem, "Christmas-Night in the Quarters," with its metrical polish and accurate conception of Negro speakers and singers, nonetheless evinced no deep understanding of African Americans, only a feeling for a pastoral concept of a simple peasantry. Thomas Nelson Page's bestselling stories and novels of the 1880s were apologias for the plantation ideal. His black characters authenticated a version of the pastoral, the Old South as tragic Eden. Joel Chandler Harris's tales of Uncle Remus, which debuted in 1876, were an advance in literary depictions of blacks. This character, tricky and sly, never depends on whites for his identity and in fact uses slave folklore to subvert the ideals of the white planter society. Yet in many ways Harris's tales nonetheless idealize the old order, and Uncle Remus is not a multidimensional, fully realized character, only a mouthpiece for Harris's wry satire. At the center of such traditions were blacks as simple, rustic characters—folk figures—the only marginally favorable aspect of this stereotype. *Porgy*, therefore, could arguably be said to be the first psychologically true depiction of an African American by a white southerner.

Part of the impulse that animates *Porgy* derived from the preservation movement in Charleston in the early 1920s. Tourists discovered the old city, seemingly untouched by time, on their way to Florida during the great real-estate boom there in the 1920s or as an alternative to Europe, closed off since the war. Heyward memorializes the "old" Charleston in the opening paragraph of the novel, where he announces that Porgy "lived in the Golden Age," an age "that never existed except in the heart of youth," and "an age when men, not yet old, were boys in an ancient, beautiful city that time had forgotten before it destroyed" (11). In much of *Porgy*, Heyward writes as a memorialist for this older way of life. While the novel does depict African Americans in a nonsentimentalized way, Heyward does not propagandize for the "new Negro" in a new social order. Just as he wishes that the old Charleston could be preserved indefinitely, he is dubious about African Americans' chances for survival in the modern age. At the time, Heyward thought that African Americans were the unfortunate victims of freedom. In places the novel suggests this lapsarian view of history: in the movement from agrarianism to industrialization (or woods to town), blacks move from the natural world into an artificial society controlled by whites. Heyward had made this point in "And Once Again—The Negro," in 1923. He wrote that African Americans were "blissfully oblivious of the impending advancement that [was] being prepared for them by their solemn and consecrated white neighbor." "Are they an aeon behind, or an aeon ahead of us?" Heyward wondered. "Who knows? But one thing is certain: the reformer will have them in the fullness of time. They will surely be cleaned, married, conventionalized. . . . Their instinctive feeling for the way that leads to happiness . . . will be supplanted by a stifling moral straightjacket" (41, 42). Heyward situates Porgy and the other inhabitants of Catfish Row in this pivotal historical moment, between slavery and a "free" white world for which, as the opening epigrammatic poem of the novel suggests, they are not yet prepared:

> Now in your untried hands
> An instrument, terrible, new,
> Is thrust by a master who frowns,
> Demanding strange songs of you.

To Heyward, Negroes were in danger of losing those innocent virtues that the modern white world no longer possessed.

Heyward was unique in this literary venture. A similar impulse animates the work of Julia Peterkin, who wrote of life among the Gullahs in the South Carolina plantations. Heyward's characters, however, convey a larger sense of the exotic and the heroic than do Peterkin's, and ultimately, although

Porgy is not a work of social protest, Heyward was concerned with social change more than was Peterkin. Another novel by a white southerner that broke with stereotype was *Birthright* (1922), by Tennessean T. S. Stribling. Unlike Heyward, Stribling saw Negroes as a subject for propaganda. The novel concerns a "noble Negro" of mixed blood who betters himself with a Harvard education, returns to Niggertown to help his people, but is mistreated by the white citizenry and denied his true paternity. The book thus demonstrates the potential for an educated Negro middle class. Yet Stribling repeats most of the timeworn clichés of the Negro, perpetuating comic and bestial stereotypes as well as "truisms" about the Negro: indolence, dishonesty, odor, love of color, and sexual promiscuity.

Porgy may seem to repeat these same stereotypes, but Heyward actually focuses on scenes of dignity and heroic triumph. For example, he stresses the Negroes' racial memory, a link with their cultural heritage. In his craps games, Porgy cups the dice, fondles them ritualistically, and tells them, "Oh, little stars, roll me some light! . . . Roll me a sun an moon!" (18) Porgy has moments of moral victory, too, as he kills the murderous Crown, who has come to steal Bess. As Maria listens across the courtyard, she hears "a sound that caused her flesh to prickle with primal terror. . . . It was Porgy's laugh, but different. Out of the stillness it swelled suddenly, deep, aboriginal, lustful" (172). This scene evokes a complex, even eerie reaction. Even in the comic scenes, Heyward avoids stereotype and ridicule. Porgy's flight from the police in his goat cart is comic but is deepened and exalted by the pathos of man's fight against insuperable odds. Thus, too, in the hurricane scene when the Negroes gather in the great ballroom and barricade themselves against the onslaught of the storm: "You an' me, Bess, . . . We *sho'* is a little somet'ing attuh all" (148).

Although less so than other southern writers, Heyward saw himself as something of a Menckenian iconoclast in writing *Porgy*. In "The New Note in Southern Literature," Heyward criticized southern readers for demanding propriety and good taste in letters, to the exclusion of anything new. The new southern writers were fortunate, he claimed, since their audience was already cultivated: "It knew and demanded good English in what it read. It was conservative, and was uninterested in sensational filth." But this audience also demanded "strict adherence to its code of good taste, and the code which it prescribed was that of the Victorian drawing room—not art." The task that now confronted the South was "to readjust its standards of good taste. Good taste in manners, if you will. But for art, its own code of good taste, based upon a fearless and veracious molding of the raw human material that lies beneath its hand" (153).

Liberal-minded but not necessarily revolutionary, Heyward intended to present a sympathetic view of African Americans simply by portraying them realistically. But in so doing, Heyward learned more about African American culture and the way it touched on his own history than he could ever have imagined. Placing himself imaginatively in Porgy's world, Heyward saw much about African Americans that he admired, envied, and saw lacking in white culture. In telling Porgy's story, Heyward obliquely commented on parts of his own history and Charleston's white culture.

Writing about the Gullahs was a way of gaining access to a type of life that Heyward could otherwise never experience. The novel is filled with scenes of celebration that suggest an intense vitality among the Gullahs, which the narrator envies. Heyward evokes a primitive, spontaneous approach to life—an ethos that confounds Puritan morality.

Analogues to this experience can be seen in the pictorial arts of Charleston in the '20s. Heyward's work most closely resembles the work of Alfred Hutty, who adroitly salvaged the picturesque antiquity of Charleston and mixed it with the intense racial identity seen in Gullah life. The description of the Jenkins Orphanage Band in *Porgy,* for example, in which the theme of liberation is linked to racial character, depicts verbally what Hutty did visually: "Bare, splay feet padded upon the cobbles; heads were thrown back, with lips to instruments that glittered in the sunshine, launching daring and independent excursions into the realm of sound." Yet the improvisations always return to the "eternal boom, boom, boom of an underlying rhythm" and meet "with others in the sudden weaving and ravelling of amazing chords. An ecstasy of wild young bodies beat living into the blasts that shook the windows of the solemn houses" (113).

In this and other scenes, Heyward shows that Porgy's strength comes from community—a collective faith emanating from Catfish Row. Its inhabitants are bound to each other emotionally and psychically, intensely aware of their roots and their beliefs. In contrast, Charleston appeared to Heyward to be only loosely bound by distant social relations, by hospitality, but not necessarily by true fellow feeling. Heyward also envied the Gullah people their robust health and strength. Crown, for example, has "the body of a gladiator" (16). The stevedores all possess "vast physical strength in a world of brute force" (41). Heyward had always equated virility with triumphing over high odds. His physical frailty was a hindrance that he fought all his life to overcome.

Ethnicity is also a prominent feature of Heyward's Gullahs. This element is not much in evidence in the work of Stribling, Roberts, and other early southern renaissance writers. As such, *Porgy* aligns less with white writers' depictions of black characters and more with black writers' work, notably that of Toomer and later Zora Neale Hurston. Although the voice of *Porgy* is unmistakably that of the white aristocrat who is only mildly receptive to social reform, Heyward depicts Porgy as representing southern Negroes' African roots, their racial uniqueness, and their non-Western exoticism, untouched by white culture. It is remarkable that a genteel white southerner should be writing about these elements of black culture in 1925 with such empathy and intensity.

Heyward focuses on primitivism by employing nonsanitized Gullah dialect, spirituals, and group emotions and by highlighting the Negro's savvy in outwitting the white man. Contact with the white world is minimal. In like fashion, Toomer and Hurston, for example, both emphasize community rather than history. Their characters speak a glittering metaphorical language and embody a folk spirit that is conveyed through oral tales, folklore, popular music, blues, jazz, and spirituals. Toomer, in particular, focuses on a black-centered identity and its ethnic roots as well as on class distinctions among blacks (something Heyward touches on in *Porgy* and develops more fully in *Mamba's Daughters*). Hurston, like Heyward, presents the language and voice of the folk in narratives that retain the oral quality of storytelling.

Yet in *Porgy* Heyward also came to terms with an ostensibly paradoxical cultural situation: racial dualism as oneness. Once Heyward examined the Gullah world with sympathy and depth, it seemed not so very different from his own, confirming W. E. B. DuBois's observation in *The Souls of Black Folk* (1903) that the Negro and the American existed within the same individual. According to DuBois, to deny either of the two was to deny the essence of one's being. After the Civil War, Charlestonians withdrew into a narrow world in which poverty reigned on both sides of the color line. Charlestonians felt imprisoned by that restrictive environment and rued their fate, whereas the Gullahs reveled in an atmosphere of liberation and mobility. Porgy's goat cart symbolizes this mobility; in the opera (which offers a somewhat more optimistic view of Negroes than the novel does), it gives him the ability to pursue Bess, thus making him a heroic figure as he challenges the prevailing odds and the dominant cultural opinion that his race would be forever denied opportunities to advance.

A fear of sudden tragedy also hangs over the Gullah community in ways similar to Heyward's white society. This fear created similar black and white cultures of ritual and memory based on shared emotions and beliefs. The two communities also shared a reverence for Providence (recall Janie's constant ruminations on the mystery of the divine plan). These beliefs gave rise to superstitiousness among blacks and whites. Heyward seems to lightly mock his characters' belief in the validity of omens (the buzzard that alights outside Porgy's room after he murders Crown; the belief among the blacks that the last man to leave the graveside service will be the next to be buried [32]). *Porgy* was among the earliest works by white authors to explore conjuring—a complex system of magic created by a syncretistic blend of Christianity and African old world religions, deeply rooted in African religious views about magic, the universe, the spirit world, and the nature of existence. Such beliefs were created by the same impulses that drove the interest in spiritualism among the white elite at the turn of the century. Heyward and his mother believed in the validity of signs (many of them related to illness and death). Janie regularly consulted palmists and other types of "readers." And one evening at the family's guest cottage on Sullivan's Island, Janie staged a seance that, according to one report, was successful in contacting the dead.

The most important element of black culture that Heyward observed, however, was its preservation and transmission of mythology through story and song. Spirituals occupy a central structural and thematic role in the novel (a role that grew in the stage and operatic versions of the story). The vitality and faith, the strength of character, and the expression of self-worth that Heyward admired in the Gullahs, whom he saw as artist figures, is conveyed through song.

The ties to a community ethic that the spirituals created for the Gullahs fascinated white Charlestonians in the 1920s. One of the most interesting cultural phenomena to emerge from the preservation movement in Charleston was the Society for the Preservation of Spirituals. Heyward was a charter member of this group, which visited plantations and country churches and wrote down the slave songs being preserved by their slave descendants. The group then performed the songs (in authentic plantation dress and on ante-bellum stage sets) for white audiences. The performers replicated the black manner of singing, not to parody but to convey historical authenticity. They mimicked the original performers' variegated rhythmic emphasis and phras-ing, arranging the sonorous melodies in a chorale setting. This group achieved national prominence, selling out tour dates in New York, Boston, and other northern cities. Newspaper editorials in those cities eventually remarked that their citizens obtained their image of the South from this group's concerts.

In 1935, just weeks before the premiere of *Porgy and Bess*, Heyward and the group gave a command performance at the White House. Newspaper accounts noted the marked absence of "sophisticated renditions"; each num-ber appeared to come to the singers "as though under a spell. The leader feels the inspiration first and the others gradually become imbued with the sentiment of the words and the magnetism of the rhythm until they sway as one in perfect unison." To a great extent these white performers were explor-ing the roots of their cultural heritage. As DuBois had noted, the white heri-tage was black as well as white, and vice versa.

The absorption and mimicry of black art forms by white artists in Charles-ton ran parallel with the co-opting of black musical forms by white musicians in the North. When Heyward arrived in New York in 1926 for the staging of *Porgy*, he found a cosmopolitan, mixed-raced society whose interests resem-bled his own. In the post–World War I decade, as Americans repudiated English and European cultural traditions and became fascinated with their own cultural resources, they discovered that their deepest cultural roots lay in the unacknowledged but long exploited African American folk traditions of story and song. Both became essential factors in America's dawning global hegemony in the fast-growing field of popular culture.

White artists and intellectuals recognized the transcendent power of black music. White involvement in this key cultural index of African Ameri-cans crested in New York, where white urbanites frequented the more than 125 Harlem nightclubs, among them the Cotton Club and Connie's Inn, to "go slumming"—that is, to participate voyeuristically in what was palpably the most exciting, because "primitive" or "exotic," subculture that had ever existed in America. One observer of the nightclub scene described its appeal: "When the floor show has ended and the evening is over, one can slip back into one's hat, coat, and niceties, and [be] once again . . . staid, proper, and a community pillar." Two famous analysts of cultural mythology, Constance Rourke and Gilbert Seldes, both friends of Heyward's, frequented these nightclubs and each gave a central place in their writings to minstrelsy, the earliest form of African American music publicly performed for white people. It was new and vital to American self-expression.

Like the members of the Spirituals Society, white performers in New York absorbed African American art and performance styles. Popular white singers like Helen Morgan and Fanny Brice became famous for blues-based "torch songs"; blues, of course, descended from the slaves' oldest work songs. The white bandleader Paul Whiteman, the self-billed King of Jazz, specialized in lightly jazzing or "ragging" the classics. To rag was to place the rhythmic emphasis in a word on a normally unaccented syllable. One of Irving Berlin's most popular tunes was "Alexander's Ragtime Band." Al Jolson, a veteran of the minstrel stage and America's most famous blackface performer, was classified not as a jazz singer but as *the* Jazz Singer, and he held himself to be the equal of Enrico Caruso, the legendary opera star. The Gershwin brothers' most famous early hits were "Fascinatin' Rhythm," "I Got Rhythm," and a plantation-type number, "Swanee," performed by Jolson in blackface.

Ragtime is perhaps the most interesting of these American arts with an African heritage. In an early musical called *Ladies First*, which debuted in New York in 1918, the Gershwin brothers introduced a song with the telling title, "The Real American Folk Song [Is a Rag]." Ragtime, with its strong rhythmic and percussive elements, moved American piano music even more into the Negro idiom than before. (Eubie Blake, a black pianist and composer, once said that the piano stood in for the African drum.) Rag, like jazz, also favored the pentatonic, or five-note, scale, instead of the more Western diatonic, or seven-note, scale. To play a C scale in the diatonic mode requires one to use only the white keys; to play it pentatonically requires one to use what Berlin reputedly referred to as the "nigger keys," tipping his hat to the Negro influence on his compositions.

Most telling, the Charleston, the white dance craze that swept New York in the early 1920s, was a Negro dance that debuted in the musical *Runnin'*

Wild. The dance conveyed feelings of liberation and abandon. It suggested a reckless throwing off of the cultural fetters of Puritan restraint. It symbolized vitality, its mode was celebratory, and its roots lay in African tribal rhythms.

Writing *Porgy* showed Heyward a cultural gateway which he eagerly stepped through. Abandoning history, Heyward instead embraced the concept of story as it was demonstrated to him by Charleston's Gullah Negroes. Heyward explored this concept in ways that paralleled national interests. His success confirmed for him the wisdom of expanding his artistic horizons beyond Charleston.

He did not know exactly how wide those horizons would become, but given white artists' interest in primitive cultures, especially in music traditions, it is no surprise that early in the summer of 1926, *Porgy* found its most interested reader. One evening George Gershwin came home late from rehearsals for his new musical, *Oh, Kay!*, and was too worked up to fall asleep. He picked up a copy of *Porgy*, a novel he had been meaning to read since it had first appeared on the best-seller lists. Gershwin became so entranced by the novel that he stayed up until sunrise to finish it.

Fascinated by the story's multicultural themes and intrigued by its author's sensitivity to music and rhythm, Gershwin quickly wrote to Heyward proposing an opera based on *Porgy*.

Chapter Four

Porgy on Stage

B Y 1924 GEORGE GERSHWIN was a household name, the most famous of popular songwriters and a versatile practitioner of many musical forms—ragtime, jazz, and blues as well as symphonic music and Broadway songs. Gershwin had recently written and produced a one-act vaudeville opera, *135th Street,* which yoked a story of poor black life with music in the American vein—a blend of jazz, blues, and a ragtime recitative. To Heyward, this show seemed much in line with his conception of a musical version of *Porgy.* Heyward was therefore thrilled to learn of Gershwin's interest in his book. Gershwin's letter asked Heyward to telephone him right away, but when Heyward reached Gershwin, all he offered was a vague promise to do the opera sometime in the future. Gershwin was still enchanted with *Porgy,* but at the moment he had too many projects and too little time.

The delay was fortuitous, because it enabled Heyward and Dorothy to write a nonmusical stage version of *Porgy,* which premiered in New York in October 1927. *Porgy: A Play* revolutionized the American theater and set Heyward's career on a new trajectory. Like the other revivals of interest in native resources that followed World War I—the new poetry and the southern renaissance—the theater of the 1920s was a hotbed of innovation and experimentalism. Heyward tapped into this climate by combining scenes of black life in the urban South with melodious black spirituals, a combination of elements that brought white Manhattanites flocking to the play. Heyward gave southern drama, essentially dormant since the Civil War, a renewed national appeal. And by employing an all-black cast, Heyward encouraged the nascent Negro theater movement in New York, creating opportunities for black actors that at the time did not exist. Staging the play helped broaden Heyward's increasingly liberal sympathies toward African Americans.

The mid-1920s was the most exciting period ever in American theater. Seventy-six theaters were in business, staging some two hundred new plays and revues each year. Many of the offerings were light: Ziegfield's Follies, the comedy of W. C. Fields, Fanny Brice, and Will Rogers. There was also the Gershwin brothers—their *Oh, Kay!* and *Funny Face* competed with such musicals as Jerome Kern's *Show Boat,* which generated the biggest box office of them all. The early Noel Coward and Cole Porter musicals were also just starting to appear.

Dramas were marked by experimentalism. Maxwell Anderson and Laurence Stallings's *What Price Glory?*, Sidney Howard's *They Knew What They Wanted,* and Elmer Rice's *Street Scene* were among those plays that tried to represent life through abstractions: space and movement were manipulated, dream sequences attempted to blur normal perceptions of reality. This impulse, most often called expressionism, gave playwrights limitless freedom to dramatize their imaginings. Although some of the most successful techniques of expressionism were found in comedy, where exaggerations and absurdities were frequently employed, the sum effect in such a play as Rice's *The Adding Machine* (1923) was to satirize native stereotypes by exaggerating them in character and setting. Thus, the standardization of life in business and of morality in conventional middle-class life is lampooned in the character of Mr. Zero, a soulless automaton whose modern life is entirely clichéd. In e. e. cummings's *Him* (1927), the two characters are also types: Him is an artist-creator, Me is his mistress. Central to these plays is the quest for self-knowledge, the breaking down of stereotypes, and the realization of self. Missing from these dramatized matrices of selfhood and human relations was the Negro.

Of course, African Americans had had a presence in American theater since the abolition of slavery made it possible for them to participate— through minstrelsy, the first truly American contribution to the stage. Like African American spirituals, work songs, and folktales, minstrelsy originated on the plantations and featured blacks in stereotyped roles: happy-go-lucky or shiftless, full of "natural rhythm" or bumbling and incompetent. Yet even during the height of minstrelsy, in the 1870s and 1880s, African Americans were never fully accepted as part of a profession, and it was impossible for African Americans to preserve their dignity while behaving merely in a manner in which white audiences expected them to behave. Role playing, then, literally and metaphorically became a refuge and a defense mechanism whereby African Americans could exercise their creative talents.

Black theater in the 1920s was confined to Harlem. A surge was noticeable—there were black revues and vaudeville, a "little" theater movement, and some stock companies that performed for black audiences. But there was no black company with the qualifications for acceptance by Broadway's white theatergoers. All-black musicals like *Shuffle Along, Plantation Revue,* and *Runnin' Wild* showcased black performers such as Eubie Blake and Josephine Baker. And some performers, including Paul Robeson, Frank Wilson, and others associated with the Provincetown Players, were honing their craft and gaining recognition. But the majority of black stage roles were still stereotypes, and no new avenues for moving into more serious roles were being created. The offerings largely perpetuated northern and southern clichéd conceptions of African Americans. Only in the work of Eugene O'Neill did black actors find outlets for serious work—*The Emperor Jones* (1920), *All God's Chillun Got Wings* (1924), and *The Great God Brown* (1926) are notable examples.

Like O'Neill, Heyward saw the gap between white and black theater. Early on he had speculated that *Porgy* could be adapted for the stage, especially given the theatrical innovations of the time and northern interest in black culture. Heyward also had never limited himself to specific modes of writing—he had tried stories, then poems, then novels. Moreover, playwriting and acting had always appealed to him. He doubtless saw himself as the heir of a rich Charleston tradition of playwriting. Perhaps this was one way of satisfying his need to blend his intense desire to be an artist with the social requirements of being a Charlestonian.

In the eighteenth century Charleston vied with Richmond for the title of theatrical capital of the colonies. Both cities performed dramas, but only Charleston fostered a group of native dramatists, the first such movement in the South. After Reconstruction, Charleston again took the lead as theatrical groups sprang up and original works were performed there. Charleston exported word of its ethnic-rich culture to the North through native dramatic works and contributed to innovation in the theater by portraying black life.

Heyward foresaw that the depiction of black characters would be a major element in the renascence of southern drama, as would racial tensions and violence, elements of his later plays, *Brass Ankle* and *Mamba's Daughters.* Heyward was not alone in this venture. A North Carolinian, Paul Green, was also beginning to explore the possibilities of folklore in theatrical writing with his play about southern black life, *In Abraham's Bosom,* which premiered in 1926, one year before *Porgy.*

The parallel careers of Heyward and Green demonstrate much about the South's contribution to twentieth-century theater. Both authors enfranchised black actors and encouraged their career aspirations. Both broke down the false stereotypes of the Negro through works of social criticism. Yet despite their efforts, by 1933, southern theater was still struggling to represent non-stereotyped characters: Erskine Caldwell's stage version of his best-selling novel, *Tobacco Road,* for example, succeeded largely because its characters seemed to exemplify southern backwardness. Later, both Green and Heyward became disillusioned with New York theater and transferred their energies to regional drama—Green with the Carolina Playmakers and outdoor dramas, Heyward with the Dock Street Theatre and its playwriting workshop. Both foresaw the decentralization of Broadway, a return to the earlier nineteenth-century pattern in which regional theater provided opportunities for new playwrights.

In 1926, however, Heyward was enthralled with writing for the New York stage, and he set about dramatizing *Porgy* with gusto. Dorothy invigorated the project: she drew up a draft script and tutored her husband in what was to him a new writing mode. For a time, Heyward worried that a dramatic version of *Porgy* might obviate possibilities for an opera with Gershwin. Gershwin, however, saw no conflict. He told Heyward that having a play precede the opera was actually beneficial: there would be a firm stage structure already in place, and one would not have to be created from the more amorphous form of the novel.

The Heywards revised Dorothy's script and submitted it to theatrical producers. Dorothy added much dialogue to the script, since the novel had so little; she took Heyward's Gullah dialect and molded it into more recognizably English speech patterns. Heyward then took her modifications and made them somewhat slangier, to capture something of the Gullah characters while keeping their words understandable.

The Heywards finished revising the play in the early summer of 1926 and mailed it off to three producing organizations in New York. To their astonishment, in little more than a week, the play was accepted by all three. The Heywards selected the Theatre Guild, a fairly new professional group made up of aspiring playwrights, actors, directors, and producers. The guild had been formed in 1915 but had fallen apart rather quickly due to poor acting and directing talent; after the war, Lawrence Langner, an attorney and part-time playwright, had revived the group, and during its first seasons in the 1920s it quickly earned a solid reputation with productions of Shaw, Strindberg, and Molnar. Missing from its repertoire, however, were distinctly American works. So noticeable was the omission and so widely known were the producers' desires to stage an American work that one wag dubbed the Board of Managers "Six Characters in Search of an American Author." When the script for *Porgy* came to them in the mail, then, the managers must have thought it divinely sent. Its native character was just what they had been looking for, even if, in their private opinions, the play had little commercial potential.

The guild's lack of confidence in the broad appeal of *Porgy* illustrates much about the gulf in the 1920s theater world between the "new theater" movement, with its focus on innovation and experimentalism, and black theater, which at the time was largely confined to musical-comedy revues. *Porgy* wedded the different impulses of these two forms, thus paving the way for black material in the legitimate theater, a surge that would later account for the Negro units of the Federal Theater Project (1935–39), the American Negro Theater group of the 1940s, and the later work of such playwrights as Lorraine Hansberry, LeRoi Jones, and August Wilson.

When the Heywards came north in September 1926 to assist in the production, they realized that the chances of the play being produced that season were slim, because they wanted to introduce another innovation—almost a heresy. The guild wanted to do what everyone else was doing on Broadway and hire white actors who would perform in blackface. Such had been the custom since the founding of American theater, but the Heywards insisted on black actors for the roles. *Porgy* was an realistic native drama, not a musical revue like *Runnin' Wild*.

Nonetheless, in America at that time it was unthinkable for blacks to be thus accorded "white" status—in the arts or in any other endeavor. In addition, "serious" black performers were few and far between, which posed a problem. Those available were mostly nightclub performers, chorus-line hopefuls, or just amateurs. The guild had also assigned the direction of the play to someone who was not much interested in doing it. After trying half-heartedly to find a black cast, the director put the play aside for another project. Then, in December, the guild manager who was most in favor of *Porgy* resigned, and so the play was left without a champion. Heyward felt deeply disappointed, for he had seen *In Abraham's Bosom* at the Garrick in February and was "bowled over" by the work: "My hat is off to you for your bravery as well as your art," Heyward wrote to Green. *Porgy*, Heyward thought, had the same possibilities, but the project seemed cursed. That fall, Heyward also had a face-to-face meeting with George Gershwin in Atlantic City. With Dorothy and Gershwin's brother, Ira, trailing them at a discreet distance, the two men strolled the boardwalk and talked animatedly about a native folk opera based on Heyward's novel. Gershwin was still interested but also still overcommitted. No plans were made.

Then in mid-February 1927 the Heywards learned from Theresa Helbrun, the Theatre Guild's liaison with its playwrights, that a new director, Rouben Mamoulian, had been assigned to *Porgy* and that he expected to go into rehearsal in September to open the guild season that fall. *Porgy* had received a second chance.

Among the surprises that greeted Heyward in New York was the vogue of being a white southerner who wrote realistically about poor black life. The vicarious interest in blacks among white New York socialites in the 1920s made Heyward, as a white "interpreter" of black life, a true curiosity to this set. He and Dorothy were in and out of New York in early 1926, dropping in on cocktail parties given by people they did not know, being feted and lionized by these crowds as token southerners—novelties, like the African Americans about whom they wrote. "There are so many things to sap strength and interest" here, Heyward wrote to his mother: one night a get-together with old MacDowell Colony friends, another night dinner with John Masefield, still another a party at which they met Nella Larsen. Heyward was more than a little bewildered. A young writer then making his way in

New York as a critic, Herschel Brickell, fell in with the Heywards and some-times accompanied them to these soirees. Once the three left a party to-gether and decided to go to dinner, but they had no idea where the "in" places were for rising young writers in Manhattan, so they ended up eating in a run-of-the-mill diner. "We were all outlanders," Brickell recalled, "two from the south and one from the Middle West, and all not quite recovered from the strangeness of New York."

Heyward had, however, lost a good deal of his provincial worldview and had broadened his social attitudes. What he saw in New York that fall brought out his inchoate progressivism, for the great artistic flowering among Negroes, the Harlem Renaissance, was then in full bloom. The influx of black writers to Harlem from the South had begun during World War I, when labor shortages in northern industrial areas prompted blacks to move there from the economically depressed South. During this "great migration," Alain Locke observed, "a railroad ticket and a suitcase, like a Baghdad carpet, transported the Negro peasant from the cotton field and farm to the heart of the most complex urban civilization." Although blacks left the agrarian South in search of new opportunities (both social and economic), they did not leave behind their racial heritage—folk customs and beliefs. Thus, Negro writers such as Countee Cullen, Langston Hughes, James Weldon Johnson, and Jean Toomer took a great interest in *Porgy*, with its honest realism and its celebra-tion of ethnic values.

Many of the Harlem group sought out Heyward. Larsen, in particular, was impressed: "Isn't Mr. Heyward interesting to meet?" she remarked to a friend. Another admirer was Johnson. Heyward had written to Johnson the previous year to thank him for a supportive review of *Porgy* that gave Hey-ward "more satisfaction than any of the reviews that the book ha[d] had." During the fall of 1926, Heyward called on Johnson and found him "in a huge office, surrounded by secretaries [and] stenographers." Heyward had a "deeply interesting talk with him" about poetry, "the negro question," and Heyward's "own writing on the Negro." When Johnson's wife entered the room and "joined in the cultured talk," Heyward found the experience "strange" and "unusual." "What would Grannie have said?" he asked Janie in a letter describing the scene. In fact, many ironies came to the fore as Heyward consorted with artists and writers in New York. At one speaking engagement there, he was introduced by a host who had not actually met him as "a southern Negro of the old school and a member of Harlem's intellectual colony."

In fact, Heyward had only just begun to develop more sensitivity to cultural and ethnic differences. He had now started traveling more widely than he had before. He and Dorothy were living a good bit of the year in New York; the rest of the time they spent in Hendersonville, North Carolina. Heyward obviously felt that the best way to write about his region was to live outside of it, to gain the necessary artistic distance with which to represent it fictionally. In this sense his career parallels that of Thomas Wolfe, who had a similarly critical view of his hometown, Asheville, North Carolina, which he satirized in *Look Homeward, Angel* with the boosterish slogan "Prosperity and Progress." Heyward's movement away from the South can be likened to other southern writers exploring regions beyond their own: Allen Tate and his wife, Caroline Gordon, also lived in New York and parts of Europe, as did (at various times) William Faulkner, Zora Neale Hurston, Lillian Hellman, Ellen Glasgow, and Richard Wright.

Heyward also began traveling abroad. Although he made no extended pilgrimages as Wolfe or others did and did not consort with the expatriate group in Paris, he did absorb the culture of some other countries. The experience led him to reflect further on both the provincial nature of his white upbringing and the relative "exoticism" of the Gullah Negroes. His first trip, with Dorothy, was to the coast of England.

In the summer of 1927 they lived in Polperro, a picturesque fishing village that appealed to Heyward immensely. "Everywhere one looks is a composition for a painting," he wrote to his mother. He was especially fascinated by the villagers. He and Dorothy attended Easter Sunday services in a "little Norman church" where they heard the fishermen's choir: "It is composed of forty weather-beaten fishermen clad in their blue jumpers and blue pants. . . . They made a really moving type of music with their big, untrained voices." Heyward saw affinities between the ethnic homogeneity and community spirit of such an environment and the spirituals sung on plantations in his native South—even though this performance relied too much on "rather Moody and Sankeyish stuff." Another comparison of a different sort occurred to him. He told his mother of a "colony of retired families living on a great cliff overlooking the sea." They looked like "the stiffest Britishers imaginable," but when Dorothy chatted them up, their somewhat frosty exterior melted. "Just like Charlestonians in their cordiality after being assured that the visitor is of their own class," Heyward wryly noted. The couple eventually developed "quite a circle of acquaintances."

This experience was similar to one two years later, in the spring of 1929, when the Heywards traveled in the Mediterranean, visiting parts of the Holy Land. In Jerusalem, for example, most places struck Heyward as distastefully commercial. His letters home inveighed against the "obvious fakes" set up for unsuspecting tourists: "You either feel like laughing or else [being] ashamed at the way the beautiful old legends are distorted and made to support a lot of dirty Jews and Arabs." The revered sites associated with Christianity prompted only a sense of "high pressure sight-seeing," but in the mosques Heyward saw "a certain bare dignity and spaciousness that's a relief from the crowded and tinseled ornamentations of the churches." He wrote to Laura Bragg that the Muslims seemed "a shade more self-respecting" than the Christians or the Jews. Away from the tourist-oriented areas, he found Tiberias looking as though it had "not changed for centuries," and he delighted in the "dusty ancient little villages" and the "naked youngsters splashing in the warm waters." Near Cannes, they motored through the different villages by coach. In one they saw a pageant that depicted scenes from the settlement of the French colonies. (It may later have inspired a scene in *Star Spangled Virgin.*) "The Negroes were magnificent in their savage dances," Heyward wrote to Janie.

During the Heywards' stay in England in the summer of 1927, Mamoulian embarked on his own journey of exploration. He went to Charleston to absorb the atmosphere there and learn what he could about Gullah culture. Like Heyward, Mamoulian wanted authenticity in the production. Thus was word of Charleston's Gullah community eventually exported to the New York stage. Mamoulian was a good choice to direct the play, because he was sensitive to the problems of race. He also had innovative ideas about stagecraft, in particular the rhythmic properties of dialogue, something that Heyward had captured especially well in *Porgy.* Mamoulian was born in Russia in 1898. Trained as a lawyer, he had given up that profession for his true love, the theater. Unhappy with the new Bolshevik regime, Mamoulian and his sister had emigrated to London, where the young man gained experience working in West End theaters. He later accepted an offer from George Eastman (of Kodak fame) to help establish the American Opera Company in Rochester, New York. There, Langner of the Theatre Guild spotted Mamoulian and offered him the job of directing *Porgy*.

Heyward suggested to Mamoulian that he contact John Bennett, who could aid the director considerably in learning about Gullah culture. Consequently, Mamoulian, accompanied by the play's set designer, Cleon Throckmorton, spent two days with Bennett in early August 1927. First they visited the leader of the Spirituals Society, who explained the history and purpose of the group to Mamoulian and played for him some of the songs that they had collected. In the evening, Bennett showed Mamoulian photographs from his "collection of Negro types and scenes" and gave him information as their to "costumes, customs, and . . . psychology."

The following day, they "sallied out" again, navigating "the most picturesque and disreputable sections of the city," according to Bennett, where they found "much richness, scenery and personality: boys gambling under the fig-trees, Negro men loafing in indescribable purlieus, and women in costumes that soothed [Mamoulian's] soul." They ended the expedition at the Jenkins Orphanage, a municipally funded home for young black children. In the 1910s the Reverend Daniel Jenkins, its founder, had formed a band from among the children. Like the Spirituals Society, this group of amazingly talented musicians performed up and down the East Coast to rave reviews. The orphanage eventually became known in the jazz world as the cradle of musical genius, as many of its residents grew up and went on to play with Duke Ellington, Jelly Roll Morton, Count Basie, and Lionel Hampton. Bennett arranged for a private performance by the band after supper that night. During the impromptu concert, the children played, and several women sang spirituals. Mamoulian was charmed by the "infinitesimally small darkey boy who led the band" and by the "melodious discordance" of the band itself.

The director was so taken with the group that he persuaded Jenkins to hire them out for the *Porgy* production. In the play, the band led the procession, "Sons and Daughters of Repent Ye Saith the Lord," to Kittawah Island in act 2. By the end of the evening, Mamoulian was already imagining the staging, arranging in his mind such "night-sounds" as would accompany a scene on the island. Mamoulian and Throckmorton left Charleston a day later with a firm sense of the atmosphere they wanted to evoke in the play.

Casting began in early September. Mamoulian had been scouting actors that summer—combing through Harlem revues, black theater groups, and cabarets, encountering the same casting problems that his predecessor had. Those black actors with whom he spoke were wary of a nonvaudevillian production with a black cast. It seemed suspicious to them, and many who were tapped for auditions never showed up. With so few actors from which to choose, Heyward later recalled, casting resolved itself into simply hiring those who were present. Yet even with experienced actors, Heyward was unhappy with the selections. Porgy was to be played by Frank Wilson, the star of *In Abraham's Bosom,* whom he thought too young for the part. Similarly, Evelyn Ellis, chosen for the role of Bess, was "young, slender," and possessed a "radiant charm"; but "the Bess of my novel," Heyward said, had been older, "a gaunt, tragic figure," like he had seen on the Charleston waterfront in his youth. African Americans such as Wilson and Ellis were more refined than those Heyward knew. As his sympathies toward Negro advancement broadened and he began to align himself with the social reformers, Heyward noticed the difference between his "new" self and his former identity in Charleston society: "I wonder what [my friends] in Charleston would have said if [they] could have seen me singing at the piano with the cast today, and calling them ladies and gentlemen?" he later wrote to Janie.

Perhaps as a symbol of this change in attitude, Heyward and Dorothy scripted a new ending to the play. In the novel, Porgy stares disconsolately off into the distance when he learns that Sportin' Life has taken Bess away to Savannah. In the play, Bess takes off for New York instead, and Porgy, as the curtain falls, pursues her in his little goat cart. This change, which carried over into the opera, exemplifies Porgy's indomitable spirit and independence of will. It is one of the essential features that make him a heroic figure and that suggests Heyward's optimism for Negro advancement. The Heywards also rewrote parts of their script, making changes in the characters. The director thought Porgy needed to be more mystical, more of the abstract figure he was in the novel. In addition, an earlier, stronger attraction between Porgy and Bess needed to be suggested.

Early rehearsals tended to be diffuse, even unruly. Mamoulian, known as the "mad Armenian" because of his frantic energy, had to lean on his cast to make them accept his direction. The cast would not take the play seriously: "they had no conception, at first, of the significance of their work," Mamoulian said. According to Mamoulian, the actors would arrive late at rehearsal, go up on their lines, and forget their blocking. Moreover, as vaudevillians, they were used to looking directly at the audience while speaking—even breaking into the Charleston, or some other high-spirited dance, when asked to register high spirits. Few understood the significance of this daring new undertaking in theater. However, when Mamoulian persuaded them to deliver the lines in a more serious manner, they lapsed into their ordinary city-bred selves, which were too sophisticated for the primitive life of a Charleston slum. "I suppose everything was going too well to hold up to its start," Heyward wrote to Janie at the end of September. At a rehearsal for the guild directors, "everything went wrong. The Negroes got rattled and left out important lines. When they remembered them they said them woodenly like school children reciting."

These black performers' behavior illustrates the role playing in which African Americans sometimes engaged as a culturally accommodating strategy. The new Negroes of the 1920s had only tenuous claims on mainstream America's attention or sympathy. If they displeased their white patrons, blacks knew they would be cut off and eventually put out of work. To keep working in theater, these performers therefore had to walk what they perceived as the fine line between white society's cultural expectations of them as exotic primitives and that same society's desire that they accommodate themselves behaviorally and culturally to the requirements of legitimate theater. Should one be clowning, as in blackface, or aping whites? The guidelines and expectations were not clear.

The directors then thought that "the play should be made more obvious"—perhaps in consequence of the black performers' consciously not getting right the manner of their characters—so that it would "get over," as Heyward put it. The guild also "wanted lots of changes that would make it less artistic." After the rehearsal, the group went into a five-hour conference, and the Heywards went back to work on the script. Heyward thought that in the end they had "saved most of it, and, frankly, built up some bits to advantage," but in many ways the revisions destroyed "some things that we wanted to handle subtly": "The cast is scarcely more than amateur" and could not convey "fine distinctions," he told his mother. They learned "terribly slowly" and forgot overnight "what Mamoulian bangs into them each day. . . . [It] is going to be a terrifically hard thing to pull over." Heyward confessed himself "a poor hand at this rewriting work," but Dorothy was "wonderful" and had "done most of it."

On a happier note, when Throckmorton's huge main set, the courtyard in Catfish Row, arrived at the theater, the Heywards were astonished. "It actually breathes Charleston," Heyward wrote to Janie. The set lent such an air of realism to the rehearsals that Mamoulian now was able to polish the pacing of the show. He believed that in the timing of the action and speeches in the play there was a rhythm similar to that in music. Thus, in the last scene, for example, which begins at dawn, he had the characters appear one by one, going about their daily tasks. The sound volume on the stage would rise, noises would be heard (such as the tolling of church bells), and the rhythm would increase. To help the actors render the sound of Gullah speech, especially in the spirituals, a friend of Heyward's came up from Charleston to coach them. And one cast member, who had grown up in Charleston, remembered an old crab vendor who roamed the streets. The actor was commissioned to create this character, and it has remained in the play (and opera) ever since.

Between the end of September and the middle of October, when the play opened, the Heywards' confidence in the play alternately rose and fell. Heyward kept Janie abreast of all the developments: "We have all worked like galley slaves this week. Yesterday they rehearsed from 10 AM to 12 midnight. How the cast stood it I do not know—they all looked sick this morning. . . . I felt better today than they did. Mamoulian has been superhuman. . . . I do not see how the play can fail to be impressive. It will probably get some criticism, and it will be for things we can't help—inexperienced cast, etc. But there are several scenes that will be unique in the American theater, and are enormously moving. The wake scene, with its drama, and spirituals . . . rises to the final curtain with a shouting spiritual, a hidden light in the foot lights shoots up on them and suddenly throws gigantic black shadows on the wall behind them. It is simply breath taking. If it had gone on a week ago it would have failed. Now it should succeed artistically at any rate."

Even with its stress and seemingly irremediable hardships, Heyward truly loved the theater. The production enabled him to come out from behind the anonymity of fiction without shining the spotlight directly on himself. Theater offered a mask behind which he could see his artistic self enacted in the words and deeds staged before him. A naturally reticent person who wanted to indulge his creative impulses, Heyward found the theater to be the perfect forum. As his career advanced, Heyward would spend more and more time writing for the stage. The venue illustrated his view that art should be public and communal.

Still, rehearsals did not bode well for the play's success. Watching Mamoulian drill a line with an actor who could not get it quite right, one guild manager moaned, "Not again! I can't stand it!" and walked over to Theresa Helbrun, the guild's liaison with the Heywards, who was sitting in the darkness beside Dorothy. Not seeing Dorothy, the manager whispered to Helbrun, "How much have we sunk in this damned thing?" "Too much to go back now," Helbrun replied, gesturing toward the expensive set.

To remedy what were thought to be flaws in characterization, the Heywards kept adding material to the play until eventually it ran to two and a half hours—much too long. The Sunday before opening, they sat up until one A.M. cutting it. Heyward told Janie he thought the play "would be most unusual and effective now." But doubts still lingered.

In the darkened theater on opening night, the Heywards sat expectantly, wondering about the fate of their creation. The performance seemed solid. All went as planned, except for a few missed cues. But when the Heywards noticed that critic Alexander Woolcott left his seat before the last scene, their mild nervousness turned into outright anxiety. As Woolcott strode heavily up the aisle to the exit, he seemed to Heyward "forty feet tall, thirty feet broad," his mouth set like "a medieval executioner." The following morning, their anxiety slid into depression when they read Brooks Atkinson's *New York Times* review—not unfavorable, but not enthusiastic either, and with some significant complaints. Atkinson, who had admired the novel, said that the adaptation was not as "crisp" as the book and was "only spasmodically vivid."

Although other reviews were more positive, the guild managers asked the Heywards to rewrite the last act. "For two days Dorothy and I have been writing ourselves blind," Heyward told Janie on 13 October. He was pleased with the revisions but did not know whether the managers would be. That evening, they went to the theater, new script in hand, in the hopes that it would salvage the play. As they passed by the ticket office, people were lined up at the window, standing under umbrellas in the pouring rain. The Heywards were mildly curious, but were so focused on their new script that they did not wonder why. When they entered the office and presented the manuscript, Langner looked at them blankly and said, "You're crazy to change it. We're a hit."

The Heywards evidently had not paid very close attention to the reviews, which were more favorable than Atkinson's hedging compliments. Moreover, Atkinson himself (perhaps influenced by his fellow reviewers) had eventually warmed to the play in his Sunday follow-up column, which the Heywards had not seen, since they had been locked in their hotel room rewriting the last act. Atkinson was now calling *Porgy* "an illuminating chronicle of American folklore" and urging everyone to see it. Woolcott, in spite of missing the final scene, had praised Mamoulian's direction as "more resourceful and more outstanding" than anything he had yet seen in American theater. All reviewers commented favorably on the "dilapidated grandeur" of Throckmorton's set. And the spirituals, sung with "the fervor, the hysteria, the emotionalism, and the curious abandon that must accompany such outbursts," were thought to be worth twice the price of a ticket.

By 20 October, *Porgy* was standing room only. The show ran for 217 performances in New York, then went on an extensive road tour. It returned to Broadway at the end of the April 1928 season for 137 more performances, then went into stock.

The play differs from the novel in many notable ways. The subtlety and meditative mood of the novel are replaced by a much more action-oriented plot (as one might expect in a stage performance). The play is presented in nine scenes, and the sequence of events in the novel was altered, apparently to give the story a quicker pace. Yet the sense of mass rhythms that Heyward said he wanted to convey in the stage version is more prominent than in the novel. The Catfish Row group as an ethnic entity is emphasized; almost every scene opens with a picture of the mass, a sort of tableau vivant that emphasizes the homogeneity of Gullah community—the craps game, the saucer burial, the hurricane. (Only the picnic scene on Kittiwah Island opens differently, perhaps to underscore the coming separation of Bess from the Catfish Row community that gives her moral support and her temptation by Crown.) The rhythm element is reinforced by the abundant use of songs and spirituals. At least two scenes (the saucer burial and the hurricane) seem designed as musical set pieces, somewhat to the diminishment of the story. Yet the songs serve the essential function of conveying the Gullahs' emotions (as folklore does in the novel), just as they did real life, as Heyward noted in an introduction to the play.

The intense action of the play distinguishes it from the novel. The play is coarse, violent, and primitive in sometimes garish ways that diminish the mystical and philosophical qualities of Porgy's original character. On stage, Porgy is much more a man of action than a speculative, quiet person. This change is certainly apparent in the altered ending, in which Porgy pursues his lost Bess.

The characters in the play, however, are "thinner" than their original versions. Porgy, Bess, and Maria lack the philosophical depth with which Heyward originally invested them. Only Sportin' Life, perhaps because he is so theatrical a character in the book, comes alive more on stage than in the original text. In the play, he is more melodramatically villainous, more obviously evil than he is in the novel. Other characters, too, seem to be presented as stereotypes, as they were not in the novel. A good example is the Lawyer Frasier (Simon Frazier in the play), who "sells" Bess a divorce from Crown. In the novel, Frasier is sly and calculating, an intelligent if disreputable character. In the play he is clownish, a comic stereotype pared away from his fuller character in the novel.

Although the stage characters did not always present as ennobling a portrait of blacks as Heyward's novel did, the majority of the black press still reacted positively to the production. James Weldon Johnson, perhaps overlooking some of the bad to highlight the good, praised the show's use of more than sixty black performers, unheard of on Broadway at that time. *Porgy* established an important precedent for black actors, paving the way for them to win nonstereotyped roles in legitimate theater. The experience of Charles Gilpin, the award-winning star of O'Neill's *The Emperor Jones* in the 1919–20 season, is representative. Gilpin was dropped from the London run of *The Emperor Jones* for changing some of the play's more racist lines and epithets. In 1927 he was fired from a Hollywood production of *Uncle Tom's Cabin* because he refused to play Tom as a stupid darky. No further film roles came his way. Thus, after reaching the peak of achievement by a black performer, Gilpin reportedly had to go back to work operating elevators when the show ended its run. He explained to a friend how hard it was "to get a chance to play even Negro parts in regular companies": "I played such a part in one company, and some of the actors used to stand outside my dressing-room and talk about me, evidently intending me to overhear them. 'Why did they get a nigger for that part?' they would say. 'A white man could play it better than any nigger that was ever born!' " In subsequent years, the number of black performers awarded starring or significant roles in Broadway productions rose steadily. "In *Porgy,*" Johnson wrote, "the Negro removed all doubts as to his ability to do acting that requires thoughtful interpretation and intelligent skill."

Even more than the novel, the play version of *Porgy* brought Heyward fame and bought attention to the Carolina low country. At the box office, *Porgy* beat its close competitors, O'Neill's *All God's Chillun Got Wings* and Green's *In Abraham's Bosom*. *Porgy* appealed to the Manhattan intellectuals and urban socialites who had fallen victim to postwar cynicism and malaise. Unsure about the mass industrialization that inaugurated the machine age and pushed Americans steadily toward uniformity, these audiences "discovered" the African American through such plays as *Porgy*. They saw in the show all the sensuousness and life rhythm that white America had lost. Black actors and playwrights began to receive critical and financial support from wealthy white artists. Later in the decade, for example, the white establishment sponsored a literary contest for black writers. The judges were Van Wyck Brooks, O'Neill, and African Americans Johnson and Locke. Hughes and Hurston won prizes that helped further their careers. Such Negro organizations as the National Association for the Advancement of Colored People and the Urban League promoted artistic excellence among blacks, and white foundations such as the Rosenwald Fund also awarded grants to subsidize the black arts movement.

Yet the situation of *Porgy* also reflects the ambivalence, conflict, and compromise that black artists of the 1920s underwent. Most African Americans were pleased that attention was being brought to black artists and hoped that race relations might thereby improve. But many also recognized that the new Negro was merely a jazz-age version of the old plantation darky, almost a pet rather than a person.

Some black intellectuals and artists were wary of this white fascination with black culture. It gave rise to unending debates over whether these explicitly sympathetic portrayals marked any real improvement over the racist caricatures that had previously dominated America's cultural landscape. The so-called talented tenth felt that African Americans should show that, given the right conditions, they could be as respectable as whites. Conversely, black artists such as Claude McKay and Hughes thought that black art specifically should not ape whites but should celebrate blacks' own special qualities and cultural gifts.

African American novelists like McKay in *Home to Harlem* and Toomer in *Cane* wrote of black life in ways that appear to reinforce the essentialist assumptions of what Hurston later named "Negrotarian" fiction. However, others such as Walter White, Jessie Fauset, Hughes, and Larsen questioned the basis of racial identity and asserted the inseparability of economic, social, and cultural processes.

Among black dramatists of the 1920s and '30s, a similar tension existed between politics and culture: African American art as protest or as accommodation. Insisting on immediate full rights for Negroes, W. E. B. DuBois urged that art be used as protest. Booker T. Washington was the most famous proponent of the other goal: he emphasized traditional values. This separation is clearly seen in the playwrights of the Harlem Renaissance. Propaganda plays, political in character, were numerous, yet there was also a well developed array of African American talent that excelled in folk drama. Many southern Negroes had gravitated to Washington, D.C., home of Howard University, where Montgomery T. Gregory and Locke, both admirers of Heyward and Green, appealed for plays that would ignore racial tensions and explore the undiscovered fields of black culture. Associated with Howard University was a remarkable group of women dramatists who furthered the folk drama in the 1920s: Hurston was the group's most famous member.

Hurston admired the work of Heyward, seeing it as well meaning in its portrayal of blacks, but she did not think it was realistic enough, and thus she undertook an ambitious program of realizing true Negro drama, the best example of which is *Mule Bone: A Comedy of Negro Life,* composed in 1930 in collaboration with Hughes. This comedy, with its depiction of authentic customs unknown to white dramatists like Heyward, is provocative and arresting; however, Hurston could not get the play staged, and it was not performed until 1991, almost thirty years after Hurston's death. Hurston's aims, while strongly applauded today, were sometimes assailed in her time by such black writers as Richard Wright, who felt that her work was not political enough and that in such plays she pandered to white audiences by using folk material and dialect humor in too self-conscious a manner.

Other black artists, dependent on white support, thus found themselves compromising their beliefs in return for success in the white world. DuBois applauded the *Porgy* production as a necessary first step toward black nationalism in the arts, but he quickly urged that black artists move on to produce black drama "About us . . . By us . . . For us . . . and Near us." By "near us," DuBois meant the establishment of Negro neighborhood theaters, but such an advance was far in the future. And despite a handful of black productions, white playwrights did the most to sustain whatever serious black drama and acting existed in the 1920s.

In contrast, serious black performers were respected in England and Europe. *Porgy* toured there in the spring of 1929 and drew sizable crowds. The Heywards were jubilant over this success. In Paris the novel was appearing serially in French newspapers and was selling well in its French edition, in which West Indian dialect was substituted for the Gullah. Later that spring, in London, the Heywards were virtually bombarded with invitations to teas and dinners. Unfortunately, they were there so briefly that they missed an invitation to tea at Buckingham Palace. ("What a final wreath of romance it would have been to the impossible facts of Porgy and DuBose!" Bennett gushed.) Meanwhile *Porgy* captivated audiences at the Pavilion Theatre every night. Its run was extended through June, and there was talk of further Continental engagements.

The success of the play abroad may be credited to the widespread fascination there, following the war, with virtually all things American. American movies, advertising, clothing, automobiles, skyscrapers, and jazz were subjects of great European curiosity. If that culture was a vast museum of the elite arts, then America in the 1920s emerged as the creator and exporter of the mass arts. Popular entertainment was distributed by a new mass media, something that Europe lacked. American films were sweeping European markets. In Great Britain, even the American vernacular was popular. One London paper, noting the large crowds that *Porgy* was drawing, expatiated on the malign influence of American movie dialogue. Londoners feared that "the young will talk like New York's East Side, or, from *Porgy*, Charleston's water-front."

Those forms of American music that were thoroughly American—jazz or ragtime—were also in vogue. James Reese Europe, a pioneering musician and composer who headed the Harlem Hellfighters, a band attached to an infantry regiment during the war, captivated Paris audiences. Florence Mills, whom Johnson described as an "exotic . . . pixie radiant [with] a naivete that was alchemic," sang and danced in numerous venues in Paris and London and in a series of plays and revues (among them, Gershwin's *Blackbirds*, which ran in London in 1926). Speaking of his first visit to London around this time, Ellington noted how "amazed" he was that people in Britain were "so well informed . . . about us and our records."

A particular fascination was associated with Josephine Baker. In 1925, a craze swept Paris when the lithe black performer presented her bare-breasted "danse sauvage" in the "Revue Negre." African American dance and music was celebrated in such places abroad, partly because European countries did not have large groups of racial Others within their boundaries; in such an environment, racial prejudice had no incentive to develop. Until the 1920s, as far as the rest of the world was concerned, with a few pictur-esque exceptions America had no culture. When the United States finally exported cultural commodities to the Old World, its most marketable assets were black.

Porgy's run in London furthered this new fascination with Aframerica, and Heyward was seen as an avant-garde purveyor of American exotica. One bizarre, impressionistic perception of Heyward was offered by the British novelist Louis Golding, who reported in the London papers on a recent trip to New York. Golding related how he "went black" and "hung out" in Har-lem, where he claimed he met a "coal-black Negro Jew": "the man . . . described to me as the most charming gentleman in the whole American continent, the Negro literary man DuBose Haywood."

Porgy's stage run was a chrysalis in which Heyward shed his conservative social views and became a moderate but active advocate for African Ameri-cans. He used the theater as his platform, bringing new opportunities for black drama and encouraging the use of black folk materials. He saw the possibilities for art as a stimulus for social conscience, and he recognized that despite his own and other white artists' efforts, a solidly optimistic message for blacks in the world of art still needed to be heard. Heyward's progressivism then grew. In his next works, Heyward would more openly become a social reformer and adopt a more critical view of race and class in the South.

Chapter Five

Evolution of a Social Critic

I N   T H E   L A T E   1 9 2 0 S   and early 1930s Heyward aligned himself
with the Chapel Hill group of social reformers, establishing what could
accurately be called a mutual admiration society. Paul Green, Gerald
Johnson, Howard W. Odum, and later Wilbur J. Cash publicly applauded
Heyward's moderately heterodox views, as Heyward did their more extreme
views. The University of North Carolina practically became Heyward's institutional champion, giving him an honorary degree in 1928; publishing his
writings in the *Reviewer,* which relocated there from Richmond; and inviting
him to speak and attend university-sponsored writers' gatherings.

After deploring social uplift, Heyward shifted to encouragement of Negro
aspirations in *Mamba's Daughters.* He next censured prejudice against the
mulatto in *Brass Ankle* (1931), then the power of conformity to stifle free
thought in *Peter Ashley* (1932), and later the exploitation of the artist by the
new southern plutocracy in *Lost Morning* (1936).

Oddly, as the Great Depression created social dislocation, and most authors gravitated toward themes of social protest, the major figures of the
southern renaissance as it emerged in full flower at this time—William
Faulkner, Thomas Wolfe, Allen Tate, and others—tended not to use their
fiction didactically. Thus, in the fiction of social commitment in the South at
the time, Heyward's work belongs more with that of Harry Harrison Kroll,
T. S. Stribling, Lillian Smith, and Erskine Caldwell. Like these authors, Heyward became increasingly concerned with agrarian reform, industrial
change, social deracination, and, most of all, race relations. Like many of

these writers, too, distancing himself from his own region allowed Heyward to see Charleston and its culture with a more critical eye.

Heyward's tendencies toward social criticism emerged fairly early—in 1926, with *Angel,* a novel he wrote as a quick follow-up to *Porgy. Angel* is a pastiche of previously published work—a story, "The Brute," and several poems from *Skylines and Horizons:* "The Girl," "The Preacher," "The Woman," "The Blockader," and "Black Christmas." Put together, the poems possess a loose narrative continuity and depict the hardscrabble life of the people living in the North Carolina Blue Ridge Mountains. "The Brute" provides the central dramatic element: a cuckolded husband's attempt to murder his wife's lover by dynamiting the side of a mountain. *Angel* is not a sophisticated novel—its plot and characters are paper thin, and there is a rushed quality to the story (it is barely 60,000 words long), but it anticipates much later southern fiction and reveals glimpses of Heyward's potential as a critic of the South.

The plot allegorizes the myth of the fall of man and uses imagery that evokes the garden, bathing as baptismal activity, and temptation by lust, liquor, and riches. As the novel opens, Angel, the young daughter of a preacher, Gabriel Thornley, is bathing naked under the waterfall at Thunder Cove. A neighbor, Buck Merritt, sees her from a distance and is inflamed with lust. Ashamed, he feels as though the azaleas are "a tangle of fire about his feet" (12) and "a dull red" grows beneath the "weathered brown" of his face. Against the wishes of Angel's father—a fanatical Calvinist who reminds one of Faulkner's McEachern in *Light in August*—Angel sneaks off to a village dance, where she is wooed by Buck. They eventually become lovers. The act takes place as Angel leads Buck to the falls. Heyward employs imagery of descent and darkness to describe the event: "The apple trees wove a black net between them and the moon" (46–47).

Learning of his daughter's sin, Thornley takes his revenge on Buck, a moonshiner, by informing on him, and Buck is imprisoned. Angel's father, whose first name suggests that he is God's emissary of judgment, then banishes his daughter from Thunder Cove by forcing her to wed Stan Galloway in Beartown, ten miles away, over the ridge of mountains that separates that village from Thunder Cove. Galloway is an alcoholic and is many years Angel's senior. Thus exiled, the no-longer-innocent Angel and her baby are consigned to a gloomy existence of hard work for little money and are cut off from the paradisal environs of Thunder Cove.

Heyward treats Angel's banishment sympathetically. She is doomed by purblind destiny to an existence over which she has no control, reminding one of Hardy's Jude Frawley, or Tess Durbeyfield. Angel also evokes the sympathy seen in her prototype, the "mountain woman" of Heyward's poem. Punished for doing something that her community considers a sin, Angel, like Hawthorne's Hester Prynne, must endure ignominy and ostracism. She is an admirable woman with whom Heyward empathetically identifies; she is a forerunner of the similar sympathetically drawn female characters in *Mamba's Daughters.*

In fact, Angel's only companion in the isolated mountain region is Myra Kent; her husband and Stan are partners in a bark-stripping business that, along with moonshining, supplements their income as farmers. The two women forge a bond borne of their isolation, but keep it as a private treasure, never risking the pain that might come of revealing their guarded emotions. Angel loses even this small bright spot in her gloomy existence when Myra moves to Misty Valley, where Stan Kent signs on with the highway company for a higher wage. Galloway takes a job with the company as well; his task is to use explosives to clear the area near Beartown for highway construction.

In the postlapsarian scheme of the novel, the highway bridges past and present, connecting the isolated mountain region with the mainstream valley. Like the railroad and other examples of industrialization in Victorian fiction, Heyward's highway also symbolizes a machine in the garden and thus the spoiling of innocence and the destruction of the pastoral ideal. The highway brings modernity to Beartown and to Angel's simple existence; thus, in the novel Heyward continues the theme from *Porgy* about the passing of one way of life for another. The highway—or its metonymy, the dynamite—is also an instrument of destruction, since it is with the explosives that Galloway wreaks his revenge on Buck Merritt, who reappears late in the novel. Merritt survives the "accident," however, as Galloway does not, and by the close of the story, the newly united lovers, like Adam and Eve, are setting off in their wagon, child in tow, for a new existence in a new world.

The novel also critiques the social conditions that keep the poor white so benighted. In certain ways Heyward was adopting Mencken's views. In *Angel,* Heyward sees little of value in the area and seems to discount all religion as harsh fundamentalism without any genuine worth. Like Mencken, he offers no solutions, only diagnoses; he sees inadequacies with few virtues. Yet this same social criticism, when directed at the upper class in *Mamba's Daughters* and *Peter Ashley*, is effective. There, it is more sensitive, sophisticated, and varied in its treatment of the South's "defects."

Mamba's Daughters: A Novel of Charleston, published in 1929, may well be Heyward's best novel: it signals an advance in his thinking about the difficulties of African Americans in the modern age. The story, which spans ten years, concerns three generations of Gullah women in Charleston. As the novel opens, Mamba, the grandmother, insinuates herself into the household of the Atkinson family and persuades them to take her on as their mauma. She does so to gain respectability as a "white folks' nigger"—that is, a household servant, as opposed to a "waterfront nigger" (the type Heyward observed as a youth in the Bay Street district). With that income Mamba will provide a better life for her granddaughter, Lissa. The focus, however, is on Hagar, Mamba's daughter and Lissa's mother. This physically imposing woman is a complete primitive. Prone to violent outbursts and vulnerable to liquor, Hagar is so disadvantaged by her lack of education that she lives cowering in the shadow of white society, which she fears above all else.

Hagar is taken on as a laborer at a phosphate mining camp—a triumph, since the mine has never before hired a woman to do a man's work. Here she meets the villainous Gilly Bluton, whose life she saves—at much peril to herself—when Bluton is knifed in a fight. Years later, Lissa, now a teenager, falls in with Bluton, who now calls himself Prince. Hagar discovers Prince's real identity and murders him when he tries to rape her daughter. She tries to bury Bluton's body in the swamp, but in the sky she sees several bad omens, signaling to her that she is doomed. She thus confesses to the murder and then kills herself, so that Lissa will be unharmed.

Heyward interweaves a subplot involving white society with the story of Hagar, Lissa, and Mamba. This other plot focuses on the autobiographical character of Saint Wentworth, the male heir to a dispossessed Charleston family for whom Mamba works for a while. When she leaves the Wentworths for the nouveau riche Atkinsons, Mamba remains friends with Saint; they are secret conspirators in mocking the farcical and sometimes pathetic behavior of the Atkinsons and other white families in Charleston who put on airs and strive for recognition of their superior social status. Saint is hired at the mining camp and eventually becomes manager. At the end of the novel, Saint temporarily takes charge of young Lissa in New York City, where he has taken his family on a combined business and pleasure trip; Lissa has gone there to study opera.

The great promise of Mamba's daughters reposes in Lissa, who gets her break in the New York musical world and sings the National Anthem of the American Negro at the conclusion of a performance at the Metropolitan Opera House. Her performance stirs a predominantly white audience to astonishment and awe that such beautiful, "cultured" music could be presented by an African American woman. The audience also realizes that a new type of art is evolving: part white, part black, "but first, American" (302). This ending to Heyward's story is optimistically predictive of his own ambitions and those of African Americans. It uncannily foreshadows the production of *Porgy and Bess* six years later, and it affirms his faith that, through the arts, African Americans could achieve more than they had thus been able to.

Heyward sympathizes with the plight of the black women he has drawn. A large measure of his admiration is given to Mamba. She is complimented as an "opportunist" (10) who knows the "vulnerabilities" (14) of white society and uses them to her advantage: she was "born of a race that owed its very existence to its understanding of the ruling white" (14). Mamba sees that "t'ings is change' now, t'ings is change' " (9), and so she presses her relationship with her white employers to provide future opportunity for Lissa. As she instructs Hagar, "Yo' an' me, Hagar—what de hell is we? Nuttin'! But Ah ain't no fool at schemin', an' yo' gots de strength. Look like we ought fuh gib dat gal a chance 'tween us" (93). Another of Mamba's strengths is her adaptability. She evolves in the novel from someone without a distinct identity to someone who is a composite of various castoff personalities from the white people she attaches herself to and "absorbs." At the end of the novel, she is simply herself, a distillation of present and past, and an instrument that ensures a future for her granddaughter. Her "separate identities" ultimately merge "into the new ego that they were destined in the future to express" (35).

Mamba's actions are contrasted with opportunism of a different sort, that expressed through her white counterpart, Mrs. Atkinson. A nouveau riche from the North, Mrs. Atkinson desperately desires entrance into Charleston society but is consistently denied it because she is not savvy enough to see the "proper" method of attaining it: "She had made the fatal mistake in the beginning of assuming that wealth was, as a matter of course, an effective weapon, not realising that, with a number of the old families in straitened circumstances, simple living had become the criterion for good taste, and the ostentation had become, by contrast, mere vulgarity" (115–16). Thus while Mamba is a brilliant field general, Mrs. Atkinson is a pathetically "misguided tactician" (117). Her behavior is mercilessly lampooned by the narrator, but she also can be vindictive and bitter. She remarks of one person that so "great a fool could never have made such a success of his life" and belong to the social circle to which she thinks she is naturally suited (118).

Heyward depicts the old-new conflict within the Gullah community as well as the white. A class structure exists within the Gullah world. Certain clubs admit African Americans whose skin is not of a darker hue than the color of the club door; membership in the Negro Reformed Church means high society for Lissa, who wishes to advance, whereas Mamba's church exists at the bottom of the social ladder. The conflict is most tellingly symbolized in the differences between two black ministers. There is the educated northerner, Thomas Grayson, who comes to South Carolina on mission work, but because of his lofty standing in a quite different African American world he is unable to relate to his new parishioners. In contrast is Quintus Whaley, the resident minister, who is a drunkard, a hypocrite, and the pawn of the white mine owners. Nonetheless, the black community flocks to hear him preach, because—like the white community that also charitably overlooks the sins of its brethren—they are willing to sit "protectively over their own flasks . . . let bygones be bygones and . . . hurry the present into the past with song" (100).

The thematic dichotomies of old versus new and white versus black are treated in other forms as well. In one pair of scenes, for example, the stodgy, formal types of dancing that take place at the St. Cecelia Ball are contrasted with the freewheeling and liberating new Negro dance, the Charleston, that takes place at a church social. The narrator reminds us that this dance had African American origins and was created by lowcountry blacks who existed on the periphery of white society. Heyward thus uses class structure to show that whites and blacks, both poised at the moment of changing times, have cultural commonalities. An eventual fusing of some of these commonalities—

such as Lissa's performance at the Met—is the key to changing with the times.

Hagar symbolizes the middle phase, the giving way of past to present. Given a choice between Grayson's church and Whaley's church, she chooses Grayson's—the future—not because she understands his high-toned rhetoric but because, as she tells him, she senses an imminent change and she needs instruction in how to cope. She is lonely, just as he is. When in her first encounter with Gilly Bluton she decides to take the injured man to a hospital, she knows that she runs the risk of being presumed guilty of attacking him herself (an ironic foreshadowing of later events), and on the perilous journey she stands, literally, at the crossing of two roads: "But here was Bluton—she could not let him die now. Sweat burst out on her face, cold and clammy in the night air. With the odd instinct of dumb animals, the horse had sensed her hesitation and stopped in the middle of the road. She mopped her streaming face. Then, with a decisive gesture, she slapped the animal's back with the slack lines. She'd have to gamble on her luck. . . . She was on the main road now, and the going was good" (106).

Hagar's act is self-sacrificing. Not being able to care for Lissa because to do so would prevent her daughter from moving in higher social circles, Hagar spends "her starved maternity" (104) on the reprehensible Bluton and risks jail. In a separate scene, Hagar similarly "debase[s] herself" by helping an old Negro who works beside her in the mines, propping up "his toppling dignity" by assisting him, in open defiance of the hoots and jeers of their fellow workers. "She was full of tenderness for him," Heyward writes (84).

But Hagar's compulsion, as a result of instinctive love for Lissa, to murder Bluton later in the novel demonstrates most deeply the conflict of humanity that Heyward addresses in the novel. He writes movingly and suspensefully of Hagar's desperate attempt to slog through the marshland with Bluton's corpse atop her shoulders, a colossus-like symbol, strapped with the burden that she must bear: "She bent forward and shifted the [body] from her shoulder to her arched back. Then she set off as briskly as possible, tearing a way through the matted growth with her right hand while she steadied the body with her left." As Hagar advances with her head lowered, her eyes fix on the pools of shallow water through which she is wading: "she became aware of the reflection of an object that projected over her shoulder and looked down into the water, as she was doing. She paused, and the reflection did likewise.

DUBOSE HEYWARD

*A Charleston Gentleman
and the World of* Porgy and Bess

*The young widow, Janie, age 27;
DuBose, age 7; and Jeannie, age 3,
Christmas 1902*

Heyward in the early 1920s

*John Bennett, "Master"
and "Hypercritic"*

"Hansel and Gretel lost in a wood":
Dorothy and DuBose Heyward

A tour abroad: DuBose and
Dorothy in Egypt, 1929

"The little house that
looks at the dawn":
Dawn Hill,
Hendersonville, N.C.

*Crown braves the hurricane in
the original play version of*
Porgy, *New York, October 1927*

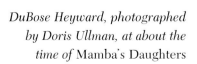

*DuBose Heyward, photographed
by Doris Ullman, at about the
time of* Mamba's Daughters

George Gershwin and Heyward in Charleston, photographed from the balcony of Josephine Pinckney's house, summer 1934 (above)

"Charleston was Charleston": the Heywards with Gertrude Stein, outside the Villa Margherita, 1935 (left, top)

"Here's hoping our collaboration is an 'always' thing": Heyward with the brothers Gershwin, spring 1934 (left)

Porgy and Bess: *Program for the Boston tryout, October 1935*

The Catfish Row fishermen greet the new day: Cleon Throckmorton's more elaborate set for the opera, 1935

George Gershwin during fifteen minutes of applause. Heyward stays out of the spotlight, just to the right

A New Life: Porgy and Bess *returns to New York, 1953*

Dorothy and DuBose Heyward, mid 1930s

Heyward in Nassau, 1936

Robert Frost, Hervey Allen,
and Heyward, Miami, 1938

Then she recognised its cause as the head of the corpse which hung over her shoulder close to her own. . . . With a heavy splash her burden fell from her back and commenced to settle slowly into the semi-fluid ooze" (273–74).

When Hagar sees a buzzard in the sky, she gives up, defeated. She returns to the camp store and signs with her mark a dictated account of murdering Bluton. She then releases herself from the bonds that have held her in servitude her whole life. She gives everyone in the store her pocket money and proclaims, "Ah's done wid money. Ah's free now . . . free as Gawd" (285).

The balance of the money that Hagar has earned, secreted in a bank, is passed on to Lissa in New York, along with a newspaper clipping that Saint sends her relating the account of her mother's murdering Bluton. Lissa can now realize the potential denied to her mother and grandmother and advance in life. But she does not choose this route automatically. In Lissa's conflicted self, Heyward explores most deeply the conflict he himself felt about the evolution of African Americans from the plantation to the modern world. To Heyward, Lissa is "two separate entities" (236)—one a product of the older age that neither he nor she wants to shed completely, with its strong sense of heritage and ethnicity. The other entity embodies the future—the new Negro, educated, empowered, and moving among whites with full equality.

Heyward depicts this conflict within Lissa through music. In *Mamba's Daughters*, singing is an even more essential method of expression than in *Porgy*. Early in her social climb, Lissa is accepted into a set of educated African Americans who host a weekly salon. (This scene is one of the earliest depictions of such a class in American fiction.) At one meeting, a group performs "Swing Low, Sweet Chariot," in which the singing is held down "to a technical demonstration" and nothing seems to emanate from the soul (213)—rather like the Polperro fishermen Heyward had observed the year before, giving whitewashed performances of once-lively folk songs. These people, Lissa later tells Mamba, "seem to spend all their time . . . trying their damnedest to be white" (224). By contrast, in Lissa the music ceases "to be a thing, external, apart" and instead becomes "a fire in her body taking her suddenly like sheeting flame about a sapling, cutting her off from the others, possessing her, swaying her irresistibly forward toward the players." The music eventually possesses her, body and soul: "her sinuous body [was] a fluid medium through which the maddening reiteration of the rhythm beat out to the listeners and forced them to respond, her voice with its deep contralto beauty the very spirit of youth, yet shading the edges of laughter with a shadow of a sob" (237).

At the novel's end, when Lissa sings at the Met, she realizes that to advance, she need not divorce herself from her roots as an African American. She should sing soulfully, stirringly, as her instinct tells her to do, and thus at the same time demonstrate to the white world the wide-ranging gifts of song (and other forms of art) that the African American community possesses and can offer to the world.

Lissa's conflict is paralleled with that of Saint Wentworth, a stand-in for Heyward himself. Saint wants to be liberal minded and progressive, but he is burdened by his duty to uphold traditional standards of behavior in society, as all Wentworths before him have done. He sees injustice—such as his black assistant's being wrongly accused of a petty theft by white people who know the man did not commit the crime—and speaks out against it, but when he is reprimanded for meddling in a private system that is self-governing and, so the thinking goes, fair to African Americans in the long run, he backs down from his outrage and decides not to upset the status quo. Just as Lissa reconciles her conflict, so too does Heyward, through Saint, seem to reconcile his own. Saint decides that "the practical thing to do" is to stay in Charleston, "observe the conventions," and give African Americans "a leg up one at a time" (160). This thinking is echoed elsewhere in the novel by Mr. Atkinson, who also sees racial inequities around him and realizes that Mamba and Hagar are "individual entities battling with destiny" just "as he was—his wife—his children." He decides that "individuals—human beings—[are] the answer, perhaps. Can't lift the mass" (71–72).

Heyward therefore stops short of propagandizing for African Americans in *Mamba's Daughters*, but the novel nevertheless marks a giant step forward in his thinking about race. As a poet at the beginning of his career Heyward thought that certain elements of African American culture, such as jazz, might be used in a limited way by white artists. Of African Americans themselves, early on Heyward could only rue the white person's determination to "civilize" a race of free spirits and mourn the passing of their uncomplicated world with "wistful envy." Curiosity about such an alien world compelled him to write *Porgy*, but in creating the novel and the play that followed it, Heyward looked more closely at this alien society and saw the commonalities between its people and his own. In the novel and play versions of *Porgy*, Heyward adopted a rhetorical strategy that enabled him to depict racial inequality obliquely, through implication and subtle rhetorical gestures. In *Mamba's Daughters*, Heyward pressed his views more directly, explicitly depicting the differences and similarities among blacks and whites. He also confronted white Charleston society head on by satirizing it in the novel. Most important, in discerning the universal commonness between the races, Heyward saw that the crucible in which equality could be forged was art. This idea he would hold in mind and develop more fully as he worked toward *Porgy and Bess.*

In *Porgy*, Heyward's vision of race relations was somewhat idealized; his depiction of Charleston society was tinged by a nostalgia for a chimerical era that existed more in imagination than in fact. By the time he wrote *Mamba's Daughters*, Heyward had traded this vision of race relations for a more realistic, even sociological, view of class and color issues that in certain ways approaches the work of southern proletarian authors. Although Heyward's post-*Porgy* fiction is not specifically committed to a revolutionary social vision like that of Olive Tilford Dargan or Grace Lumpkin, it does transmute the old agrarian themes into reformist ones, especially the plight of blacks in the South. Although not a militantly antiracist novel, *Mamba's Daughters* bears comparison to Lillian Smith's 1944 novel, *Strange Fruit*, in its treatment of a black woman and a white man innocent of the world's meanness. Like *Strange Fruit*, *Mamba* effectively presents the social, ethical, and economic impact of white on black, black on white. To Heyward, the issue of race relations was the sine qua non of the socially committed fiction writer.

Heyward even tried his hand at a novel with a specifically proletarian thesis. This uncompleted novel dramatized the highly publicized textile workers' strike in 1929 in Gastonia, North Carolina. Its main character, a single mother, is dehumanized by the grim working conditions in the mill, preyed on sexually by one of the managers, and punished for her outspoken condemnation of the factory's labor policies. Parts of the fragmentary novel are quite bold by prevailing southern standards of 1930–31, when Heyward seems to have worked on it; this element of the novel in ways anticipates Caldwell's unrestrained method in *Tobacco Road* and *God's Little Acre*. Heyward's targeting class relations in the novel indicates his ability to embrace left-leaning social attitudes, although he would never commit himself to a revolutionary social program.

It is perhaps a cultural irony that the more liberal Heyward became in his novels, the more fame and wealth the novels brought him. Heyward was a true celebrity by the end of the 1920s. First *Porgy* then *Mamba's Daughters* had secured his place as one of the most prominent southern writers. The dramatic version of *Porgy* had made him and Dorothy quite well known in the New York cultural world. It had introduced Heyward to some influential people and made him something of a star, with his name often appearing in the literary pages of newspapers and sometimes in the gossip columns.

Heyward had also become linked in the public mind with social causes, particularly race relations. He accepted a position on the advisory board of the Association of Negro Writers and was also elected to the Writer's League against Lynching. He was more than ever in demand as a speaker and could pick and choose where he wanted to appear. And five years after giving his first poetry reading at Vassar College, where Hervey Allen was now teaching, Heyward returned for another appearance. Five years after its original publication, *Porgy* continued to sell well, spurred on by the success of *Mamba's Daughters. Porgy* was released in Swedish, and a new translation in Japanese was undertaken: the novel now appeared in five languages. In addition, *Mamba's Daughters* was appearing in translation serially in the Paris newspapers, as *Porgy* had before it.

Honors seemed to be bestowed on Heyward virtually everywhere he went. In November 1930, *Vanity Fair* magazine nominated him for its "hall of fame," not just on the basis of his recent successful books and plays but because he was "one of the most important figures in the literary renaissance of the south." Back home, he was made an honorary Phi Beta Kappa of the local chapter at the University of South Carolina. Sometimes, however, the old lack of confidence surfaced. The following year, Sewanee, the University of the South, asked Heyward to give that year's commencement address, but he politely refused. Famous or not, Heyward still felt insecure around "superior" intellects, such as he expected to find at the college, and he did not want to draw attention to his own lack of formal education. "It was simply out of my depth," he told his mother. He did, however, accept the College of Charleston's offer of an honorary doctor of letters degree at their commencement exercises on 14 May 1931. A hometown degree was perhaps easier for Heyward to accept—a local boy who had made good.

With the earnings from the play and from the *Mamba* serial, scheduled to begin running in June 1928, Heyward had a new home built on his North Carolina property. Dawn Hill, as the residence was eventually named, was a large white house set on extensive grounds with a huge garden and a swimming pool. On one side a two-tiered veranda ran the width of the house and faced the hills. In the woods to the rear, far enough away to be out of earshot from the telephone and any other distractions, were two small studios, one for Heyward and one for Dorothy. Their routine was to work here alone from nine to one each day; after lunch each took a nap, then a walk, and then read or had friends in for dinner at night.

The house was a long way from the drafty cabin in which Heyward had written *Porgy,* and it symbolized his success at a career in art. When he visited Bennett in Charleston earlier that year, he told his friend that he never dreamed such money "would be possible in the Heyward family," especially from writing, and he sported new clothes of "the latest London make," a malacca cane, buff spats, and a new car. Bennett, however, did not think Heyward affected. He felt Heyward actually seemed "simpler and more himself" now than he had been just after his initial success with *Porgy.*

The graph of Heyward's life, however, was always a pattern of peaks and valleys, highs and lows—much like Charleston, in fact, with its cycles of boom and bust, felicity and tragedy. In an unusually unguarded moment in 1928 he had written to Josephine Pinckney, "I am by way of being dirty rich these days, dear old Joey." But his life had never, in his words, let him "meet one thing at a time," and so that same year he and Dorothy were devastated by the birth of a stillborn child: "it has all been terrible," he wrote to Pinckney. Sadly, too, much of his earnings from *Mamba* were erased by the slump in stocks that followed the financial panic of 1929. But in February 1930 his and Dorothy's fortunes seemed again to reverse themselves with the birth of a daughter, Jenifer, a delight to them both.

Heyward was now clearly enjoying the authority of fame and, in particular, his celebrity status among Charlestonians. He felt confident enough to offer advice, write blurbs, and attend gallery openings. He took a mentoring interest in Elizabeth O'Neill Verner, as Bennett had done for him years earlier. He commissioned Verner to do an etching of Catfish Row for the frontispiece of the French *Porgy*. He told her that "the publication would not pay much" but "would place your name before a lot of artistic people in Paris and on the continent." More honors redounded to Heyward in June 1928 when the University of North Carolina presented him with an honorary doctorate of letters.

In fact, Heyward and the university circle there developed a cozy friendship. Whereas Heyward had earlier separated himself from these crusaders, he now read the *Journal of Social Forces* with keen interest, especially articles on such issues as Negro education and racial equality. He praised Odum and Johnson for their courageous stands on Negro issues, and when the Richmond-based *Reviewer* was transferred to the university and to Green's editorship, Heyward singled the journal out for praise. At Chapel Hill he was often entertained by Dean of Arts and Sciences Addison Hibbard, whose influential syndicated book column, "The Literary Lantern," had praised Heyward; Heyward in turn had applauded Hibbard's *Reviewer* essays in their calls for criticism of current life in the South.

These figures uniformly praised *Mamba's Daughters* as evidence of Heyward's new socially correct thinking. In contrast, one of the more traditional-minded Fugitive poets, Donald Davidson, objected to the novel on precisely the grounds that Heyward (like Wolfe) had become a "New York writer." Once a local colorist, Heyward was now writing like some "fly-by-night millionaire novelist from the Riviera . . . who put his yacht into Charleston harbor for the winter season and picked up enough local color to fill out his contract for a fifteenth best-selling novel." Davidson liked the sympathetic treatment of Hagar but objected to the scenes of life at the mining camp. He thought Heyward was merely railing against an "unholy system" by which workers were kept under the thumbs of the evil bosses, a "doctrinaire" attitude that Davidson could not tolerate. The success of Lissa as a singer was an unbelievably "pat echo of the Harlem school of rhapsody and propaganda," Davidson wrote. He thought, in sum, that Heyward wrote like a "latter-day abolitionist."

As the Fugitives became the Agrarians and penned their 1930 manifesto, *I'll Take My Stand,* they became allied against the new southerners like Green, Odum, Johnson, and Cash, whose *The Mind of the South* would appear in 1941. As the Agrarians called into question the notion of progress and proclaimed their preferences for a traditional, agrarian civilization rather than a modern, industrial way of life, Heyward by contrast responded to the call issued by the social critics, moving from sweetness and light to a confrontation of hard social realities. Defending Heyward, Cash said that he was pleased to hear that *Mamba* had met with disfavor from traditional southerners. That the story was "both pointless and untrue to the Southern Negro" indicated to Cash that "Mr. Heyward's portrayals fit neither the Uncle Tom formula nor that of the vaudeville buffoon" and that a major social critic was thus in their midst.

Brass Ankle certainly leaves no doubt about Heyward's reformist views. This play was his boldest confrontation yet of the race question. The play is more melodramatic than anything else Heyward wrote, and for that reason it was his least successful work. He seems to have intended it to be a shocker from the outset; when he began writing it, in the fall of 1929, he told Bennett that he was "starting into some fairly intense stuff," a description that in retrospect seems an understatement. Perhaps because of the sensationalistic material—the title refers to a familiar southern epithet of the time for people of mixed-race blood, usually African American or Native American—Heyward also was downright secretive about the project. When Bennett pressed Heyward for more information to publish in the Poetry Society yearbook, he replied, "There isn't an awful lot to report. . . . [P]ersonally I wish to avoid as much preliminary cack as possible. The safest thing is to be mysterious." These statements indicate that Heyward well knew how radical this material was. All Heyward would say was that "Unlike *Porgy*, the play is presented with a white cast, and has no spirituals. It is almost unmitigated realistic tragedy."

The play is in fact brutally realistic. It concerns Larry and Ruth Leamer, a young couple with a little girl and a new baby on the way, who live in the fictional Rivertown, a village on the edge of a swamp somewhere in the Deep South. Larry is a respected local leader. He is a member of the school board and a likely candidate for mayor when the village incorporates into a town and continues on its program of civic improvements—an event expected to take place soon. These "improvements" include segregating the schools. The impetus for the plan is the discovery that a local family, the Jacksons, has Negro blood. The village leaders want to remove the Jackson children from the white school and send them to the school for Negroes. Larry has researched the Jackson family tree and discovered documents that confirm the family's Negro ancestry.

Ironically, however, Larry discovers that his wife, Ruth, is herself a "brass ankle," though she did not know it when they married. This makes their young daughter, June, technically a Negro; moreover, when Ruth gives birth to their baby son, the child turns out to be a genetic throwback to Ruth's Negro ancestry: the boy is dark-skinned, with pronounced Negroid features. Once the town learns of the baby's appearance and Ruth's "tainted" blood, Larry is ostracized. Ruth wishes to save him and their daughter from shame. Various reasonable plans are discussed, but the option she finally chooses is shocking and ludicrous. She gathers the villagers in her living room, feigns drunkenness, shows the baby so that everyone can see its race, and then proffers an improbable confession that she slept with a black family servant (now conveniently dead), whose son she is now holding. She then loads a double-barreled shotgun, sets it down with a gesture that invites her husband to shoot her and the baby, and then goes to her bedroom. Larry takes up the gun, kills his wife and new baby (offstage), and the curtain falls. Heyward implies that Larry will not be prosecuted because of the racist attitudes inherent in community law, and his daughter June can continue to be considered white.

Heyward had difficulty getting this play produced because of the boldness of its subject matter. Miscegenation, treated by black writers since the early novels and slave narratives of pre–Civil War times and reaching its peak with Harlem Renaissance artists, was to that point rarely addressed by white writers. (Green's *White Dresses* employs the topic mostly for its melodramatic value.) Heyward used the theme to explore racial attitudes and behavior. One must remember that in the 1920s and '30s the idea of romantic interracial unions was thought of as a colossal cultural transgression. The producers of Eugene O'Neill's 1924 drama of miscegenation, *All God's Chillun Got Wings,* had to avert a riot when the playwright cast the white actress Mary Blair opposite Paul Robeson and word got out that Blair was to kiss the black man's hand in the play. Groups lobbied to close down the show before it even premiered. O'Neill had to make his white heroine go crazy before she kissed the black character's hand, thus making the scene palatable to white theatergoers.

Heyward offered *Brass Ankle* first to Theresa Helbrun at the Theatre

Guild, but even that innovative organization balked at the material. Helbrun tried politely to ignore the play, hoping that Heyward would not press the matter. But Heyward felt strongly about the play and wrote to Helbrun to chide her: "I feel that the month that has elapsed since you have had the play under consideration has given you ample time for the exclusive first reading that I agreed to give you at the time we signed up for *Porgy.*" When the guild rejected the play, Heyward took it to New York director Guthrie McClintic, who took out an option but then let it lapse. The play was finally taken up by James W. Elliott Productions, and it was presented it on 23 April 1931. Alice Brady, a famous stage actress, starred as Ruth Leamer.

It is likely, however, that Helbrun and McClintic balked at more than just the frank material in the play. They doubtless also were appalled at the low quality of the work. The play is sheer melodrama with little thoughtful consideration of the issue it confronts. The plot is predictable. The paper-thin characters speak in clichés that merely mimic timeworn expressions of cowardly narrow-mindedness: "What I say is black's black an' white's white"; "Keep 'em where they belong"; and "That's what I say—the bastards are all right in their place" (43; 42). The dialogue and the blocking are wooden, and the playing out of the action is so bald and inept that one would think Heyward lacked even the slightest understanding of subtlety or indirection. He took a profound social problem of confused racial identity and merely sketched it. This theme was handled more thoughtfully by Faulkner, particularly in *Light in August,* as well as by Heyward's Charleston friends Samuel Gaillard Stoney and Gertrude Shelby Matthews in a novel published just before *Brass Ankle* appeared on Broadway, *Po' Buckra. Brass Ankle* also resembles Wolfe's early drama *Welcome to My City* (which had lost to Dorothy Heyward's *Nancy Ann* in the 1923 Harvard competition), a play about a small southern town's attempts to oust Negroes from their neighborhoods.

Nonetheless, much should be said in Heyward's favor. First, he confronted the issue of miscegenation with candor—courageously and unapologetically for someone of his background and social position. If Heyward meant to shock his audience, he succeeded. The tawdry atmosphere of the village and its lower-class whites is repellent. The character of Larry is also repulsive in its unmitigated bigotry and belief in white supremacy. *Brass Ankle* is also arresting in its confrontation of a people so overwhelmingly intolerant of differentness and cultural diversity. In the play, too, Heyward continues his interest in the fate of African Americans in a new world, and his interest in race issues became even deeper and franker than in *Mamba's Daughters*.

However, the play lacks a sensitivity to aesthetics and to theatrical plausibility. Heyward constructed a scenario so horrific that his failure to cope with the social problem presented, and his failure to present a plausible resolution of the plot, is unsatisfying. His failure to offer some solution to the Leamer family's dilemma could not be excused in so tragic a situation. In his earlier works, such as *Porgy* and *Mamba's Daughters*, Heyward could evade grappling with race issues because those scenarios were not as brutal; they were more complex and less sensationalistic. Moreover, Heyward offers life for Porgy and Lissa elsewhere. In *Brass Ankle*, he offers no hope for anyone, a nihilistic conclusion that is too pat to accept.

Brass Ankle closed after only forty-four performances, but the reviews blended praise and criticism—not at all the panning that one might suspect the play would receive. One reviewer said it deserved the Pulitzer Prize, and another put it on his list of the ten best plays of the season. Nobody ignored it, and many excused Heyward his inelegancies, saying that perhaps he merely intended to draw attention to the miscegenation question and write a shocking story about it. Heyward gave his own assessment of the play to Allen, but even it is ambivalent. Heyward said that he "felt that it would never run [anyway], and with a perfectly desperate season [on Broadway] it languished. I am sending you a copy; and when you read it you will understand many things. Why I am not so hot with the old guard at home, and why the press ran the whole gamut. . . . From a rather sour one in the Times to unqualified praise from some of the other top-stringers. At any rate, I am happy to have done it."

Perhaps in consequence of his frankness in *Brass Ankle*, in his next major work, Heyward was more restrained though no less sweeping in his critiques of race and class. *Peter Ashley* is one of his finest works, along with *Porgy* and *Mamba's Daughters*. The novel was published by Farrar and Rinehart in 1932, after being serialized in the *Woman's Home Companion*. Heyward had wanted to write a novel about the Civil War since as early as 1926. At that time, he told Allen that it was one of many ideas percolating, but Heyward did not yet feel prepared to start it. Just before beginning *Mamba's Daugh-*

ters in 1928, Heyward again thought about the idea, telling South Carolina historian Yates Snowden that to write an "epic novel" was his greatest ambition, but Heyward again could not push through with a draft. Finally, in 1929, with *Mamba's Daughters* completed, Heyward came up with a story idea, the period just before and during the war, and began his work in earnest. Heyward "put in a hard spell of study" for the book in the Charleston Library Society in the fall of 1930, immersing himself in accounts of the events in Charleston by reading newspaper clippings and private documents, such as the letters and diaries of those involved. Some elements of the research, such as that into the French-English civilization of South Carolina, were laborious.

Heyward's method liberated him from several restraints that typically governed writers of historical fiction. He confined himself only to the information and the knowledge that a Charlestonian would have had in the time period of the novel—the beginning of the Civil War. Thus, unlike in many southern novels about the war from that period (Evelyn Scott's *The Wave* [1929] or Stark Young's *So Red the Rose* [1934], for example), in *Peter Ashley* there is no view of the internal affairs of the Confederacy or of different military campaigns—readers see only what Peter observes with his own eyes. Moreover, as Heyward said in an essay he wrote about the novel for *Publishers' Weekly*, he aimed not to catch history "in a post-mortem sense" but to capture the temper and spirit of the time as revealed in "the daily papers, reports, diaries [and] first-hand descriptions of men still living." This was an innovative method. It enabled Heyward (most of the time) to avoid the excesses of the archromantic, cloak-and-sword historical novel, particularly about the antebellum South, that was then so commonplace: what exists in parts of Allen's *Anthony Adverse* and Margaret Mitchell's *Gone with the Wind*. Finally, the technique also allowed Heyward to jettison the pretentious voice of the enlightened Charleston aristocrat, as heard in *Porgy* and in parts of *Mamba's Daughters*.

Heyward's views of his southern heritage had deepened and broadened considerably since he had begun writing in the early 1920s. In *Peter Ashley* Heyward criticizes the South more overtly than in any previous work—a boldness made possible by his confronting the race issue so directly in *Brass Ankle*. In *Peter Ashley* Heyward addresses such issues as the family (under attack from both private and public forces), the inadequacy of the traditional order to tolerate dissent and change, and, of course, slavery. In *Porgy* Heyward seemed never for a moment to question the rightness of the aristocracy. That view changed in *Mamba's Daughters,* a novel that was quite critical of the white Charlestonian elite. Further, *Porgy* and its play version had introduced Heyward to a new world, in which many of the old standards were no longer in place, in which color did not matter, in which the challenge of human achievement was open to all. In *Peter Ashley* Heyward casts his eye back over the southern baronial past and finds it lacking in critical judgment and sensitivity to human rights. In this novel he writes one vast elegy for the way of life that from birth he had been taught to cherish. Heyward does not lambaste the aristocracy or indict Charleston and the South as evil. He sees much that is admirable: grace, honor, tradition, determination. But Heyward also sees the results of extreme fidelity to those elements in the face of plain sense. Although in the end the protagonist chooses complacency and belonging over dissent and rebellion, he is painfully aware that he has compromised his values in so doing. That ambiguity reflects Heyward's own persistent questioning of what it meant to be a Charlestonian.

As the novel begins, Peter Ashley is returning to Charleston after studying at Oxford. Peter has been sent there by his uncle, Pierre Chardon, his guardian since Chardon's wife and children perished in a typhoid epidemic and the Ashley family allowed Chardon to raise Peter as a surrogate son. Chardon, in the true spirit of his Huguenot ancestors, is a philosopher and an aesthete. He is a nonconformist in a culture dominated by tradition. Chardon has raised Peter to follow in these footsteps, so when Peter arrives in Charleston as the Ordinance of Secession is being signed in December 1860, he is flung into a conflict for which he is unprepared. In his youth with Chardon and later in his studies at Oxford, Peter has come to question the accepted southern orthodoxies, especially the issues of slavery and the wisdom of separation from the Union.

Like Saint Wentworth, he wishes to pursue a life of the arts. Full of idealistic ambitions, Peter intends to strengthen Charleston's vibrant literary culture, which has grown up around the Russell's Bookstore group of William Gilmore Simms, Paul Hayne, and Henry Timrod. But when Peter arrives in Charleston he finds that secession fever has gripped the city, including its writers, who with everyone else have unhesitatingly endorsed disunion. Peter manages to keep his artistic and political principles intact and distanced from his hometown's secessionist spirit, particularly through a difficult stint writing for the local newspaper, which forces him to pepper his articles with anti-Union sentiments, and in a duel with the vulgar Archie Holcombe, who has publicly called Peter an abolitionist. But eventually the force of tradition and the need to belong pull Peter back into the fold of family and society, and he joins a local regiment just in time for the artillery duel with the Union forces at Fort Sumter. He weds a local woman named Damaris Gordon, puts his objections to war aside, and goes off to fight.

Heyward aims most of his shafts of criticism at the aristocracy, which, through Pierre Chardon's point of view, the author views as sterile and sometimes foolish. The scenes during Race Week, a Charleston tradition, depict this community as lacking individuality—in appearance and in manners but by extension also in thinking and in mores. In one passage, the narrator notes that everyone looks "remarkably alike, bearing as they did the marks of their class." Their eyes bespeak a candid intelligence, but they are "not the eyes of analysts"; they are the eyes of "a people with an enormous capacity for faith in its accepted beliefs. Faces singularly free from the marks of mental conflict" (80).

To Peter, this class now seems incapable of or unwilling to entertain introspection or independent thought. In one particularly memorable line, a friend tells Peter that a southern wife need not be intelligent but merely possess "a superficial brilliance." Later, Peter reflects on the impossibility of changing the thinking of a society so wedded to tradition and custom: "Generation succeeding generation in the same surroundings, facing the same problems, old faces fading away at the hunting club dinners, the race meets, their places filled by young faces varying little from the hereditary mold" (135). Having been abroad, Peter finds distasteful the puerile provincialism that many of his countrymen evince. He recalls a letter once sent him by his Uncle Porcher, when Peter was at Oxford, asserting that nowhere in the world compared to the Carolina lowcountry.

Peter no longer fits in with the society to which he has been bred. The book then becomes a meditation on how difficult it is for a Charlestonian, then as well as in Heyward's time, to choose a life of art, of the mind, of philosophy, instead of a life of conforming to tradition. Heyward aligns himself intellectually with Peter and Pierre. When, for instance, Peter tells his father that he wishes to make poetry his life's work, his father tells him, exasperated, that "even for a bookworm there were dignified alternatives—medicine, the law, statecraft. 'But great God . . . not a poet! I have done nothing to deserve that!" (31) Peter's dilemma is to choose between individualism and the mass, between acting on principle and acceding to conventional wisdom. According to the narrator, Peter "must conform or he must be destroyed." The temptation to conform is strong: "He has but to march into camp and lay down his arms. He is acclaimed a hero. He at once surrenders his will to the mass. . . . And for the nonconformist—what? Only the approval of a small, stubborn, inner voice that will not be silenced" (103).

Passages like these, however, are balanced by a recurring ambivalence about the southern character—a reflection of 'eyward's own ambivalence. Like Pierre Chardon, whose heterodox views are always colored by a tinge of sentimentalism, Heyward could never give himself over completely to iconoclasm and reform. For example, Peter eventually reconciles slavery and Christianity on the dubious principle of "good form": he knows that the slaves at his family's plantation are "well treated" and that some masters are even guilty of "pampering their Negro yards." Yet he has also heard of "the horrors of the cane fields in the deeper South." What standards, he wonders, "could be so elastic in [their] application?" He concludes that "good form" is the explanation—the same code that "surrounded the institution of dueling, or behavior upon a ballroom floor." In the master-slave relationship, "there were certain decencies to be observed," and if a gentleman failed, "there were deflections in every social order." This code allows Peter "to reconcile conscience and necessity. It buttressed the threatened edifice with certain Christian virtues and endowed the impending conflict with the indispensable elements of a crusade" (70–71).

An experience at the slave market just a few pages later seems to confirm to him the validity of his theory. Peter joins his friends in outbidding a villainous slave trader ("a nigger splitter," one who breaks up slave families by selling each family member off to a different master), so that the slave for sale can work at the Ashley plantation under humane conditions. Peter's actions enable his friends to point out that he is not a rebel after all: "I am glad to see that you are still one of us," they say (82).

Peter's feeling of belonging is affirmed by Race Week, where his sense of the neighborhood's "common personality" and "solidarity" appeal to him. Then, when Holcombe charges that Peter is a traitor, he is absorbed into the "rhythm of the crowd," which pounds in his blood: "His town, his state. And these men about him, waiting, headstrong, blind perhaps, but generous, impulsive, passionate, surrounding him, pressing in upon him with the weight of a single unalterable idea" (207–8). Peter finally senses that his fate is predestined when near the end of the novel he accepts from Damaris the gift of a slave, the same man that he had helped rescue from the slave trader.

There is, of course, irony in these statements. Heyward's tone almost always undercuts the complacency that Peter voices in deciding to belong rather than to rebel. Peter can see the fallaciousness of his change in thinking, and Heyward makes clear that what Peter ends up doing does not reflect what he truly thinks is right. Peter—and, by extension, Heyward—is symbolic of the transition between the closing of the southern mind in the contradiction between slavery and Christian values in the nineteenth century and the recovery of memory and history by the southern renaissance in the twentieth century.

Peter Ashley received mixed reviews. Many critics praised Heyward's handling of Peter's "rebellion." Pointing out the irony with which Heyward handled this issue, the *New York Times* reviewer commented at length on Heyward's sympathy with Peter and concluded that ultimately, "the mores" of Charleston society "become the ironic hero" of the book. This reviewer compared Heyward's method with Stephen Crane's in *The Red Badge of Courage*. But the critics generally thought the novel was flat, pointing out a lack of truly full development in the character of Peter, a perfunctory love story; and the "atmospherically pat" quality of the descriptions. Several reviews noted that Heyward did not seem to have as much command of the psychology of the white man as he had of the African American.

Charlestonians, according to Bennett, were "puzzled" by the novel. They had expected Heyward to put an "entire, uncritical approval of everything southern" into Peter's character. Bennett told Heyward, "I think, had you shown him galloping into St. Michael's on a coal-black stallion, full panoply of gray, singing at the top of his golden voice, which rang through the historic structure like a bugle stirring the south . . . to action . . . 'The Bonny Blue Flag,' or the chorus of 'Dixie,' they would all have sunk back into their easy chairs with a happy sigh of relief and instant approval." But "the suggestion that there was any whose heart grew doubtful, or who perceived the bitter thorns among the roses of that old life . . . makes some hearts twitter still.

You know some of those which twitter at the mere mention of shadows in the past." Bennett's remarks indicate that Heyward was still seen by some quarters in Charleston as a defector to New South thinking.

More accurately, *Peter Ashley* shows how a Charlestonian like Heyward could manage to become a liberal in a way acceptable to himself and not completely at odds with his social training. Like Peter Ashley, Heyward tried to preserve tradition while effecting change. Only a Charlestonian could do so because of the city's relationship with the past, one quite different from that of other southern cities. In the popular conception of Charleston, the haven of charm and grace to which Mitchell's Rhett Butler returns, the city is unreflecting, awash in its idiosyncrasies and sense of self-importance. To outsiders, the cultural desideratum of charm is seen as a blight that impeded the development of great art. Belonging to a tradition and preserving continuity are important elements that must not be sacrificed. Thus arises the image of Charleston as a city frozen in time (the image that Heyward evoked in the opening of *Porgy*), immobilized. In contrast, the project of most modern southern literature is the comprehension of change. It is little wonder, then, that Charleston has often seemed marginal to modern literature.

Yet in 1930, as in 1860, when *Peter Ashley* takes place, Charleston was changing and was fully aware of doing so. As Michael O'Brien points out, the change differed from that affecting the Deep South, the region inhabited by the Agrarians, for example. Tate held that the best southern literature would be created by steering a middle course between alienation and belonging to tradition. Yet Tate, as with Faulkner and Wolfe and other modernists, invariably chose alienation as the driving force of literature. Charlestonians chose belonging. Their circumstances made it difficult to do otherwise.

Pinckney adumbrated the situation in a 1934 essay on southern conservatism written for a Chapel Hill symposium and published as *Culture in the South*. Pinckney pointed out that Charleston was and is a more concrete place than anywhere else in the South. It survived the ravages of war with most of its institutions intact. She characterized the "local divergences" among such southern cities as Birmingham, Vicksburg, Chattanooga, and New Orleans. Charleston was "a trifle more austere" than New Orleans, for example: "the English culture absorbed the French to a surprising degree, and after all the Huguenot was the French Puritan." The city's "peculiarities," she continued, "are sympathetic to neither French nor American culture." And, she added, the South considers Charleston "most peculiar." Moreover, the most pervasive Charleston tradition was that of family, emblematic of the South ever since the Civil War. As Heyward well knew, in Charleston more than in the South generally, name was seen as a continuation of tradition, a bulwark against the horrors of the modern world.

The semitraditionalist among the Agrarians, Davidson, said as much in a 1949 essay, "Some Day, in Old Charleston." He praised Charleston's stability, its "subtle balance of persistence and innovation." The secret was "the old southern principle that material considerations . . . are means not ends, and should always be subdued to the ends they are supposed to service." To that statement Davidson might have added the unusual concreteness of Charleston as a place. Such was the buffer against modernity's tendency toward abstraction and alienation.

Receiving an intact tradition, as Charlestonians did, and a broken one, as did the writers of the southern renaissance, are quite different propositions. The problem Peter Ashley faces, as Heyward himself faced, is neatly, albeit starkly, put: how to effect change while restoring and preserving tradition.

As modern southern views of race relations, *Mamba's Daughters* and *Brass Ankle* are fascinating. Heyward's ability in *Peter Ashley* to turn inward and analyze himself and the culture that produced him is equally notable. By the mid-1930s, in his novels and plays, Heyward had deeply explored both sides of race and class issues, as perceived by the Negro community and by the white aristocracy. After *Peter Ashley* Heyward may not have been able to write of the South as he once had. As Heyward came to question the dictates of heart, family, and community, it may have been difficult for him to envision another novel set in Charleston.

In *Lost Morning* (1936), Heyward's last major work, he continued to critique southern ideals and to reflect on his status as a southerner in a changing world. But the novel takes place in the South Carolina piedmont region, and it concerns none of the commonplace southern institutions. Heyward's new subject was a virtual first in southern fiction: the artist in the South. (Ellen Glasgow had treated the subject in her first novel, *The Descendant* [1897], but did so with little success.) Heyward addresses the exploitation of the artist by the new southern plutocracy, and he returns to the theme with which he began his career, the conflict between art and commerce. The novel is not a roman à clef, but it does possess autobiographical resonance.

Lost Morning seems more the work of John O'Hara or John P. Marquand rather than Heyward. The scene is laid against a backdrop of swank—country clubs, highballs, and roadsters—in a medium-sized city called Exeter. The setting is about as different from Charleston as could be imagined. Unlike Charleston, Exeter represents the emergent New South: white-collar businessmen and professionals comprise its society—an ersatz gentry, as opposed to Charleston's true aristocracy. These conventional-minded people assume a patrician pose, but they are not, like the Charlestonians with whom Heyward was familiar, to the manner born.

In this atmosphere of the high-powered southern nouveaux riches Heyward places his protagonist, Felix Hollister, an artist. Twenty years earlier, Hollister underwent his apprenticeship in Paris, studying under no less a figure than Matisse, who trained Hollister in painting and clay modeling. However, under the influence of Miriam, his business-minded wife, Hollister gave up that work to become an etcher, working in a medium that yielded quicker results for his work as well as a substantial profit, primarily among the tourist trade. Hollister's specialties are quaint scenes of historic areas, such as Charleston, New Orleans, and Williamsburg.

Despite his financial success, the ironically named Felix Hollister (unhappy and hollow) has never been pleased with how his life has turned out. For one thing, he is married to a shrew; Miriam's self-centeredness and the ithyphallic control she maintains over the rather weak-willed Hollister reminds one of Ernest Hemingway's Margot Macomber or Sinclair Lewis's Fran Dodsworth. Hollister also lives and works in a region that Heyward describes as impersonal and insensitive to the higher values of art and learning. Finally, Hollister is forced to face up to his cowardly abandonment of high art for the lure of money by his secretary and studio assistant, Leslie Morgan, who urges him to discard his present life and pick up where he left off twenty years previously.

Leslie Morgan becomes the symbol of Hollister's lost morning—his wasted opportunity. (Her name sounds like "lost morning"; *morgen* is the German word for morning; *Leslie* suggests less, a diminution, or loss.) Whereas Leslie encourages Felix to do what he wants to do, Miriam commands him to do her bidding, manipulating him under the false guise of improving him. In fact, Miriam has arranged a business deal that would bring her husband's artistic self-esteem to an all-time low: she is proposing to have a series of Hollister etchings accompany an advertising campaign for a cigarette manufacturer. (Tobacco represents the loss of pure agrarian ideals to New South commercialism.) The etchings would be seen everywhere from billboards to smutty men's magazines.

On the evening when Miriam proposes her plan to Felix, he flees the house, half in fear, half in revolt, and ends up at Leslie's apartment, where for a moment in time he is assertive and free. She in turn confesses her amorous feelings for him, and they kiss, but then Felix weakens, still trying to balance the conflicting demands of heart and head, of Exeter, Miriam, and stability versus the wider world of Leslie and artistic freedom. He flees again.

The rest of the plot is a mix of unsatisfying contrivances and genuinely deft touches of deliberate ambiguity. Feeling spurned by Felix, Leslie packs up her belongings and intends to leave Exeter right away. She writes a note to Felix, resigning from his employ. She then walks across the street to mail the letter, but in so doing she is struck by a hit-and-run driver. When Leslie's body is discovered the next morning, suicide is assumed, and her neighbors place the blame on Felix, having witnessed the two embracing the evening before. a scandal is about to erupt but is forestalled by the capable machinations of Miriam, who manipulates the coroner and other city officials and establishes an alibi for Felix. No one, including Felix, knows the truth—that Leslie did not commit suicide over Felix.

Leslie's alleged suicide is the impetus for Felix finally to break with Miriam, with Exeter, and with the commercialization of his talent. He divorces Miriam and moves to New York, where he takes a studio to do clay modeling. But he also allows a partial compromise by securing a monthly stipend from the cigarette advertising deal to provide him with an income while he redis-covers his artistic self.

It was natural for Heyward to choose an etcher for his subject, because drawing (and later painting) were his own early loves. Hollister shares many other characteristics with his creator. Physically, Hollister resembles Hey-ward: he is "a tall man with a loose, angular frame and broad thin shoulders carried slightly forward in a premature stoop," a characteristic that "should have suggested an age greater than a man's mid-forties" but was, "paradoxi-cally, quite the reverse": "adolescence, a co-ordination not yet mastered rather than one which was breaking down" (5). Hollister is also not a good self-promoter; this task he gladly leaves to his wife, who has pushed him to the heights of his success. He is also absentminded, like Heyward, and nervous. He dislikes driving, a trait that Heyward expands into a motif in the novel, contrasting Hollister with his wife, who is an aggressive driver, exerting a "masculine grip" on the steering wheel. Hollister also never drives with Miriam; he is thus "driven" by her. ("Felix . . . is good for sixty miles per hour when I . . . throw him in gear," Miriam says [77].) And finally, Hollister has not "kept up with modern trends" in art during his self-induced exile in Exeter (62).

Like Heyward early in his career, Hollister also finds himself pinioned uncomfortably between two different worlds, the world of business and the world of art. Moreover, he sees the difference between his provincial world and the wider world of art beyond Exeter. In a scene with Jarvis Maxton, the cigarette manufacturer, Hollister feels that he must treat with Maxton with false bonhomie, to "hide" his artistic nature (78). Another philosophical similarity between Heyward and Hollister is their belief that God is manifest in nature, and thus their worship of God through art rather than through more traditional forms. Hollister does not care for the formality and ceremony of Episcopalianism (94).

The autobiographical resonance of the novel can best be seen when its theme is viewed as conflict and compromise, recurring issues in Heyward's life and work, especially since *Brass Ankle*. The conflict is art versus craft or high art versus commercialism. Hollister has chosen etching, a form of art that can be mass-produced. He has aimed, like Heyward, for a wide, popular audience. And he has remained a strictly regional artist—one with a national audience, to be sure, but nonetheless one who rarely strays outside the boundaries of his artistic home base. Like Heyward, Hollister also understands the differences between what he does and what other artists do. He is aware of the differences, and like Peter Ashley, has made his choices consciously and rationally. Hollister's philosophy is that "every man finds his level" (14). The successful man, according to Hollister, realizes his limitations early on and stays within them.

Against this set of premises Heyward places an opposing philosophy, one that pulls his character in the other direction, the same tension that Heyward felt. This conflict is seen in the series of chapters leading up to the novel's midpoint. These chapters are set on the Sunday morning following Hollister's first frustrated visit to Leslie's apartment. Feeling that he has sold out to commercialism, he resolves one Sunday morning to go to his studio and create what his heart tells him to paint. Instead of the austere black lines against the white background of his etchings, Hollister has now created a distinctively rebellious, nontraditional work of art that is a riot of color— "red, purple, magenta, in violent conflict." In the foreground, there is a bed on which lays "the exaggerated breasts and long white limbs of a woman": "Hanging over the figure, with rudimentary hands that held back heavy purple draperies, was a form, obese, lewd. There was the rondure of a pendulous belly, above it twin half moons that suggested flabby male breasts, and out of the purple shadows a spheroid that hung inward over the supine figure, with a great beak of a nose showing in perspective." The figure represents "lust incarnate, unleashed and gloating over its prey" (109). The painting was inspired by Hollister's visit to Leslie the previous night, and the "passionate conviction" that she expressed in him, as well as by his previous summer's visit with her in the mountains, when her "young confident body" leaned "outward against the weight of the wind," like the Winged Victory of Samothrace. The fragmented and disjointed representation, however, more closely recalls some of Picasso's drawings, and the lewd situation it depicts also seems an allusion to the myth of Leda and the swan.

Miriam is horrified by the painting and throws a sheet over the canvas to hide it from the bewildered gaze of the dinner guests she has brought home from church. She suddenly sees in her husband "something sinister, enigmatic . . . that in all these years she had never guessed" (109). The guests repulse Felix: they are the moneyed philistines for whom he feels he has prostituted his talent. He flouts Miriam and her carefully arranged publicity event by moving a press out of the way for his visitors, staining his white suit with the colored ink, and walking out on Miriam, who has violated the sanctity of his holy inner temple, his studio, and has invited the money changers into his place of worship.

When Hollister makes his break, the conflict between art and commerce is imaged in another way—the motif of clay modeling. Earlier in the novel, Hollister defends his choice to be an etcher to his daughter, Felicia. Like Leslie, Felicia feels that Hollister has sold out, and she urges him to give up etching for clay modeling, his first love (59). At this point, Hollister desires to model Felicia, in whom he sees himself at a young age, before his talent has been compromised. At the end of the novel, when he revolts, it is fitting that he works in clay, a malleable substance, so that he can remake himself in a different image, recast his identity, become another man.

Hollister does so by making his break with Miriam, with Exeter, and with etching, and as the novel closes it appears that Hollister will be happy reliving his former life as the archetypal starving artist in New York. *Lost Morning* is thus on the one hand an embellished retelling of Heyward's own 1924 break with a life he did not want. Heyward takes as his epigraph for this novel a statement from Sidney Lanier's notebooks that served as Heyward's talisman in the early 1920s: "a man does not reach any stature of manhood until, like Moses, he kills an Egyptian . . . and flies into the desert of his own soul." In *Lost Morning*, Hollister slays his Egyptian. Like Heyward in 1924, Hollister sees "how small a difference there is between freedom and exile. If you could stand alone, fight through and win, you were free. If you had overestimated your power, and failed, you were lost, an alien in a strange land" (259). Heyward could say with some satisfaction that he had won and was free.

But on the other hand, the conflict in the novel is resolved through compromise rather than a rebellious repudiation of everything that was once true and dear to Hollister. The same, of course, might be said for Heyward. In the 1920s he had tutored himself in the ways of the world outside Charleston, and he grew as a person and artist. But with all his successes doing something that was unusual, even shocking, for a white southerner to do, Heyward could never bring himself to abandon Charleston completely or to embrace uncritically the new progressive social philosophies of the modern world. Thus like *Peter Ashley*, wherein Heyward signaled his disapproval of southern thinking yet still asserted that he belonged to the South, *Lost Morning* also places its protagonist squarely in the field of compromise.

From his rise in the New York theater world with the play *Porgy* through his candid self-examination in *Lost Morning*, Heyward had undergone a personal odyssey. He left much of his youthful reticence behind and became emboldened, tackling with sympathy and candor issues such as race, class, the burden of history, and the role of the artist. While Heyward's most lasting contributions lay in his work about the southern Negro, those writings should be placed within the context of his moderate reformist views as they grew to maturity during this time. Only an artist with a socially mature outlook and the ability to foresee a more enlightened future for a disenfranchised and misunderstood race could produce *Porgy and Bess.*

Chapter Six

Man of Letters

WITH SUCCESS CAME the leverage for Heyward to broaden his ambitions and try his hand at film writing and more playwriting. As a man of letters in the modern South, Heyward also took part in other literary endeavors, notably gathering southern writers together in the 1931 and 1932 for major conferences. These events turned Heyward's mind to the topic of southern self-consciousness and the role of the southern writer, the topic Heyward treated in *Lost Morning*. The trajectory of his career follows that of other southern writers as they "professionalized" at this time and branched out, working in a variety of genres. Unlike his peers, however, Heyward was never fully comfortable among the literati and thus never matured into the role of elder statesman of southern letters, as might have been expected.

Throughout the 1930s, magazine editors frequently asked Heyward to write on Gullah culture (apropos of *Mamba's Daughters*) or on old Charleston (apropos of *Peter Ashley*). At this time, readers by the millions turned to the image of the Civil War as depicted by southern writers as varied as Margaret Mitchell, Stark Young, and Andrew Lytle. As Heyward had seen in writing *Peter Ashley*, this subject was often presented merely as entertainment, and authors sometimes could be indifferent to standards of literary skill or historical authenticity. Heyward routinely turned down these magazine offers because he was not interested in producing ephemeral writing and preferred to save his creative energies for long-term projects. One editor at *Cosmopolitan* finally persuaded Heyward to write an article on the Gullahs in early 1932, but the piece apparently was killed before it reached print. Heyward was also pursued by rival book publishers. Russell Doubleday, for one, wanted to bring Heyward into the firm's stable of authors. Doubleday pursued Heyward with great determination, but Heyward was loyal to John Farrar for taking a chance on *Porgy* in 1925.

Heyward did lend his name and his time to the first-ever conference of southern writers, which gathered at the University of Virginia in October 1931. The recently installed president of the university, James Southall Wilson, asked Heyward to organize the meeting. This gathering, which has rarely garnered more than anecdotal commentary in books about those who attended it, was significant. The goal of the conference was to examine southern self-consciousness and to explore what made southern literature peculiarly southern.

The guest list, thirty-four writers in all, was luminous: William Faulkner, Sherwood Anderson, Paul Green, Amelie Rives, James Branch Cabell, Ellen Glasgow, Donald Davidson, Allen Tate, Stark Young, and Emily Clark, among others. Heyward and the organizing committee had proposed the topic of "The Southern Writer and His Public." To the chagrin of the other participants, Glasgow took the lead in the first roundtable discussion and held forth almost without interruption, except for an occasional unconvincing "I agree, I agree" from Faulkner. The debate was revived, however, when Green weighed in with his opinion that the machine age would "do no harm to the creative mind," a view quickly challenged by Tate and Davidson, who took their stand against the encroachment of industrialism on traditional agrarian values.

The meetings subsequently became more loose and informal. Heyward wrote about the conference, "there was an almost militant spirit present against organization, and especially sectional organization and identification," but there was also an awareness of southernness: the question of what distinguished these writers from their peers in other parts of the country dominated the discussions. The consensus was "the possession of a common point of view toward life . . . a sense of values opposed for the most part to the conventional standard of American success." Heyward was echoing the views of Tate, who had said that the southern attitude differed from the dominant American one, which he defined as a social point of view rather than a literature of conviction and experience. Heyward also noted, giving voice to his own feelings as much as those of his peers, "Isolated by distance, many of us may have mistrusted these values. Meeting, we were able to discover that we were not alone, and we have returned home wondering if, even in the face of overwhelming contrary opinion, our scale of values may not endure." The meeting again confirmed for Heyward his view that art could best be created in a group setting. Earlier that year, he had written to Josephine Pinckney of his isolation in the North Carolina mountains, "I need to see something of my own kind now and then." Yet when the sequel to the Virginia conference took place the following year in Charleston, a "Southern Literary Houseparty," as Heyward termed it, a much different spirit prevailed.

Heyward and his committee—Glasgow, Cabell, Green, Young, and Thomas Wolfe—drew up an initial list of thirty people to invite, but Heyward had to fall back on the second choices when many of the invitees sent regrets. Prospects for a first-rate gathering dimmed further when, in early September, Heyward, having learned that even some of the second-stringers could not attend, had to confess to Wilson that he was "dipping deeper into the well."

None of the members of the organizing committee even attended the event. Some had legitimate excuses, but many of the Charlottesville conferees had felt that the previous year's meeting, contrary to Heyward's rosy description, had not amounted to much more than cocktail-party chitchat. Archibald Henderson spoke for this opinion when he sent his regrets to Heyward: "I trust the 'glorified house party' of Charlottesville, gracious and pic-nicky as it was, will not be repeated." Henderson wanted a more concrete and structured agenda: "A program, some constructive ideas, a group of major objectives." But no such plan developed, and the conference was not repeated the following year. Heyward ended up with a meeting much like the previous one, more social than literary.

Davidson was particularly disappointed. On returning to Nashville, he wrote to Pinckney congratulating her and Heyward on the event, but his comments belied a deep dissatisfaction, some of which slipped out when he noted that "it would have been a wry sort of pleasure to stir up all the sleeping dogs and have a tremendous barking and biting that would all come to nothing." Privately, he assessed the meeting's outcome more candidly to

Tate: "The Charleston meeting was delightful on the entertainment side, but in other respects completely uneventful. There was no fighting at all; there was almost no discussion. My impression was that . . . Heyward . . . had judiciously oiled the wheels and arranged that there be no discussion. . . . There was a little light chatter, and then we went to lunch."

Davidson thought that the whole literary culture in Charleston lacked rigor and debate, because rancor was considered impolite. Intellectuals like Davidson must have found such an atmosphere unusual given the trend toward self-scrutiny of southern life and letters and the rise of the critical temper then occurring. The Agrarians' southern manifesto, *I'll Take My Stand,* published in 1930, was charged with conviction and disagreement; it translated the developing southern literary consciousness into a public statement about the social, economic, and political conditions for a coherent southern culture. Moreover, the *Journal of Social Forces* was being published in Chapel Hill, and the university there had established the Institute for Research in Social Science, which promoted another view of the new social order, a defense of the assumptions of modernity as they applied to the South's economic and social conditions. Southern historiography was also undergoing a transformation: revisionist works on such topics as Reconstruction were already published or were underway, including Ulrich B. Phillips's *Life and Labor in the Old South* (1931), a book with which Heyward was familiar. C. Vann Woodward, William Alexander Percy, and, of course, Wilbur J. Cash produced treatises on southern identity.

Davidson's assessment of Heyward's character was correct: Heyward's natural tendencies toward reticence surfaced in his native Charleston, and they colored the meetings. There, once again, literature became for him more a social art and less a socially conscious art. Moreover, he seemed ill at ease among other "literary people." To John Bennett he commented on "the utter futility and waste of about ninety-nine percent" of the "new social contacts" that arose from such meetings. He now concluded that he simply did not fit in with the "writer crowd": "They would suck you dry if you let them, and give you not one God's thing in return. It is the old ones that count, and to these I would always return." He confessed his fondness for "the people who used to put up with [me] when I was a dumb insurance agent, and not those who want to take a look into my innards now" to see how a writer thinks and feels.

A similar feeling of exclusion can be seen in Heyward's hosting of Gertrude Stein when she visited Charleston three years later. With her companion, Alice B. Toklas, Stein addressed the Poetry Society in February 1935. Her appearance was part of a six-month tour through the United States. Stein had been living in Paris since 1903 and had not returned to the States in more than thirty years. An enigmatic woman, Stein had, in typically imperious fashion, decided to march across her native land on a mission to do nothing less than "tell very plainly and simply and directly . . . what literature is."

Heyward had been curious about Stein since he had seen a performance of her "native opera," *Four Saints in Three Acts,* in early 1934. The work, with words by Stein and music by Virgil Thomson, had enhanced Stein's celebrity status (as had the 1933 publication of *The Autobiography of Alice B. Toklas*) and had drawn attention to the relative absence of authentic American works for the musical stage.

If Stein's Charleston audience was expecting a byzantine presentation, they were not disappointed. Heyward was not only upstaged by Stein; he was quite nonplussed by the whole event. The oddness of the evening began when Heyward announced from the platform that the speaker had requested she not be introduced. An observer reported that Heyward then "walked the full length down the hall, and reaching that point, turned in behind Miss Stein, who sailed voluminously about two feet in front of him inveloped [sic] in [the] convolutions and folds of her brown skirt." Heyward was "quite lost in the back-wash of it and arrived at the dais just in time to have her ignore his proffered assistance." Stein then "immediately whipped open her manuscript and without so much as a good evening in acknowledging the presence of those who had gathered to hear, began."

As the talk progressed, Stein "kept throwing out little chunks of wit and if you got it you did and if you didn't, you didn't": for example, she said, "Now, sentences are not interesting. Paragraphs are. Sentences are not interesting because they are not emotional. Paragraphs are because they are emotional. I learned that by watching my dog drink water." The dog, she explained, drank in gulps by making the form of a cup with his tongue—"paragraphs" instead of "sentences." Accordingly, nouns were not interesting. Neither were adjectives. Verbs and adverbs were a little more interesting because they "change to look like themselves or to look like something else."

Prepositions attracted Stein the most strongly: "they make nothing but mistakes, but this makes them interesting, if you feel that way about mistakes." Stein continued in this vein for more than an hour, reading from her script in a slow, monotonous manner.

The audience was by turns amused, confused, and irritated: people did not know whether they were listening to a writer or to a character from an Ionesco play. Another attendee reported that "nobody there" had "even the vaguest idea" what Stein was talking about. . . . I thought she was simply having some quiet fun for herself" by hoodwinking "the intelligentsia." When the lecture ended, Stein, Toklas, and Heyward all "beat a retreat toward the exit. No word of greeting, no thank you or anything. Just rudeness and business."

Appearances to the contrary, however, Stein truly enjoyed her visit to Charleston. She told a local reporter of her pleasure in speaking to the Poetry Society. And she was very taken with Heyward. She confided to her diary that Heyward was "a gentle man . . . like his Porgy." She later saw a stock production of *Porgy* and wrote to Heyward to tell him how good the production was and to praise him as a playwright. Heyward was gratified, telling her in reply that "we liked you in Charleston, tremendously—even if we did not always understand you."

Just as Heyward was not always comfortable among the literati, he also made little of his two sojourns in the world of moviemaking, the new industry to which writers flocked by the hundreds. Heyward was a skilled screenwriter, however, and the one screenplay for which he was sole author, *The Emperor Jones,* was a solid piece of work. The film later became a landmark in movie depictions of African Americans.

Eugene O'Neill had sold the film rights of his play to John Krimsky and Clifford Cochran, a team of innovative moviemakers from England. O'Neill had seen the stage version of *Porgy* in 1927 and had been impressed by its treatment of race. He was also impressed by the play's director, Rouben Mamoulian, whose successful integration of rhythm into the play O'Neill envied, as he himself had strived for such rhythmic pacing in his own plays. Through these connections Heyward was hired to write the screenplay for *The Emperor Jones.* In the spring of 1933 he flew down to Sea Island, Georgia, for a story conference with O'Neill. The latter was sufficiently impressed with Heyward's ideas to sign him to a contract, and in April Heyward began drafting a scenario.

Heyward was not a facile writer. As a self-described "slow moving novelist," it is no wonder that Heyward could not adapt himself to the rushed rhythms of moviemaking life. He estimated that to do the screenplay he would have to write a thousand words a day: he usually considered five hundred "a good crop." Nonetheless, he plugged away at the script and eventually put together a polished product. In June and July he then had to dash back and forth between Hendersonville and Long Island, the scene of the filming, at the whim of his employers, who, "with the usual hecticness of movie companies . . . did not make up their minds they wanted me until they were almost ready to begin filming." Heyward found the experience exasperating and tiring and the final product rather a compromise with his and O'Neill's intentions. He complained to Hervey Allen of having put "about a years [sic] work into . . . six weeks" and to Green of being unable to tell whether the film would turn out "good, bad, or indifferent. I do know, though, that it is different from the usual run."

Heyward's assessment was accurate. The producers signed Paul Robeson to play the lead and Dudley Digges, one of Broadway's finest character actors, to play Smithers, the white Cockney trader. But after Heyward had finished his script, others tinkered with it, and the end product was flashier and more action oriented than what Heyward had originally written. The result was a compromise, neither wholly artistic nor wholly commercial. The director was Dudley Murphy, a first-time amateur whose only experience was a series of all-Negro shorts.

The story concerns Rufus Jones, an ex–Pullman porter and fugitive from justice who has become the self-appointed ruler of a small West Indian island. He has hoodwinked the natives into thinking he has supernatural powers by brandishing such accoutrements of modern "civilization" as a pearl-handled revolver. When the natives revolt, Jones, much like Kurtz, the protagonist of Conrad's *Heart of Darkness*, flees deeper into the jungle, on a metaphorical journey into the recesses of the human soul. Hounded less by his enemies than by frightful images of his criminal past, Jones at last reverts, Kurtz-like, to the primitive condition of his Congo forebears. O'Neill intended a comment on white exploitation in the area as well as an allegory of the dictator Jean-Christoph in Haiti, a matter made all the more topical by recent events in Germany.

Shortly after the film's release, Heyward wrote about the project. The stage play begins with Jones as emperor, fleeing from the palace revolt. The action of the play covers a single night in nine scenes, during which flashbacks provide glimpses into Jones's criminal past. Heyward added a longish section (nearly half the film's running time) that preceded the action in O'Neill's play—what Heyward described as "a piece of straight creative writing which . . . merge[d] with the play without any break or jolt in story or characterization." In constructing a framework of Jones's early life, Heyward added the character of the earlier Jones, as the author imagined it: "By throwing this character into contact with the disintegrating power of our white civilization," Heyward wrote, he "broke Jones down from the rather simple Southern Negro to the shrewd, grafting Negro of the play."

In Heyward's version of Jones's early life, he is first a pleasure-seeking Harlem partygoer who one night steals his friend Jeff's sweetheart. Through a combination of Machiavellian determination and obsequiousness (a mimicry of whites and a playing up to their stereotyped conceptions of blacks), Jones has risen in the ranks of Pullman porters to the president's private car, thus gaining an advantage over Jeff. Always listening for important intelligence that might be discussed by his white employers, Jones learns of a forthcoming financial merger and invests his meager savings in a scheme that yields considerable profits. When his new girlfriend mocks his ambitions, he abruptly abandons her. She then sees him at a cabaret in the company of another woman and stirs up trouble by goading Jeff into challenging Jones. Jones ducks out of the ensuing fight but later encounters Jeff again in a gambling house in Savannah, where Jeff cheats Jones with loaded dice and then tries to kill him. Jones, however, overpowers his former friend and kills him in self-defense.

Jones is sentenced to prison for ten years. He eventually becomes a trusty, but when he refuses a guard's order to whip a Negro boy who has fallen over from heatstroke, Jones revolts, killing the guard and taking refuge in the stokehold of a boat bound for the West Indies. En route he jumps ship and swims to a nearby island, where he outwits the tribal chief and becomes emperor of the land. From there, Heyward followed the original play. The first half of the film thus appears to be all Heyward, the second half largely

O'Neill. Heyward's parts of the story recall elements of both *Porgy* and *Mamba's Daughters:* the gambling-inspired knife fights, the unjust working conditions for black laborers, and the questionable morality of killing in retribution.

The film is notable for its technical accomplishments. A series of close-ups of Jones emphasize his human relationship to people in his past. Other close-ups give dramatic emphasis to unfolding events, such as the shot of Jeff's hand as it draws the "button" knife from his pocket and springs it open. Lap-dissolves, gradual changes of one scene into another, abound. The initial dissolve—the beating of the drum—has the effect of an overture, which suggests the rhythmic character of the story. Music here, as in the stage version of *Porgy,* intensifies mood and atmosphere. Several authentic spirituals ("Walk Right in an' Sit Down," "O, I Want Two Wings," "Now Let Me Fly") are employed to interesting effect.

Heyward's screenplay ultimately is most interesting as a continuation of his increasingly ironic, critical, and even jaundiced view of whites. Heyward's point here is the same as that in an earlier novella entitled *The Half-Pint Flask:* the narrator of that story, a white resident of one of the Carolina sea islands, entertains a scientist-friend who, over the narrator's protests, violates a local taboo by taking a valuable old flask from a Negro grave. Destructive supernatural forces begin to erupt on the island, and the two men just barely escape by returning the relic to its original resting place. In the story, Heyward's theme is the destruction of a "pure" civilization by the corrupt machinations of white society. In *The Emperor Jones,* however, the point is made more emphatic by racial role reversal, as William Slavick has noted. Jones is a black Horatio Alger figure, an embodiment of the "virtues" of white society that, in the end, become vices, which he exports to an untainted community: gambling, drinking, and, most important, the abuse of power by one class in control of the other. Heyward later said that the most enjoyable part of his task was making Jones "a black counterpart of our own big business pirate." The significance of Heyward's sardonic views was not unnoticed by his fellow Charlestonians. When Heyward suggested that the filming be done on nearby Folly Island, the residents there threatened to leave en masse.

The film flopped at the box office, although the reviews were generally appreciative. The critic for the *New York Sun,* in particular, praised Heyward's injecting some "pictorial variety" into O'Neill's stage play. While the film lacked the play's "concentrated power," the cinematic values obtained by shifting from the South to Harlem, from the ship to the island, and so on, were singled out as innovative dramatic effects.

One year later, Heyward accepted another screenwriting assignment, this time in Hollywood. Thus for a brief period, Heyward joined the hundreds of other novelists, story writers, and playwrights who had flocked to California to work as contract writers for the screen. The depression had cut severely into authors' royalties, and many publishing houses could no longer even offer their writers advances. In contrast, by the 1930s moviemaking had become one of the ten leading American industries; writers thus thought of Hollywood as a promised land, a Mecca of economic prosperity and artistic potential.

Heyward was hired as scriptwriter for Irving Thalberg's MGM film adaptation of Pearl Buck's *The Good Earth*. The movie, which did not follow very closely Buck's best-selling 1931 novel, was a story of humility and bravery in which the wife of a poor Chinese farmer remains steadfast and loyal as her husband and son are led astray by a young woman and as famine and natural disaster threaten the family's livelihood. When the film was released in 1937, $200,000 had been spent on its production, Thalberg was dead, and some twenty other writers had followed Heyward. Although the major writing was done by Heyward, the credit went to others.

The comic-opera overtones of Heyward's experiences with the *Emperor Jones* production alerted him to what he might expect in Hollywood. He regarded the six weeks he spent there with bemusement and cynicism. More than anything, he wondered why he had received the assignment. He recalled, "When I arrived on the lot [I] asked why I had been offered the job, [and] it was made perfectly plain to me. Negroes were not a Caucasian people. Neither were Chinamen. I wrote understandingly of Negroes. It was obvious then that I would understand the Chinese." "I suspect," Heyward noted, "that before my engagement closed their faith in their reasoning power was shaken. But I gave them my best."

The experience that summer taught Heyward a good deal about screenwriting and broadened his understanding of the movie industry, an experience not shared by many other southerners. Erskine Caldwell, Faulkner, and Lillian Hellman all worked for MGM, too, at one time or another. All three reaped quick profits in exchange for their artistic pride, and like Heyward, they found the experience unsettling. Heyward liked the look and feel of Hollywood—the climate especially as well as the low cost of living. Since he could pick where he wanted to work, he installed himself on the top floor of the Beverly Wilshire Hotel. He wrote to Dorothy that he was settling down, "though . . . in solitary," and that it was "the most healthy life imaginable. I have nothing to do but work and take care of [my]self." He enjoyed the quiet of the hotel, the good climate, and the accommodations: The room was "real swank" and "not expensive. The best picture people stop here. Nearby eating places are cheap. Last night after dinner I walked for an hour through beautiful moonlight streets with lovely houses and flowers all about." But he was offended by the contrast between the decadence and extravagance of the filmmakers and the rest of the community, which lived in a series of shanties and homeless camps. Heyward found this view of the haves and the have-nots painful, one reason he did not fully take to the movie industry.

Heyward also seems to have received preferential treatment from Thalberg and company, an indication of the staying power of *Porgy*, with which Heyward most continued to be associated. Other, less commercially successful novelists who had been hired by the studios were not in as comfortable a position. Novelist Nathanael West complained of the pressure-cooker atmosphere he had encountered the previous summer as a writer at Columbia: "There's no fooling here," he told a correspondent. "All the writers sit in cells in a row and the minute a typewriter stops someone pokes his head in the door to see if you are thinking." Heyward, in contrast, dined at the Brown Derby, went to the movies in the evenings, and strolled the beach.

Also unlike most screenwriters, Heyward had access to Thalberg, already a legend in the still-young industry. Thalberg possessed rare taste and self-assurance. Thought by some to be the intellectual high priest of Hollywood, Thalberg, although brighter than most studio heads, was nonetheless commercially motivated. In *The Last Tycoon*, F. Scott Fitzgerald's Thalberg-like character, Monroe Stahr, tells an associate, "I never thought I had more brains than a writer has. But I always thought his brains belonged to me—because I know how to use them." Heyward met with Thalberg almost immediately after arriving, desirous of learning Thalberg's reaction to how Heyward proposed to treat the story. He had been told in advance that Thalberg was "the best man" in Hollywood, but Heyward's illusions quickly burst. He was chagrined to discover that the studios were controlled entirely by commercial considerations and that the producer wanted merely a "slick, sentimental piece of Hollywood picture stuff."

However, Heyward did find Thalberg "pleasant" and guardedly open to the writer's ideas about the picture. Thalberg would let Heyward try some of them, "and if they go, so much the better for me," Heyward told Dorothy. When Heyward arrived at his studio office, he happily found that MGM had provided him with a secretary—a true "college graduate secretary," Heyward wrote to Dorothy, "one who reads books, and knew all about me." They are "rare out here, I understand," he wryly added. Later, he watched background footage that the production company had shot on location in China. Heyward intended to make the setting of the movie "very real." He also befriended the head of the scenario department, a Mr. Marks, "a charming fellow" who knew of Dorothy's work and was an "intimate friend" of the Gershwins. Marks provided Heyward with a sympathetic sounding board for his ideas about the script. Heyward asked for some research data on religious ceremonies and other tribal customs in China, and Marks happily ordered the work done, telling Heyward that if other writers were so conscientious, the studio would probably get better scripts. But despite these promising signs, when finally released in 1937, the film was standard Hollywood issue.

Heyward had also hoped to make contacts in Hollywood, thus establishing connections that might later bring him more work. A fellow Charlestonian who had belonged to the Poetry Society, Dwight Franklin, and his wife, Mary, had done so successfully. Both were screenwriters earning a good income at Warner Brothers. They introduced Heyward around, but he seems not to have made the necessary connections. He probably did not pursue them strongly enough; he confided to Dorothy that he was pretty well satisfied to write and rest instead of work the cocktail-party circuit. He also may not have been quite savvy enough about studio politics. He even annoyed his agent by working "too rapidly" on a job for which he was being paid a weekly wage. Heyward was simply too forthright to work the studio system adeptly enough to fit in and make a living from screenwriting. He concluded that motion pictures were "great art" but were "not a satisfying medium for a literary artist."

Heyward's experience in Hollywood, then, was quite unlike that of other writers who successfully adapted their talents to the new industry. Heyward was bothered by the cog-in-the-wheel environment; he felt he was but a tiny part of a huge process that operated beyond his control. Further, there was no stability: the people he met at MGM seemed unreliable and capricious. There was endless socializing, but Heyward could not fall in with the crowd of self-consciously intellectual, voluble writers; they seemed to belong to one big country club at which he was merely a guest.

Heyward also tried to broaden his playwriting skills during these years. A friend of Bennett's, George C. Tyler, contacted Heyward in April 1932. Tyler, a New York theatrical agent who had been James O'Neill's business manager at the end of the actor's career and had produced two of Eugene O'Neill's early plays, had asked Bennett to pitch an idea of his to Heyward, a play about African Americans who fought in World War I. Bennett was eager to do so; he probably felt that he was reliving his happier days mentoring Heyward.

Bennett described the idea as an African American version of *Journey's End* and *What Price Glory?* He thought the focus should be on African Americans' "disappointments and small rewards" for being put somewhere they did not belong, "to do things they had for centuries been thoroughly unfitted for doing." Bennett suggested that Heyward talk over the idea with his "consultant-chief," Dorothy, and see what they might come up with. Dorothy was "enthusiastic" and thought the project had "great possibilities"; Heyward, however, demurred. "I did not see service in the war," he noted. "I did not see the Negro under fire. I have probably a fair grasp of Negro psychology. I think that I know how he would react to the experiences which he endured on the Western front. But [it would have to be] second hand." Tyler was disappointed, but he accepted Heyward's reasons. Bennett, however, was not about to give up yet: "First-hand experience be damned, my dear!" he wrote Heyward. Realism was irrelevant; Bennett believed everything was based on imagination. After all, just as Stephen Crane wrote about war without ever having been in one, so Heyward himself had written about Catfish Row without ever having lived there. But Heyward could not be convinced, and he finally ended Bennett's persistent entreaties by admitting what was probably the true reason for shying from the play: "there may be the vestage [sic] of an old inferiority complex there that inhibits me. I felt very keenly (at the time) my inability physically to go over. I took refuge in making speeches about it, and I have a sort of feeling that if I try to do a play, it will ring false. It would turn out to be a sort of black-face *What Price Glory,* and not DuBose Heyward at all."

Heyward and Dorothy also considered another theatrical project, one based on a famous episode in Charleston history and rich with possibilities for social commentary since it concerned African Americans in the era of slavery. The play chronicled the fate of a revolutionary black man, Denmark Vesey. Vesey, born on St. Thomas, had once belonged to a sea merchant who traded regularly between Charleston and the Dutch West Indies, but Vesey won enough money in a lottery to buy his freedom. He then set himself up as a carpenter, and according to folklore, amassed several thousand dollars' worth of property, including a home and several wives. He was also a prominent leader in the African Church of Charleston; an unusually educated and articulate Negro for the time, Vesey could read, write, and speak several languages. In 1822 he was implicated by other blacks in an alleged plot to rise up against the slaves' white masters and murder them and their families at night. Vesey was arrested and hanged with four other blacks, their bodies left on display for several days as a warning to others.

The Vesey story, along with Nat Turner's insurrection in Virginia, is among the most interesting of such episodes from southern history; artists have treated the Vesey incident in fiction, poetry, and music. The episode is most interesting because it may well have been an imagined threat. The truth of the conspiracy allegation has never been determined, and the question of how much the panic was the result of anxiety or misunderstanding over what information had actually been gathered also remains unanswered. The story interested Heyward for other reasons, including Vesey's intelligence and standing in the black community. Heyward found that in one contemporary report the man was a "hero, in the next a villain." Heyward was also fascinated by the black-versus-black angle: members of an oppressed minority being disloyal to the cause of their own race and informing on their brethren to whites. (In the play, George Wilson, who informs on Vesey to the city authorities, is the most intriguing character.) Finally, there was the allure of the conjure doctor, Gullah Jack, who reportedly empowered groundnuts and crab claws with the force for the revolting slaves to resist the rebuffs of their white oppressors. The slaves held Gullah Jack in such awe that even when they saw him in the white man's chains, no one dared testify against him.

Heyward may have been drawn to the story since the central conflict is one of self. Wilson is torn between rebelling at injustice and desiring to belong to his community, even if in so doing he overlooks elements of it that are obviously wrong. Wilson desires rebellion and revolution, but his blood ties prevent him from doing so. In loose terms, then, Wilson's conflict resembles Heyward's. The play is another instance of Heyward seeing in the black experience social and emotional conflicts that also played out in the minds of the white community.

Heyward arrived at the idea for the play in 1932, just after finishing *Peter Ashley*. At that time he had contracted to write a chapter on "The Negro in the Low-Country" for a collection of essays on South Carolina history and folklore being published under the auspices of the Spirituals Society. As Dorothy Heyward later told the story, she and DuBose were at Dawn Hill, sitting under the huge pine trees in the back yard, when he read aloud the scant one and a half pages on Vesey that Heyward had found in a history text. When he finished, he and Dorothy said simultaneously, "That is going to be our next play." They dropped everything the next morning and drove down to Charleston to do research at the Library Society there. Then, for unknown reasons, Heyward abandoned the idea and told Dorothy to work on it by herself while he scouted other projects.

The Heywards took up the play again in early 1939, just after the stage version of *Mamba's Daughters* debuted. More work on the script ensued, and when they had honed it to their satisfaction, they began to think of someone to play the crucial role of George Wilson. All along Heyward had Paul Robeson in mind for the role. Robeson, in London that spring, was looking for new properties. He had turned down the lead in Maxwell Anderson's and Kurt Weill's *Eneas Africanus,* reacting negatively to the patronizing story of an ex-slave's quest to find his former plantation. The actor also was offended by Anderson's cover letter, which referred to the slave as never having been able "to make an ethical decision for himself" or to accept responsibility of any kind. By contrast, Robeson was quite enthusiastic about the Heywards' treatment of the Vesey story; when Robeson's wife, Essie, read the script and seconded the idea, he told the Heywards that he was prepared to sign on. But their work stalled again, Heyward became ill, and Robeson eventually committed to another play. Dorothy later returned to work on *Set My People*

Free, as it was eventually entitled; it played in New York in 1948 but received mixed reviews and had only a short run.

Why did Heyward abandon the Vesey play? He was not losing his appetite for playwriting in general: *Porgy and Bess* in 1935 was a great accomplishment, as was the play version of *Mamba's Daughters* (1939). With so many rapid advances in black rights during the 1930s, was Heyward losing his ability to see into the African American psyche? It is possible, since his last novel, *Star Spangled Virgin,* indicates that his skill in interpreting African American life with precision and understanding was waning.

Nonetheless, Heyward's work as a man of letters in the 1930s—his screenplays of *The Emperor Jones* and *The Good Earth,* his roles in southern writers conferences, and his attempts at dramatizing new Negro material for the stage—show his versatility and his attempts to warm to the role of litterateur with which the public regarded him. Most important, these episodes prepared him, intellectually and emotionally, for *Porgy and Bess.*

Chapter Seven

Porgy and Bess on Wings of Song

ORGY AND BESS, the folk opera about black life in Charleston, is DuBose Heyward's greatest achievement, one of the most memorable icons of the American South. Yet Heyward's role in the creation of the opera has been either misunderstood or overlooked. No mere assistant to Gershwin, Heyward wrote the libretto, authored the lyrics to more than half the songs, and assisted in almost every stage of production. The work's tumultuous history is also not widely known. The greatness of the opera was not recognized at its debut in 1935, and in relative terms, *Porgy and Bess* was a critical and financial failure. Heyward and the Gershwin brothers lost their initial investment, and the work was lambasted by music critics who claimed that it was not authentic opera but a mere Broadway crowd pleaser. Today a finer distinction can be made: *Porgy and Bess* represents an important cultural moment in America, when the popular arts rose to prominence and such a "crowd pleaser" as *Porgy and Bess* could be regarded as high art. That the opera was a major production featuring black performers also makes it a milestone in the democratization of art in America.

Yet *Porgy and Bess* came under fire—and still does today—from some African Americans who felt that the opera's portrayal of black life was demeaning rather than ennobling. While many feel that the opera represents the odyssey of the African American, others regard it as a museum piece that depicts the seamy side of black life, presumably what white audiences want to see.

"I am off on a new course," Heyward wrote to Hervey Allen excitedly in the fall of 1933, "an operatic version of *Porgy* with George Gershwin." Heyward found the prospect exciting and was eager to explore "old trails again" for "spirituals and Negro material." By that time, Heyward was more than ready to do the opera, since he had been waiting seven years for Gershwin to commit. The composer had read *Porgy* in 1926 and had contacted Heyward right away, suggesting that they collaborate on an operatic version, but in the ensuing seven years, Gershwin did not seem to Heyward to be willing to make a firm commitment. Then in 1927, while Heyward was trying to jump-start the ill-fated first attempt at a nonmusical version of *Porgy,* he and Gershwin talked face to face in Atlantic City. The composer again expressed sincere interest but simply did not have room in his schedule to begin work at that time.

Off and on in the next few years Gershwin and Heyward occasionally communicated about the prospects for a *Porgy* opera, but each time Gershwin demurred, and Heyward ended up working on other projects—*Mamba's Daughters, Peter Ashley,* his screenplays of *The Emperor Jones* and *The Good Earth.* Heyward stood by Gershwin, however, never wavering in the belief that the composer would undertake the project—and with good reason, for by the mid-1920s Gershwin had become a household name and the ideal person to treat the *Porgy* story musically.

Born Jacob Gershwine in Brooklyn on 26 September 1898, Gershwin was a first-generation Jewish American whose father had left St. Petersburg, Russia, in search of a better life. Gershwin spent his childhood exploring the city, darting in and out of traffic on roller skates and taking in all the latest American crazes. One day he stopped outside an arcade where a player piano was running and heard Arthur Rubinstein's "Melody in F." "The peculiar jumps in the music held me rooted," Gershwin later recalled, and thus began his love affair with the piano.

He began playing by ear, and at age fifteen landed a full-time job as a "song plugger" at Remick's, a music publishing firm on Twenty-eighth Street, otherwise known as Tin Pan Alley. Here, in the heart of the American music-publishing business, would-be songsters and established musicians frequented the "professional parlors" of music companies, hawking their work. Producers, actors, and singers likewise milled around in search of material. "Every day at nine," Gershwin recalled, "I was there at the piano, playing popular tunes for anybody who came along." Under the influence of Jerome Kern, Gershwin came to see that musical-comedy music was more lucrative than popular songs, so he gave up Remick's for a job at Fox's City Theater on Fourteenth Street, where he played piano for the dinner show.

The head of a leading music publisher, Max Dreyfus, heard two songs that Gershwin had written for Vivienne Segal, star of a Victor Herbert and Jerome Kern musical called *Miss 1917,* and signed him to a contract. Through Dreyfus, Gershwin was commissioned to write songs for new revues, and from here he went on to create his first musical comedy, *La, La Lucille,* in 1919. Hit after hit followed—*Lady, Be Good, Oh, Kay!,* and *Funny Face.* He became nationally famous when Al Jolson recorded a one-step tune Gershwin had reputedly written in ten minutes, "Swanee."

Gershwin's interests ranged beyond popular song. In 1924 he premiered an ambitious orchestral composition entitled *Rhapsody for Piano and Orchestra.* Later retitled *Rhapsody in Blue,* the work was an attempt to bring out the musical value inherent in jazz. It showed the influence of such French composers as Darius Milhaud, Erik Satie, and Maurice Ravel, who had similarly incorporated the jazz idiom into classical orchestral compositions. Gershwin not only wanted jazz to be taken seriously by the musical world but also believed that the form was America's only genuinely native music. Toward this end, in 1924 he wrote and produced a one-act vaudeville opera, *Blue Monday* (later called *135th Street*), that evoked a Harlem mood through the use of jazz themes. Long interested in black art forms, Gershwin often visited Harlem nightclubs, absorbing Negro music. He then returned downtown and turned "Harlem straw into Broadway gold." Although *135th Street* was performed by white actors singing in blackface, as was the custom at the time, the work was innovative in its yoking of a story that concerned poor black life with music in the American vein—a blend of jazz, blues, and a ragtime recitative. But the show was an embarrassing failure: "the most dismal, stupid, and incredible blackfaced sketch that has probably ever been perpetrated," one reviewer declared. The show was a crude forerunner of *Porgy and Bess,* which would be hailed as evidence of a new American musical art. Heyward knew that Gershwin was unquestionably the right person to transform *Porgy* into a musical but wondered whether it would ever come to pass.

One of several tantalizing moments occurred in the spring of 1932, when Heyward finally thought Gershwin meant business. On 29 March Gershwin wrote to Heyward that "in thinking of ideas for new compositions," he had come back "to one I had several years ago—namely *Porgy* and the thought of setting it to music. It is still the most outstanding play I know about colored people." Heyward telephoned Gershwin, they talked enthusiastically about the idea, and then Heyward wrote a follow-up letter to Gershwin, noting tremendous interest "in working on the book with you. I have some new material that might be introduced, and once I got your ideas . . . I could do you a satisfactory story." Heyward was fairly champing at the bit to do the opera, and his overeagerness may have frightened Gershwin off. The composer let more than a month slide by before replying, saying that he was glad the rights were free and clear but that there was "no possibility" that the project could begin before January 1933. Heyward was crestfallen, but he did take some comfort in Gershwin's mentioning that he was rereading the novel "several times" to get him thinking about "how it should be done."

Soon thereafter Heyward's hopes for a theatrical version of *Porgy* were raised again by another musical star, Al Jolson. In 1932, Jolson approached the Theatre Guild with plans for a musical stage version to star himself in blackface. Jolson proposed that the music be done by Kern and the book by Oscar Hammerstein II. With this imposing trio, it was difficult for the guild to reject the idea. The guild members certainly could think of no obstacles, and they urged Heyward to accept Jolson's offer at once. Heyward, however, felt tied to Gershwin, and in September 1932 he wrote to the composer about the Jolson offer and tried to press Gershwin to sign a contract for the opera. Heyward was candid with Gershwin, laying out the facts of the situation in an usually forthright manner—Dorothy called it a "Madison Avenue letter." "In these trying times," Heyward said, an offer like Jolson's had to be considered. If Gershwin was still interested in doing the opera, could some arrangement perhaps be worked out to use Jolson in the production, Heyward asked, "or is that too preposterous?"

But Gershwin would not be rushed. He thought it was "very interesting that Jolson would like to play the part of Porgy" but really didn't know "how he would be in it." Additionally, the type of work that Gershwin had in mind was "a much more serious thing than Jolson [could] ever do." Gershwin told Heyward, "If you can see your way to making some ready money from Jolson's version, I don't know that it would hurt a later version done by an all-colored cast." Gershwin said that what he had in mind was "more a labor of love than anything else."

Heyward therefore began negotiations with Jolson but still kept open the possibility of a Gershwin opera, telling the composer that he would "like to be able to afford . . . to wait indefinitely for your operatic version, and to work with you myself without the least thought of the commercial angle," but he could not turn ready money from the door. He therefore resolved to sell the rights to Jolson but not to work on the project, thus leaving Heyward free to write the libretto for the opera when the time came to do so. Heyward hoped it would be soon: "before we wake up and find ourselves in our dotage," he half-jokingly told Gershwin.

The Jolson project never materialized. Just before *Porgy* was to go into production, Hammerstein and Kern split up. Without a composer and a librettist, Jolson was stranded, thereby leaving the door open once again for Gershwin, but he was still occupied with too many other projects to commit to *Porgy*.

Then, in the fall of 1933, as Heyward was finishing *The Emperor Jones*, his thoughts far distant from *Porgy*, he heard from Gershwin yet again. The composer flattered Heyward with promises of "something big." Heyward was so jaded by Gershwin's tantalizing but unconsummated offers that this time he replied in a gentlemanly but curt fashion. But to Heyward's surprise, Gershwin cleared his desk, a contract was drawn up, and a list of potential producers was compiled. The Metropolitan Opera House pressed Gershwin to bring the production there, but Gershwin thought that Broadway was a better home for the show. It would have a longer run there, and the potential profit was far greater than at the Met. The Theatre Guild, ready for its first full-scale musical venture, was chosen to produce the show, and on 17 October 1933, after what was for Heyward a very long wait, work began.

Heyward went to work on the opera as soon as he had finished his commitment to *The Emperor Jones*. Heyward's first task, to compose the libretto, turned out to be only one in a long line of assignments that he took on. He condensed the play, cutting it and reshaping it to conform to operatic form; he wrote the libretto, providing opportunities for arias and choruses as he went along; and he wrote the lyrics to nearly half of the arias himself and collaborated with Ira Gershwin on several more songs. Further along, Heyward assisted in casting, rehearsals, and other production details.

Heyward's first task was to reduce the play by about 40 percent and to refashion the dialogue so that it was suitable for a musical treatment. "It had to be arranged to form a new pattern," Heyward said, "to escape monotony and adapt itself to the music." Working quickly, he had the first scene cut and drafted for George Gershwin by 12 November. "I have cut everything possible," he wrote to his collaborator, "and marked a couple of possible further cuts in pencil on ms. As a matter of fact, this is now a very brief scene considering that it carries all the exposition necessary for the play." Gershwin replied, on 25 November, that "there may be too much talk, but I can't tell until I start composing just how it will work out." Heyward had decided that the dialogue should be spoken instead of rendered in recitative, the traditional operatic form. "This will give the opera speed and tempo," he argued, and it would give Gershwin a chance to "develop a new treatment, carrying the orchestration straight through the performance . . . but enriching it with pantomime and action on the stage, and with such music (singing) as grows out of the action." Also, Heyward continued, "in scenes like the fight, the whole thing can be treated as a unified composition, drawing on lighting, orchestra, and the wailing of the crowd, mass sounds of horror from people, etc. instead of singing. It can be lifted to a terrific climax." In the play version, Heyward noted, the fight "was treated with a great deal of noise. . . . That is not my idea of [the] best art."

As Heyward continued to draft the libretto, more suggestions occurred to him. He thought of a new opening, one unlike the "regular riot of noise and color" in the play. He wanted to "let the scene . . . merge with the overture, almost in the sense of illustration, giving the added force of sight and sound. The curtain rises in darkness, then, the first scene will begin to come up as the music takes up the theme of jazz from the dance hall piano [played by Jasbo Brown]. The songs which I have written for this part will fall naturally into the action and mood of the separate flashes of negro life."

Gershwin considered Heyward's suggestions carefully, knowing that his partner had an eye for dramatic detail and knew how to represent southern Negro culture. Gershwin told Heyward that he had done "a swell job, especially with the . . . lyrics." But Gershwin trusted his own instincts in music. He stuck with his original idea for recitative, not wanting to hybridize or diminish the classical form of the opera with unsung dialogue. He also wanted the production to be a true musical experience. He had thought the play version of *Porgy* did not exploit the potential of the spirituals to their fullest effect, and he was careful that the opera not be overbalanced by "too much talk."

Heyward continued to send Gershwin new scenes, questions, and suggestions throughout the fall. But Gershwin was not actually working on the project. He was preparing to embark on a tour of twenty-eight cities to mark the tenth anniversary of *Rhapsody in Blue* and to premiere some new piano compositions. By December, most of these new pieces were complete, and Gershwin planned to finish the work in Florida, where he was going for a brief vacation with his cousin, Emil Mosbacher. Gershwin proposed to stop in Charleston, stay a few days, and "hear some spirituals and perhaps go to a colored café or two." He did so, with Heyward hosting him during the visit. Gershwin tried to talk Heyward into coming down to Florida to work there, but Heyward was not sanguine about the possibility. His daughter, Jenifer, had been ill, and he also found his "creative ability practically paralyzed in a new environment. I am just getting into my stride here now, and I do not want to risk breaking it." Then in Florida on 4 January 1934, Gershwin announced to the press that he would be writing an opera "about blacks," adding that "a negro flavor will predominate." Gershwin also said that he already had an actor in mind for the lead: Paul Robeson.

Heyward pressed on with the libretto. He had recently renewed his ties to his native Charleston by purchasing a cottage on nearby Folly Beach, one of several barrier islands in the area—a "smallish" place that was "no trouble" to maintain and was "beautifully placed in a grove of palmettoes, pines, [and] live oaks." In the rear of the property was a studio where he worked. Heyward was happy to be back near Charleston—in the vicinity but not in and of the city itself. He would slowly reinvolve himself in Charleston's cultural life, but not quite yet. Heyward also sought to escape the demands of fame. He wrote to Allen, now famous as the author of *Anthony Adverse*, "You are doubtless discovering, as I did after my lucky break with *Porgy*, that a measure of success makes life infinitely more complicated. You think that with economic problems solved things ought to be . . . simple. . . . Then you get the full impact of this awful American publicity, and all that goes with it, and you almost wish you were penniless again." The Folly "shack," Heyward said, "is an attempt on my part to get back to the simplicities, and away from people."

Work on the opera progressed smoothly. When Gershwin returned to New York that spring, he had new scenes from Heyward waiting for him and more new ideas. "I have discovered . . . a type of secular dance done here that is straight from the African phallic dance," Heyward wrote at one point, "and . . . undoubtedly a complete survival. . . . It will make an extraordinary introduction to the primitive scene of passion between Crown and Bess." In reworking the play version of *Porgy,* Heyward also purged it of any "conventional Negro vaudeville stuff," aiming to make the opera even more authentic than the story's previous incarnations. "I think I have managed to get the lyrical parts to conform to the rhythms of ordinary speech," he told Gershwin, "and also the idiom, and what I have hoped to do is to ease these passages in so that there will be no consciousness of a break in the flow, and no feeling of a set song in the conventional operatic sense." But while Heyward slaved away on such details, he began once again to worry about whether Gershwin would come through and do the music. Despite Gershwin's press announcement in January, Heyward could not help recalling the composer's earlier waffling and his sometimes capricious attitude toward the project.

Heyward had particular reason to worry about Gershwin's degree of commitment when a radio show called "Music by Gershwin" premiered in March. Heyward, who did not know about the show in advance, heard it one evening and was alarmed. The next day, he wrote to Gershwin, "Swell show, George, but what the hell is the news about PORGY!!! . . . I am naturally disappointed that you have tied yourself up. . . . I am not criticizing your decision. I know well what an enormously advantageous arrangement the radio is . . . only I am disappointed. . . . I hope mightily that you have . . . plenty of time now that you are giving to [the opera]. Reassure me about this some time." Gershwin replied that he had not abandoned the opera and was formulating ideas for the score even as he was engaged in these other projects. Heyward had not yet divined Gershwin's genius and his ability to juggle several complex tasks simultaneously. After the opera had premiered, however, Heyward thought that the radio may have indirectly accounted for some of the advance interest in the opera: "Out of [twenty-five million radios] for a half hour each week," he wrote, "poured the glad tidings that Feenamint could be wheedled away from virtually any drug clerk in America for one dime—the tenth part of a dollar. And with the authentic medicine man flair, the manufacturer distributed his information in the irresistible wrapper of Gershwin hits, with the composer at the piano."

The astonishing vitality associated with American culture during the 1920s sprang primarily from the popular arts. Mass culture began to emerge in the 1920s and accelerated in the 1930s with the advent of radio, which had evolved from a mysterious curiosity to a universally accepted instrument of entertainment, business, learning, and mass communication, with few counterparts in American social history. In certain respects radio was the first truly mass medium and had the potential to democratize culture in terms of both distribution and participation.

Radio was only one facet of the vast democratization of the American arts in the 1930s, as preferences for all things European—the rage in the 1920s—gave way to new definitions of art, which now included popular or mass culture. The fine arts had become increasingly remote to average Americans, particularly in the economic hard times of the 1930s. Gilbert Seldes recognized this emerging transformation of culture in his 1924 book, *The Seven Lively Arts*. The title referred to those arts that were created to satisfy mass entertainment demands—such things as slapstick movie comedies, comic strips, revues, musical comedies, newspaper columns, slang humor, popular songs, and vaudeville. Eventually he and such other critics as George Jean Nathan, James Gibbons Hunecker, Matthew Josephson, and Marsden Hartley would expand the boundaries even more to include such arts as industrial design, Works Progress Administration theatrical productions, Bristol-Myers's roadside jingles, and the type of "Broadway opera" illustrated by *Porgy and Bess*. The popular opera might be said to have offered a new form of art, accessible culture.

Heyward had always been interested in the nexus between art and commerce: its unification seemed confirmed in this Broadway opera and its mass-culture cousins, a point made in jingoistic fashion by Seldes in a 1936 essay that proclaimed that commerce and art had been irrevocably united in American culture: "When Bing Crosby spoke the name of Marcel Proust into the microphone . . . more or less in honor of Miracle Whip, the long uneasy, half-scandalous affair between commerce and the arts was at last acknowledged." A necessary part of a program to democratize culture, of course, meant enfranchising African Americans in the creation and presentation of art, something that *Porgy and Bess* did in superior fashion.

In late February Gershwin wrote to Heyward that the first act was begun and that the composer was starting with the songs and spirituals first. When the opera debuted, the unique character of the music would be its most-discussed element. Gershwin had decided to write his own songs rather than use authentic ones. He explained that he "wanted the music to be all of one piece." Consequently, Heyward, instead of using original material, created quasi-spirituals and work songs. A persisting question about the musical compositions in *Porgy and Bess* is whether they are true arias or Broadway-style songs simply placed in an operatic setting. Gershwin unapologetically maintained that they were simply songs and that he "was not ashamed" of writing them instead of arias. "In *Porgy and Bess* I realized I was writing an opera for the theater and without songs it could be neither of the theater nor entertaining, from my viewpoint." Moreover, Gershwin contended, songs were "entirely within the operatic tradition. Many of the most successful operas of the past have had songs." Verdi's *Carmen,* for example, was "almost a collection of song hits."

The collaboration by mail continued. Some disagreements about the length of the work took place (an issue that would resurface at the show's Boston premiere). As early as 6 February 1934, Heyward had cautioned Gershwin, "Act 2, scene 1 may still seem a little too long to you, but I have reduced it from 39 pages in the talking script [the stage version] to 18 for the opera, and it is strong on humor and action." On 8 March, after receiving act 2, scene 3, Gershwin wrote to Heyward that it was a "very interesting and touching scene" but "a bit on the long side. However, I see one or two places that do not seem terribly important to the action and which could be cut." Heyward felt strongly that the script should not be too lean: on 27 March he wrote to his collaborator that "the storm scene [act 1] must stand about as it is with very few cuts in dialog. . . . [D]o not be alarmed about any inclination toward too much length. There are many places where we can cut . . . without disrupting the story."

Gershwin was impressed by Heyward's work: "I really think you are doing a magnificent job and I hope I can match it musically," the composer wrote. He began increasingly to depend on Heyward for unexpected help. For example, Gershwin did not know the rhythm Heyward had in mind for his songs and asked him to "put dots and dashes over the lyric[s]" when he sent them. Heyward had a good sense of this rhythm, a key to the authenticity of the music. He suggested to Gershwin that for a song that Jake, the captain of the fishing fleet, would sing, Gershwin should "imagine [himself] at an oar and write the music to conform to that rhythm—that will give you a better idea than anything I can write." At another point, a scene in act 3 needed cutting: "You must make sure that the opera is not too long as I am a great believer in not giving people too much of a good thing, and I am sure you agree with this," Heyward advised Gershwin, and the two men jointly worked toward eliminating any unnecessary material. In Heyward's idea for opening the show with Brown at the piano, Gershwin found a special challenge. He and Ira, he said, were working up lyrics to the music "with a sort of African chant" to them. They eventually developed a system whereby Heyward could send scenes and lyrics through the mail, then they, "after their extraordinary fashion, would get at the piano, pound, wrangle, swear, burst into weird snatches of song, and eventually emerge with a polished lyric."

Gershwin thought so highly of Heyward's talents that the composer wanted the author to come north so that they could work together— especially on the spirituals for act 1, scene 2, which was posing another challenge. Heyward agreed. He wanted to expedite the work for several reasons. One, he was running out of money. He said that he had been "letting everything else go" but the opera, and that if the show was not going to open in the fall, he would "have to get something else . . . to tide me over."

Heyward was also worried about the appearance of Gertrude Stein and Virgil Thomson's *Four Saints in Three Acts*, which also employed an all-black cast. The title derived from Stein's making each of her two main characters, Saint Teresa of Avila and Saint Ignatius Loyola, into two character aspects (one sung by a soprano and the other a contralto). But when he saw the opera, Gershwin wrote to Heyward that they had nothing to worry about: "the libretto was entirely in Stein's manner, which means that it had the effect of a 5-year-old child prattling on. Musically it sounded early 19th century, which was quite a happy inspiration and made the libretto bearable—in fact quite entertaining." In addition, no two works could be farther apart in form or content: *Four Saints* was a highly stylized, virtuosic performance that was supposed to be an allegory of the development of modernist art in Paris in the 1920s. *Porgy and Bess,* of course, was a gritty, realistic drama set in the American South.

In April 1934, Gershwin installed his friend from the South in a guest suite in his fabled fourteen-room duplex at 132 East Seventy-second Street. Heyward wrote many of his lyrics during the visit, and most were used in the opera with hardly a syllable changed: "Summertime," "A Woman Is a Sometime Thing," "Buzzard Song," "It Take a Long Pull to Get There," and "My Man's Gone Now" as well as more than half of "It Ain't Necessarily So" and "I Got Plenty of Nuttin.'" Ira Gershwin wanted to give Heyward shared credit for "Bess, You Is My Woman Now" as well, because Ira "took the title from one of the lines in the text and probably used three or four other lines from the libretto in the body of the song." But Heyward could not be persuaded, contending that the song was in essence Ira's work and denying any claim to it. In the same manner, Ira also took lines from the text to create "I Loves You, Porgy," "A Red-Headed Woman," and "Oh, I Can't Sit Down." Ira considered these songs "collaborative efforts, rather than my exclusive work" and urged Heyward to take partial credit for some so that he could be paid royalties. But Heyward simply would not do so, thus raising him even higher in Ira's esteem. "In all honesty," Ira went on, "I don't recall having had much to do with polishing any of DuBose's lyrics. True, if a scene was too long or a substitute line was required here and there in the text, I was always available and if DuBose wasn't around I would help my brother cut, edit or change," but even in such cases as these, Heyward was a full collaborative partner.

A good example is "I Got Plenty of Nuttin.'" Ira recalled that he and Heyward were in his brother's workroom: "George felt there was a spot where Porgy might sing something lighter and gayer than the melodies and recitatives he had been given in Act 1. He went to the piano and began to improvise. A few preliminary chords and in less than a minute a well-rounded, cheerful melody. 'Something like that,'" Gershwin said. Both Ira and Heyward had the same reaction: "That's it!" they said. "Don't look any further." "You really think so?" Gershwin asked. He recaptured the melody and played it again. Then, a title popped into Ira's head. (Usually, he recalled, "I sweat for days.") "I Got Plenty o' Nuttin,'" he said tentatively. Heyward and Gershwin liked the title, so Ira said he would get to work on it "later." Heyward then asked Ira if he would mind if Heyward tried his hand at it. "So far, everything I've done has been set by George and I've never written words to music," Heyward said. "If it's all right with you I'd love to take the tune along with me to Charleston." He and Ira "discussed generally the mood" and "arrived at a couple of lines." Two weeks later, Heyward sent him a version that was a solid first draft: it had many usable lines but was somewhat awkward when sung. Ira then took the lyric and polished it into the final product.

Overall, it was a happy and productive collaboration. George Gershwin later wrote that he felt that Heyward and Ira had "achieved a fine synchronization of diversified moods," with Heyward writing "most of the native material" and Ira "most of the sophisticated songs." Nonetheless, Heyward has never received his full due as cocreator of the opera. He was naturally shy, never fully comfortable with fame, and never consistently confident in his abilities. Heyward always thought that everyone was smarter or more talented than he was. His friend Gerald Johnson, writing to Josephine Pinckney the following summer about the buzz preceding the debut of *Porgy and Bess,* was exasperated that Heyward was such "a damned gentleman . . . in the most grimly literal sense": " I am thoroughly convinced that [he] has so much more than all the rest of us put together that he ought to be a whole school of Southern writers in himself." But Johnson knew that were the opera to be a hit, Heyward would never claim too much of the credit.

Heyward's tendencies toward self-effacement also led him easily into George Gershwin's shadow, considering the virtuoso aura that surrounded the composer. Gershwin was a musical genius, and, as Rouben Mamoulian noted, Gershwin "enjoyed his playing as much as his listeners did." The atmosphere at his duplex, with celebrities coming and going as if they were dropping in on an ongoing dress rehearsal, made it natural for Gershwin to dominate the room. And it led those who did not know Gershwin well to mistake his absorption in his own creations for egotism and vanity.

Heyward was happy to give most of the credit to Gershwin and had only kind things to say about him after *Porgy and Bess* debuted. Heyward felt that Gershwin's "self-appreciations were beyond modesty and beyond conceit. He was incapable of insincerity; he didn't see why he should suppress a virtue or a talent simply because it happened to belong to him. He was just plain dazzled by the spectacle of his own music and his own career; his unaffected delight in it was somewhat astonishing, but it was also amusing and refreshing."

Work on the opera continued to move forward; the creators expected to put it into rehearsal in August and have it open in the fall. Then the time came for Gershwin to make another foray south, to refresh his mind with the sights and sounds of the lowcountry and to stimulate his composing with a change of venue. In mid-June 1934, he arrived in Charleston with his artist cousin, Henry Botkin. They drove out to Heyward's cottage on Folly Beach, where Gershwin planned to continue writing the piano score for his opera, welding Heyward's words to his music. Gershwin seems to have liked the isolation of the place, preferring to stay to himself most of the time, away from the busier life downtown.

Heyward had rented a separate cottage for Gershwin and Botkin in advance, on the shore side of the street opposite his own. The lodgings were Spartan, to say the least, quite a contrast to Gershwin's opulent Manhattan digs. There were four rooms and a sleeping porch, and water was imported from the city in five-gallon jugs. In one room Gershwin slept on an iron bed. A rented upright piano stood in another room. The character of the house matched that of the island—the whole area had a battered, ramshackle look to it. Gershwin wrote to his mother, "Imagine, there's not one telephone on the whole island—public or private. Our first three days have been cool, the place being swept by an ocean breeze. Yesterday was the first hot day and it brought out the flies and gnats and mosquitoes. There are so many swamps in the district that when the breeze comes in from the land there's nothing to do but scratch."

Gershwin soon fell into a routine, rising at 7:00 or 7:30 in the morning and working most of the day. When a local reporter came to call on him early in his stay on Folly, Gershwin was dressed in a Palm Beach sport coat and an orange tie, but he soon succumbed to the rough charm of his environment, and a week or so later he was walking the beach in cutoff Bermuda shorts and sporting a day's growth of beard. At this point he befriended a local college student, Abe Dumas, who became Gershwin's driver for the summer. (Dumas did not know who this scraggly looking fellow was until one evening, when, invited back to his cottage for dinner, Dumas heard the composer playing some excerpts from *Rhapsody in Blue*.)

Dumas drove Gershwin and Heyward out to various Negro churches to observe customs and hear songs in authentic settings. Heyward recalled that nearby James Island, "with its large population of primitive Gullah Negroes," became a sort of "laboratory in which to test our theories, as well as an inexhaustible source of folk material." He thought the experience was "more like a homecoming than an exploration" for Gershwin: "The quality in him which had produced the *Rhapsody in Blue* in the most sophisticated city in America, found its counterpart in the impulse behind the music and bodily rhythms of the simple Negro peasant of the South." The two men toured in this manner for five weeks. As word spread around the churches that Gershwin was in the area, the sanctuaries became thronged with crowds, and according to Dumas, Gershwin left generous donations at each of the churches he visited, thus ensuring that he would always get a welcoming audience wherever he went.

One particular custom that interested Gershwin and Heyward was called shouting. Heyward described the technique as "a complicated rhythmic pattern beaten out by feet and hands as an accompaniment to the spirituals, and . . . indubitably an African survival." At one remote church on a nearby sea island, Gershwin started shouting with the participants and eventually, "to their huge delight," outshouted them. "I think that he is probably the only white man in America who could have done it," Heyward wrote. On another night, in Hendersonville, where Gershwin and Botkin had gone at the end of their southern tour to stay with the Heywards, the group entered a Negro meeting house, and Gershwin stopped suddenly, catching hold of Heyward's arm and holding it tightly: "The sound that had arrested him was one to which, through long familiarity, I attached no special importance. But now, listening to it with him, and noticing his excitement, I began to catch its extraordinary quality. It consisted of perhaps a dozen voices raised in loud rhythmic prayer." Oddly to Heyward, "while each had started at a different time, upon a different theme, they formed a clearly defined rhythmic pattern, and . . . this, with the actual words lost, and the inevitable pounding of the rhythm, produced an effect almost terrifying in its primitive intensity." Inspired by the extraordinary effect, Gershwin wrote six simultaneous prayers (eventually cut from the production) producing a terrifying primitive invocation to God in the face of the hurricane.

Gershwin returned to New York to press ahead with the piano score. *Porgy and Bess* was scheduled to open the Theatre Guild's fall 1935 season. Gershwin had been meeting with the guild managers to select a production team for *Porgy and Bess.* Heyward provided his input via the mails. The behind-the-scenes story of the production shows what a truly multiethnic and innovative project *Porgy and Bess* was. Mamoulian, the director of the stage version of *Porgy,* was the logical choice to direct the opera. From *Porgy* Mamoulian had gone on to direct other plays for the guild, including Eugene O'Neill's *Marco Millions* and Ivan Turgenev's *A Month in the Country.* Soon thereafter Mamoulian had moved into an even more successful career as a motion picture director, a pioneer in the emerging technology of the talkies. By 1935 he had many notable films to his credit, among them the now-classic 1931 version of *Dr. Jekyll and Mr. Hyde,* starring Fredric March, and the first Technicolor film, *Becky Sharp,* based on William Makepeace Thackeray's novel, *Vanity Fair.*

Heyward objected to the choice of Mamoulian. Heyward had found Mamoulian hard to work with in 1927—too mercurial and too harsh a taskmaster on cast and crew. Heyward's choice was John Houseman, the young director of *Four Saints in Three Acts.* But the guild's production manager, Warren Munsell, felt that Houseman was not practiced enough to take on as big a production as an opera, and Munsell urged Heyward to put aside his differences with Mamoulian: "I really believe that the values of the present version will be brought out far better by [Mamoulian] than by Houseman, and it would be greatly to your advantage, as well as to ours, to have him produce the play. . . . [W]e want to close the arrangements now so that he will hold the time open for us." Gershwin also favored Mamoulian strongly, so in the spirit of the partnership, Heyward conceded.

Mamoulian himself did not really want the job. When he had first heard that the play *Porgy* was to be the libretto for the opera, he was "shocked": "I felt the play was so pure and complete in its form, had such a direct simplicity and strength, that any attempt to translate it into operatic form might spoil it. However, my second thought was that if there was a composer in the whole world equipped by the quality of his talent to achieve this task, George was that composer." In a great act of faith in Gershwin's genius, Mamoulian signed a contract with the guild "without having heard a single note" of the opera he was to direct.

Gershwin tapped another Russian-American, Alexander Smallens, to conduct the orchestra. Smallens, an associate conductor of the Philadelphia Orchestra, had been musical director of the Stein-Thomson opera as well. Although Smallens was dubious about Gershwin's handling of recitatives when Smallens heard parts of the piano score, he nevertheless accepted the assignment. The third important production slot was given to yet another person of Russian origin, Alexander Steinert. He had been coaching the singers for the Russian Opera Company, and Gershwin was impressed with his work. He located Steinert one evening at a Town Hall reception for Igor Stravinsky and told Steinert about *Porgy and Bess*. He was so intrigued by the concept that he signed a contract with the Theatre Guild the next day. *Porgy and Bess* now had in place a troika of Russian Americans to guide it from drafting table to opening night. It was the first of many elements of the opera that signaled its true multicultural character.

Heyward naturally deferred to Gershwin when musical judgments needed to be made, so the author was not involved in the signing of Steinert, Smallens, or Eva Jessye, leader of the chorus. But in April 1935 Heyward came to New York to assist in casting the leads. Some of the same problems in casting the play recurred with the opera. According to Steinert, "nearly every day, [w]e sat for many hours, listening to hundreds of auditions. . . . Many of the colored people, born and educated in the North, hadn't the slightest trace of the essential Negro lingo, and were obliged to learn the dialect of the South." However, conditions had improved: black actors now had agents to represent them, and casting could now be made from a much larger pool of candidates. As many as a thousand hopefuls were either interviewed or auditioned.

The lead role of Porgy went to Todd Duncan, a music professor at Howard University in the Washington, D.C. Duncan, thirty-two, had been recommended to Gershwin by Robert Wachsman, the producer of a radio program of Negro music whom Gershwin had met while doing "Music by Gershwin." Duncan immediately impressed Gershwin. He wrote Heyward of having convinced Duncan to sing one Sunday afternoon and felt right away that the baritone was "the closest thing to a colored Lawrence Tibbett" (a popular singer with the Metropolitan Opera) that he had ever heard. When Heyward saw Duncan perform, Heyward thought that the singer was "an angel's baritone, and . . . a superb actor." Duncan, however, was not overly impressed by what he heard of *Porgy and Bess*. He felt that Gershwin's work, in the Tin Pan Alley vein, was beneath him. Moreover, Duncan was not sold on the opera's vision of black life: "I knew it would cause controversy among my people because of its representation of black life and music," he later said. "But, Gershwin had sold me on it right then and there!"

Duncan liked the idea of singing a story about southern blacks set in a classical form. He thought the opera, if executed properly, would elevate African Americans to a higher status in the arts. The melting-pot aspect of the production did not escape either man's notice. At a rehearsal some months later, Duncan, bowled over by the emotionalism of Gershwin's music, kidded him that the composer was more Negro than the actor was. Gershwin, in turn, joked that Duncan was more Jewish than Gershwin himself.

Anne Wiggins Brown, a student at the Juilliard School, was chosen for the part of Bess. She did not have as much stage experience as some of the other choices (like Gershwin's original favorite, Etta Moten), but her vocal range was far more impressive than her competition's, so Gershwin signed her. To give her some dramatic experience, he arranged for her to take on a small role in the London production of his play *Blackbirds* until rehearsals for *Porgy and Bess* began.

Heyward recommended Ruby Elzy for the part of Serena. Heyward knew her from a small role she had played in the film version of *The Emperor Jones*. The author struck up a friendship with Elzy, whose life history Heyward must have found to be compelling dramatic material, much in the vein of the works he had himself written. Born into a poor family in rural Mississippi, Elzy had washed dishes to work her way through a small school run by a Methodist missionary society. By great good chance, the president of Ohio State University, on an accreditation trip surveying southern schools, heard her sing and enrolled her in the music department at his school. She received scholarships to continue her training until she ended up at Juilliard, and from there she moved to the professional stage. Heyward must have been struck by the similarities between Elzy's life and that of his character, Lissa, from *Mamba's Daughters*. Elzy told Heyward that at every opportunity she rode a bus four days and four nights back home to see her parents, and she boasted that she could still "chop cotton with any of the family."

The last major character to be cast was Sportin' Life—a flashy urban hipster descended from an earlier Negro stereotype, the so-called zip coon, from minstrelsy. In the 1952 revival of *Porgy and Bess,* Cab Calloway played this part, and from that production evolved the story that the character was based on Calloway's nightly shows at Harlem's Cotton Club in the 1930s. Of course, Heyward had created Sportin' Life long before Calloway had become famous, although Gershwin did frequent the club and no doubt saw Calloway perform there many times. But both Heyward and Gershwin's first choice for the opera's cocaine-purveying tempter was John W. Bubbles, a dancer from the vaudeville team of Buck and Bubbles. Bubbles, whose real name was John William Sublett, hailed from Kentucky, where he had grown up with another boy, Ford Lee Washington. The two got jobs at a theater and put together a vaudeville act, which they would perform after the show had ended and the audience was leaving the building. The two clicked, a manager saw them, and they took to the vaudeville circuit, where they became Buck and Bubbles. Both were hired for *Porgy and Bess;* Ford received a smaller role and was billed as Ford Buck.

Bubbles's undisciplined talents presented problems during rehearsals. First, he could not read music, and so he was bewildered by the several-hundred-page score. Steinert eventually came up with the idea of Bubbles tap dancing his way through the rhythm of "It Ain't Necessarily So," but then other difficulties occurred. Bubbles was rarely on time for rehearsals, and when he did make it on stage, he often changed rhythms in midline or jumped a note higher in singing. These differences suggest the complexity Heyward and Gershwin had encountered in trying to wed black folk material to a classical form. Bubbles's roughshod manner of working through the score was completely at odds with the formal, rigid rhythms of the opera. But Gershwin stood by him. When at one point Smallens, exasperated by Bubbles's lack of discipline, threw down his baton and shouted that Bubbles should be thrown out of the show, Gershwin came running down from the back of house. "Throw him out? You can't do that. Why, he's the black Toscanini."

By this point, Gershwin had completed the orchestral score—a monumental task since, as he himself had noted, there were "millions of notes to write." The opera was scheduled to open in Boston on 1 October.

The first thing Heyward marveled at when he entered the rehearsal hall was the way that Steinert had prepared the cast members vocally. On the first day of rehearsal, they could read the score from beginning to end—not just

Duncan and Elzy, who were already proficient musicians, but also Bubbles and others who had no such training. This northern cast had also deeply absorbed the dialect and rhythmic inflections of southern Negro speech, mostly because of the diligence of Gershwin, who coached them in this aspect of the interpretation.

About the only person who was not pleased with the opera thus far was its moody director, Rouben Mamoulian. A natural pessimist, Mamoulian tended to elevate small difficulties to the level of insurmountable obstacles. Recalling his work on *Porgy and Bess*, Mamoulian later wrote, "The first day of rehearsing a play is . . . like breaking mountains of ice. The end of it leaves one completely exhausted and usually a little depressed. Everything seems awkward, disorganized, almost hopeless." That was the way Mamoulian felt after the first rehearsals. He was laying abed in his hotel room, "indulging in rather melancholy and misanthropic thoughts," when the phone rang. Gershwin's voice came over the line, "glowing with enthusiasm": "Rouben, I couldn't help calling you. . . . I just had to call you and tell you how I feel. I am so thrilled and delighted over the rehearsal today." Mamoulian was mollified; he went to work the next day as if nothing had happened.

Eventually, too, the lyrical beauty and transcendent emotion of the music washed over the cast completely and thus smoothed over any early difficulties. In describing one rehearsal, Duncan wrote, "[P]resently there rose the most glorious tones and wails with accompanying amens and hallelujahs for our sick Bess that I ever hope to experience. . . . [I] knew then that [Heyward] had put down on paper accurately and truthfully something from the depth of soul of a South Carolina Negro woman who feels the need of help and carries her troubles to her God" (60).

Before the play went to Boston, the Theatre Guild pressed Gershwin and Heyward for decisions on two issues. To this point, the working title of the opera had been simply *Porgy*. But the guild's publicity department worried that the title might lead people to think the opera was simply a revival of the 1927 play. Heyward came up with a new title, right in the operatic tradition. There had been, he said, Pelleas and Melisande, Samson and Delilah, Tristan and Isolde. Why not Porgy and Bess? And so it was. The second matter concerned using the word *opera* on the program, marquee, and publicity materials. The guild worried that *opera* might scare off audiences, but Gershwin insisted on it. Finally, a compromise was reached: *Porgy and Bess* would be billed as a "folk opera."

Opening night at Boston's Colonial Theater was a society event. The Theatre Guild had arranged for the first performance to benefit the New England Hospital for Women and Children. This charity, and the allure of a world premiere opera by the famous George Gershwin, brought out scions and dowagers by the cabful. The crowd also served as evidence of the egalitarian appeal of the opera. The society editor for the *Boston American* reminded readers that *Porgy and Bess* was unique, a "tale of work-day-Negroes" that was the first opera indigenous to American soil.

The performance was enthusiastically received. Backstage, J. Rosamund Johnson, the assistant conductor of the chorus, who also played the part of Lawyer Frazier, ran up to Gershwin, embraced him, and cried, "George, you've done it—you're the Abraham Lincoln of Negro music." At the end of the curtain call, Gershwin, Heyward, and Mamoulian came onstage to take their bows. They stood there for fully fifteen minutes while applause thundered throughout the house. Gershwin characteristically gravitated to downstage center; in a photograph of the scene, Heyward's head is just barely visible over Gershwin's left shoulder.

But there was no quibbling over credit that evening. The opera was a smash in Boston. Hopes for an equally successful New York debut soared. But before it could happen, the show needed to be shortened.

Mamoulian had already indicated so to Gershwin while the show was in rehearsal, and Gershwin knew that cuts were a foregone conclusion. He was emotionally attached to his music, and he was reluctant to let anything go. His strategy had been to launch a preemptive strike by instituting some major cuts even before the Boston premiere, before he became too tied to the work to change it. The introductory scene that Heyward had written—the atmospheric opening with Jasbo Brown at the piano—had been jettisoned in the interests of economy. The Theatre Guild did not want to have to build another set just for the opening. In addition, Gershwin had cut Porgy's tragic aria, "The Buzzard Song," from act 2 on the principle that Duncan's voice might buckle under the pressure of singing three big songs in a row. But the show was still too long, and another forty minutes needed to come out.

In consultation with Heyward, Gershwin therefore cut the six prayers he had written that were inspired by his visit to the Hendersonville church and deleted thirty-eight continuous pages of Porgy's singing from the third act. The original third-act trio, "Where's My Bess?," became Porgy's solo. It was painful for Gershwin to make these cuts, but he knew that they were necessary if the show was to be commercially viable.

The cuts compromised some of the thematic integrity of the work, and not until the 1970s was the full version of the opera performed. The elimination of the Brown scene, for example, coming after the orchestral introduction, symbolized a Negro Eden that fit the opera's essence as a parable of the inviolability of innocence of spirit in a corrupt world. Moreover, Gershwin's music for this scene beautifully evokes the blend of southern and sophisticated city themes in the work. It contrasts the piano's tawdry sophistication of Tin Pan Alley melodies with the primitive nature of the chorus. However, Gershwin ultimately thought the cuts enhanced the work rather than damaged it. After the New York premiere, the composer reportedly handed Mamoulian a rolled-up sheaf of pages from the score, tied with a red ribbon. "This is my thank you for making me take out all that stuff in Boston," Gershwin said.

In Boston they may have been wild about *Porgy and Bess,* but in New York that wasn't necessarily so. Cast and crew were thrilled with the opening night performance on 10 October at the Alvin Theater, and spirits were high during the all-night party that followed it, but the morning brought sobering reviews from the newspaper critics. White reviewers almost uniformly latched onto one issue about the show: was *Porgy and Bess* an opera or a musical?

The *New York Times* music critic, Olin Downes, noted, "The style is at one moment of opera and another of operetta or sheer Broadway entertainment." The paper's drama critic, Brooks Atkinson, also dragged the issue into his column while admitting that the production actually "lies in Mr. Downes's bailiwick." Atkinson was annoyed by the use of recitatives—"why commonplace remarks that carry no emotion have to be made in a chanting monotone is a problem in art [I] cannot fathom," he wrote. Atkinson may simply have disliked operatic form, but his point received some legitimacy from Samuel Chotzinoff's remarks in the *New York Post.* Chotzinoff, the paper's music critic, also wondered "why Mr. Gershwin continued to impose the recitative on matter that did not require it." The *Times*'s chief music critic, Joseph Swain, observed that "the drama critics objected to recitative per se and the music critics to 'Summertime,' 'I Got Plenty o' Nuttin' and other tunes which seemed 'too popular' for opera." (Ironically, Gilbert Seldes, champion of the popular arts, thought *Porgy and Bess* was without question an opera, not qualifying for his definition of accessible culture; disliking opera himself, he gave the show a so-so assessment.)

Mamoulian glancingly summed up the pettiness of the debate: "You give someone something delicious to eat and they complain because they have no name for it." Lehman Engel would later write in *The American Musical Theater* that "this annoyance with *Porgy* is far more the product of semantics than of anything Gershwin put into his score. It is as if just calling *Porgy* by the name 'opera' serves to assail the sensibilities of those who believe that such a classification is a slur on the dignity of Wagner, Verdi, and Mozart" (143). Later still Rodney Milnes would argue in a review of the opera that it was both the heir of a long tradition and an inspirer of works to come: "Its influence on [Benjamin Britten's] *Peter Grimes* grows more obvious as time goes by, and there was never any doubt of its influence on *Street Scene*. In the case of both works, the 'folk opera' or 'Broadway opera' labels were the result of managerial nervousness about potential customers being put off" (521).

Indeed, during the 1920s and 1930s in particular, critics reveled in quibbles over labels and categories. Gershwin and Heyward, while certainly wanting to elevate public taste by working in the operatic form, also respected diversity among cultural preferences. *Porgy and Bess* erases boundaries and transcends categories. The work thus mirrors the rise of such cultural democratism among American arts. In the 1920s, preferences were for all things European; the new definitions of art ("new poetry," "new theater") made possible the enfranchisement of "popular" or mass culture. In the 1930s, for the first time in American cultural history, artistic forms truly began to meld and reconstitute themselves in mixed or even amorphous media. The "status" of the opera could best be described by a phrase that Duke Ellington used to convey praise regardless of precision in form: "beyond category."

An assassin's review came from the pen of Thomson; by this point, Gershwin and Heyward must have regarded him as their nemesis. "Crooked folklore and halfway opera," sneered the composer of *Four Saints in Three Acts*. "Gershwin's lack of understanding of all the major problems of form, of continuity, and of straightforward musical expression is not surprising in view of the impurity of his musical sources and his frank acceptance of them." Although in later years, Thomson would soften somewhat in his opinion of *Porgy and Bess*, at the time he thought that Gershwin had merely served up a "piquant but highly unsavory" mixture "of Israel, Africa, and the Gaelic Isles." There was also some sense among New Yorkers that they had been handed a Great Cultural Event as a fait accompli, and they had not yet formed their own judgments. In the *Nation* Joseph Wood Krutch said that "admiring it will be one of the Things Being Done," and Stark Young in the *New Republic* was uncertain whether "the whole thing" was black or white (338).

But if the reviewers harped on the form of the opera, they enthusiastically applauded its dramatic content. Downes raved that when it came to "sheer acting" that night, "certain operatic functionaries should have been present. If the Metropolitan chorus could ever put one half the action into the riot scene in the second act of Meistersinger that the Negro cast put into the fight that followed the crap game it would be not merely refreshing but miraculous." Similarly, John Mason Brown of the *Post* wrote that the show was "compellingly dramatic."

Black critics raised a different point, that of whether the show was completely Negro. Ellington (ironically, the coiner of the phrase "beyond category") logged the harshest negative reaction: "The times are here to debunk Gershwin's lampblack Negroisms. The music does not hitch with the mood and spirit of the story. It does not use the Negro musical idiom." In like manner, Ralph Matthews, music critic for the *Baltimore Afro-American*, agreed that the opera certainly was not Negro: "The singing, even down to the choral and the ensemble numbers, has a conservatory twang. Superimposed on the shoddiness of Catfish Row they seem miscast." Hall Johnson, in the Negro magazine *Opportunity*, decided that he liked *Porgy and Bess* but granted that no white composer could ever command the "requisite knowledge or experience" needed to write in an authentic Negro musical language. Adverse black reactions to the opera grew even stronger in the civil rights era of the 1950s and 1960s.

Southerners tended initially to disparage *Porgy and Bess*. Many disliked the idea of putting black life in the spotlight at all. Still others felt that the mix of black and white art forms was so unrealistic that it negated the story's credibility. One Charlestonian told John Bennett that the opera represented "the sort of confusion which will undoubtedly keep running [in New York] because the self-sufficient visitors prefer to think that the South is like that. . . . Gershwin managed to ruin a very fine fragment of folk-lore. . . . [T]his new version . . . is a bastardized union of 'grand' opera and Tuskegee Choir singing." Another Charlestonian did not think that the opera would "add any kudos to the ubiquitous Massa Heyward" and argued that the "major credit" in this sort of production was given to a "Broadwayite like Gershwin"—in "capital letters and italics," to boot.

Porgy and Bess's inauspicious debut now seems something of an omen of its future tumultuous life. It ran for 124 performances—a long run for an opera, but a relatively short run for a Broadway musical. Moreover, the show was profitless. On 27 January 1936, the opera opened in Philadelphia as part of a four-city tour, going on to Pittsburgh, Chicago, and Washington, D.C. During this tour, more problems were created—by segregated seating. The National Theater, in Washington, was a segregated house, and Duncan and Anne Brown refused to perform under those conditions. The Theatre Guild threatened the actors with reprisals, but as Brown recalled, "We were adamant." And so, with help from other cast members and from political figures such as Mary McLeod Bethune and Ralph Bunche, they won. The National admitted African Americans to a desegregated house. After the performance, however, the management reverted to its original policy.

These problems with staging *Porgy and Bess* were omens of more controversy to come. The opera would be revived many times thereafter, and it would take on a paradoxical new life as both an ambiguous depiction of African Americans and as a stirring tribute to the will of the human spirit. Gershwin died shortly after the opera's debut, in 1937; Heyward passed away not long thereafter, in 1940. Neither man knew that they had created a permanent and controversial cultural icon.

The posthumous existence of *Porgy and Bess* was sustained by Dorothy Heyward, who survived her husband by twenty-one years. Dorothy championed the opera, often in the face of opposition from civil rights activists, and ensured its future as a world masterpiece. She fought many battles along the way, not least among them securing her late husband's claim to equal billing with Gershwin.

Plans were laid for the first full-scale revival of *Porgy and Bess* barely a year after Heyward's death. The idea was the brainchild of Cheryl Crawford, who had worked with the Theatre Guild on the 1927 production of *Porgy* and on *Porgy and Bess*. In 1940 Crawford had taken over an old movie house in Maplewood, New Jersey, and turned it into a home for summer stock. She attracted many Broadway shows after their runs in New York ended, and she decided to close the 1941 season with *Porgy and Bess*. This version of *Porgy and Bess* was considerably streamlined: the recitative, which Crawford and others had never thought appropriate, was eliminated; several minor characters were cut; the original forty-four piece orchestra was reduced by half; and the performers successfully quickened the pace of the show. It was a "snappier" production, closer in form to a Broadway musical than to an opera.

This new *Porgy and Bess*, with most of the original cast, was more favorably received by critics who had demurred at the 1935 production. The revival went on to Boston and then arrived at the Majestic Theater in New York on 22 January 1942, where it ran for 286 performances, at the time the longest theatrical revival in history. After closing in September 1942 the show went on tour for another eighteen months and then returned to New York for a special two-week engagement. It was a great success story, but Dorothy had to protect her late husband's interests: Crawford advertised the show as "George Gershwin's *Porgy and Bess*" and would have left Heyward off the bill completely had not Dorothy, who owned 40 percent of the production, pointed out the omission.

Another issue was the word *nigger*, which offended African Americans. Etta Moten, who replaced Anne Brown in the role of Bess, objected to the word in the libretto. Eva Jessye recalled that other cast members did not like the word either "but were afraid to object, that being the tenor of the times." Still, since they could not bring themselves to speak the work aloud, they "agreed to drown it out wherever and whenever it occurred. . . . The total ensemble would bombard the word with an avalanche of sounds, groans, [and] screams." Such was the way black professionals in pre–civil rights days had to compromise to be heard. Eventually the word was eliminated with the full support of Ira Gershwin, who rewrote parts of the libretto. This incident foreshadowed unpleasant conflict to come as African Americans balked at the unlettered and apparently simple-minded black characters.

One year after the Crawford revival, the opera appeared in Copenhagen with an all-white cast. The 1943 production was a great success, alarming the city's Nazi occupiers so much that they closed the show down after only a few performances. When World War II ended, *Porgy and Bess* was re-installed in the Danish Royal Opera's repertory, occasionally with Duncan and Anne Brown in the title roles.

The second revival of *Porgy and Bess*, produced by Robert Breen and Blevins Davis, was its most famous. Breen was a theater visionary who headed the American National Theater and Academy (ANTA); Davis was a wealthy theater enthusiast who sat on ANTA's board of directors. This time Dorothy not only made certain that Heyward received his fair share of the credit but also assisted Breen in scouting performers. The twenty-four-year-old Leontyne Price won the role of Bess, and the opera rescued the sliding career of Cab Calloway, who was tapped to play Sportin' Life. William Warfield, fresh from a successful film debut as Joe in MGM's *Show Boat*, signed on as Porgy.

Breen directed the production, restored many of the cuts in the Crawford version, but still managed to reduce the running time of the original. In places he also added some dialogue, drawn from the novel with help from Dorothy. Breen had high aspirations for *Porgy and Bess*. For some years, he had been striving to internationalize the theater community. *Porgy and Bess* had already played limited engagements in Denmark and Switzerland; if this new production succeeded, Breen intended a lengthy world tour. He also persuaded the Metropolitan Opera Association to book the show even though it had originally rejected the idea, usually allowing only their own productions to play in the house. But Breen knew his politics and pointed out that a rejection on the grounds of exclusivity would be unfortunate, "especially in the light of *Porgy and Bess* being a unique case in that it requires Negro artists." "We know very well indeed," he continued, "that if *Porgy and Bess* did not require Negro personnel, the Metropolitan would have long since acquired the rights for its repertoire."

The Met reconsidered and booked the show. But other problems prevented its opening there, and eventually Dallas was chosen as the first city for the tour. The opening was outstandingly successful, largely because of

Price's superlative performance. She combined the physicality of Bess as Crown's woman with the ideality of Bess as Porgy's wife, thus bringing out dimensions in the character not evident in the Crawford production. Her performance, together with the ensemble emphasis on shouting, dancing, and writhing in a jubilant group movement to the passionate rhythm of the music, led critics to conclude that this show was "blacker" than the earlier version. Reviewers were unanimous: *Porgy and Bess* had come into its own. By the time the show reached Washington, D.C., one reviewer declared, "America has grown up at last to *Porgy and Bess*. A superlative cast sang the word to an audience which appreciated and understood its compassionate revelation of Negro life in this alien hemisphere. It was one of democracy's historic moments."

Incorporated under the apt title of Everyman Opera, the Breen-Davis production went on a tour abroad in the fall of 1952 under the sponsorship of the State Department. The show played Vienna, Berlin, London, and Paris, then came back to New York for another engagement beginning in March 1953. But when the show returned to New York's Ziegfield Theater, the black press launched a vicious attack. One reporter for the *Baltimore Afro-American* reviled the opera as "the most insulting, the most libelous, the most degrading act that could possibly be perpetrated against colored Americans of modern times." Warfield, despite his role in the show, seemed to agree: "In 1952 the black community wasn't listening to anything about plenty of nothing being good enough for me. Blacks began talking about being black and proud."

This set of performances, however, eventually reversed the negative opinions of the show voiced by black performers in 1935. Ellington recanted his earlier damning of "Gershwin's lampblack Negroisms." Ellington telegraphed to Breen, "Your *Porgy and Bess* the superbest, singing the gonest, acting the craziest, Gershwin the greatest." When a reporter went backstage to ask one of the actors who played Porgy, John McCurry, why he thought African Americans disliked the show, McCurry replied that it was the media's fault: "They stir up controversy to sell newspapers," he claimed. Hattie McDaniel, who played Maria, later added, "[T]hose of us in *Porgy and Bess* saw ourselves as playing only roles, and in no way did we play them as ordinary black stereotypes. It was art, and we were artists. At the same time I have to say there was a fine line as far as my own sympathies were concerned; I could agree with the need for blacks to play roles that would provide more respect."

The European tour had once again raised the debate about how audiences perceived southern blacks based on their portrayal in the opera. The street attitude toward the show had changed as attitudes toward civil rights changed. There was now reform in place to end lynchings, enfranchise black voters, and combat discrimination in the armed forces. President Dwight D. Eisenhower praised the cast members for "what they have done for establishing good will between the countries . . . a direct answer to the communists that will destroy their charges that the Negro is enslaved." But black and white critics alike sometimes countered this view and worried that Europeans would assume that the squalid life of Catfish Row was an accurate reflection of reality and would help the communist cause by providing evidence of oppressed Negro conditions. When a new, longer international tour was proposed with State Department funding, Atkinson, *Porgy and Bess*'s longtime foe, declared that the opera would hurt international relations because it portrayed African Americans as "poverty-stricken, tattered, superstitious people, and some of them as criminals." Yet another tangled motive was suspected by American Communist Party's *Daily Worker,* which interpreted the idea as a "move . . . designed to counter Communist propaganda that American Negroes receive no recognition in the arts."

In Milan, *Porgy and Bess* played La Scala, the first time an American work and company had been invited there. Maya Angelou, who played Ruby, recalled the momentousness of "a huge cast of blacks" playing that theater. "Both audience and company were tense . . . coiled tight like a spring, wound taut for a shattering release." The audience loved the show: time and again, the people "came to their feet, yelling and applauding" as the singers engaged the elegant operagoers with their tale of the harshness of black life in the American South.

The State Department, however, now regarded *Porgy and Bess* as its most visible instrument of international goodwill, and so the company set out on a tour of the Mediterranean and Near East that included stops in Zagreb, Belgrade, Cairo, Athens, Tel Aviv, Casablanca, Barcelona, and Rome. The tour was then extended into South America, and *Porgy and Bess* journeyed on through Lima, Santiago, Bogotá, Caracas, Buenos Aires, and Rio de Janeiro. And then, in late September 1955, the visionary Breen persuaded the

Russian ambassador in Washington to arrange for the opera to come to the Soviet Union. One observer noted how impressed musically trained Russians were with the cast: the Russians had no idea that so many black Americans had such a solid grounding in classical music.

The Russians lionized *Porgy and Bess* and its cast. In Leningrad, thousands of people hoping to get tickets to the show had to be held back by police. This group included several African Americans who had emigrated to the Soviet Union (a land without racial prejudice) and had found work as farm laborers. These people were particularly eager to talk to members of the cast, to thank them for their efforts at bringing recognition to African Americans as artists.

From Leningrad and Moscow, the company went on to Warsaw, where the opera was also enthusiastically received. Truman Capote wrote an infamous account of the tour behind the Iron Curtain, *The Muses Are Heard.* The title derived from a Latin proverb that was employed in a speech by a Russian official who was announcing the breaking down of political barriers through art: "When the cannons are heard, the muses are silent; when the cannons are silent, the muses are heard." Capote's account of the tour was in most ways unconcerned with how the show played, what audiences thought, and what the performers did. Capote apparently began the trip having decided that *Porgy and Bess* was demeaning to African Americans and that the performers were Uncle Toms, prostituting themselves to an opera about slum Negroes. The resultant work was an assassin's biography of the production.

The success of the international tour generated Hollywood interest. There had been talk of making a movie out of *Porgy and Bess* as far back as 1942, but the question of assigning film rights was entangled by legal problems that stemmed from Gershwin's having died intestate. At that time, Dorothy and Ira thought the rights might fetch as much as $25,000. When bids were made fifteen years later, the price had swelled to more than ten times that amount. Thus, when Dorothy, who controlled 30 percent of any screen sale, was approached by the venerable Samuel Goldwyn in 1957, she stood to earn the most considerable sum ever on Heyward's and Gershwin's "failed" opera. But negotiations hit a snag again when Breen, who had insisted on directing the film, was unceremoniously dumped by Goldwyn and in the process alienated Dorothy. She had been on cordial terms with Breen and had trusted him to the extent that for a small sum she sold him an option, giving him the legal authority to negotiate the film rights on his and her behalf. But Breen, desperate to be the film's director, did not tell her that to seal the deal he had transferred his option to Goldwyn, who now had creative control over the whole project. Breen had assured Dorothy that she would work on the film scenario. Now she could not.

Although Goldwyn had no intention of consulting Dorothy on the film, the producer did at least show her some hospitality. She, Jenifer, and a family friend, Bill Banks, were put up at the Beverly Wilshire Hotel at Goldwyn's expense to observe the filming. But the group merely drank cocktails and lounged at the hotel pool. Whenever Dorothy went to the studio, she was told that *Porgy and Bess* was a closed set and that she would not be let in. She was furious: "They're saying the words that I wrote!" she complained to Banks.

After production overruns and costly delays, the Goldwyn film premiered in 1959 with Sidney Poitier and Dorothy Dandridge in the title roles. Poitier had not wanted to do the movie; his agent had committed him without his consent. Poitier thought the film "was not material complimentary to black people." But he was pressured by such prominent African Americans as Ralph Bunche, who thought the opera a classic, not demeaning at all. Other African American performers, such as Harry Belafonte and Lena Horne, urged Poitier to stand his ground, but he eventually gave in and did the film. From the start, the production was shrouded in scandal, secrecy, and suspicion. At one point a fire consumed the expensive curvilinear set, and the National Association for the Advancement of Colored People (NAACP) was accused of masterminding a conspiracy to do the film in. The movie lost most of the money invested in it and then was barred from public view, again by an unforeseen legal problem. Goldwyn had bought a fifteen-year lease on the rights. After that time lapse, the film could not be shown without the permission of the authors' estates, and neither the Gershwins nor Jenifer Heyward, who owned the rights after her mother's death, wanted the film shown—for whatever reasons. It remains out of circulation today.

Dorothy Heyward died in 1961. She lived to see her husband's work receive the recognition that was its due, but she died before her greatest dream for *Porgy and Bess* could be realized: a production in Heyward's native city. This great cultural irony is perhaps the most interesting twist in the opera's history; it is an interesting gloss on the artistic history of Charleston as well.

A production looked like it would take place in April 1954, when the Dock Street Theatre sponsored a local production to be presented at the County Hall with an African American cast. This would be the play's first performance in the southern United States. But *Porgy and Bess* was sacrificed to political expediency. South Carolina law, citing "historic reasons of authenticity," stipulated that there be no mixing of the races in "places of amusement." The Stagecrafters, an African American dramatic organization that was supplying the cast, suggested a compromise in which the house would be split in half, one side for whites and the other for blacks, but the NAACP objected to this arrangement, and when the media seized on the incident as evidence that an opera produced by African Americans could only be performed in a segregated theater, the production was canceled.

Finally, in 1970, to mark the three hundredth anniversary of the founding of Charleston, *Porgy and Bess* was performed in its native setting. After several other revivals following the great Breen-Davis production of the 1950s (the best of which was probably the 1976 Houston Grand Opera production, which had chosen to honor America's preeminent native opera by performing it on the nation's bicentennial), *Porgy and Bess* had risen to the level of the world's greatest musical works, and Charleston was proud to have it performed there. The cast was a group of local amateurs, and the theater was desegregated. The opera was staged again in Charleston in October 1985, exactly fifty years after its Broadway premiere and one hundred years after Heyward's birth. That year also saw the canonization of the work when it was finally presented at the Metropolitan Opera in New York. *Porgy and Bess* now belonged to the ages.

In Charleston, of course, no one had to be reminded who had written the story: Heyward's name stood out on every piece of publicity that surrounded the production, and his immortality there as the creator of *Porgy and Bess* was assured. Such was not always the case elsewhere, for example, in the 1986 production at the arts festival in Glyndebourne, England. In this production, the opera was less a folktale than a universal drama of humanity's struggle for survival. This version was thus truer to the spirit of the original novel by Heyward, but most critics ignored Heyward's role. One even attributed the libretto and lyrics to the Gershwin brothers alone. There is injustice in that characterization. But in spite of it, Heyward's story has secured its measure of fame and significance. *Porgy and Bess* has ascended into the pantheon of the universal. It is truly an opera for all people, a human document that, like *Hamlet,* has become archetypal, appropriate and meaningful to any time, any place, and any age.

Gershwin and Heyward deserve essentially equal credit for the creation of *Porgy and Bess.* Heyward authored the story and created the libretto and many of the lyrics. He also assisted in production details. Gershwin wedded Heyward's simple poetic lines to a score that simultaneously evokes passion, rage, pathos, and humility. More than merely appropriating the notes for certain musical gestures, as many critics charged, Gershwin used them creatively, extending their implications by linking them with a kind of musical organization that was typical neither of African American music nor of American popular song.

The complex character of the opera, however, still engages debate. Its portrayal of blacks certainly relies on stereotypes, yet there is an undeniably heroic character about the work that arguably mitigates the condescension that may be evoked in the characters' words and deeds. It is a tale of pathos and dignity and of the triumph of the human spirit, white or black. Indeed, the opera's blindness to racial prejudice may be the most compelling reason for its staying power today. As one reviewer said in 1935, *Porgy and Bess* is "the most American opera that has yet been seen or heard: it is a Russian who has directed it, two Southerners who have written its book, two Jewish boys who have composed its lyrics and its music, and a stageful of Negroes who sing and act it to perfection."

Chapter Eight

Return to Charleston

EYWARD ACCEPTED THE lukewarm reception of *Porgy and Bess* stoically, but it soured him on New York and even to some extent on his profession. He began to distrust the Broadway world and felt rebuffed by many whom he had once trusted. He could not get over the indifference of most critics to the bold experimentation of *Porgy and Bess,* and he was confused by some black critics' and artists' negative reactions to the opera and the seeming lack of appreciation for his work on behalf of African American art; in consequence, he began to feel directionless. He did not know what he could write next: did he truly understand the African American psyche as people had once said he did? Or were times changing too rapidly for him—could he no longer keep pace with the liberalization of artists' attitudes toward race?

The experience sent Heyward in two directions during the final years of his life. First he went in search of new material, but in his desire to find interesting subjects about which to write, he began to sacrifice quality and virtually disregard the distinction he had once carefully drawn between art and commercialism. The rancor over what "type" of art *Porgy and Bess* constituted only added to his indifference. Moreover, the way Heyward depicted African Americans in his final works, *Star Spangled Virgin* and the stage version of *Mamba's Daughters* in particular, suggests in some ways a disturbing regression to his youthful impressions of African Americans as happy in their insular worlds and not in need of opportunity or social uplift. Second, Heyward's displeasure with Broadway led him back to his artistic roots—to

Charleston and to regional theater. He devoted the last years of his life to working with young southern playwrights at Charleston's Dock Street Theatre. Heyward found that, contrary to the views of Thomas Wolfe and other self-exiled southerners, you can go home again.

Heyward had begun to long for Charleston well before *Porgy and Bess*. He had come to feel that Charleston had, after all, made him. It had given him his identity and, of course, had provided the raw material for his books. Moreover, he had a deep and profound love for the beauty of the place, as is clear from the rhapsodic descriptions of it in his early poems and in such novels as *Porgy* and *Peter Ashley*. Although he knew that he could not have earned a living from writing by staying there, he always maintained ties to the area—through friends and through the Poetry Society. In the early 1930s he had made a small concession to his feelings by purchasing the cottage on Folly Beach. In 1936 he decided to buy a home in the city proper. He chose one of the large, antebellum houses on the harbor, at 24 South Battery. The residence commanded an imposing view. It overlooked the water across the historic public garden where Stede Bonnet, the "gentleman pirate," had been tried and executed by the local militia led by William Rhett and where Citadel cadets had fired on the Union supply ship *Star of the West* the shots that some consider the opening salvos in the Civil War.

Smallish by South Battery standards, the house nonetheless looked suitably patrician. Moreover, it was still South Battery, the premier address for Charlestonians of note. At great expense, Heyward remodeled portions of the house so that Janie could continue to live with him and Dorothy, as she had at Dawn Hill. Heyward enjoyed his status as a celebrity but was melancholy for most of these last years. At times he was depressed about his writing, feeling that he had mined the vein of material open to him—that of the southern Negro—and would never produce anything equal to the quality of *Porgy and Bess*.

His celebrity status did, however, given him entrée to an interesting group that came to Charleston in the spring of 1937 in search of new experiences. This group comprised scientists, socialites, and connoisseurs of culture led by George Huntington Hartford, a famous New York art patron and sometime author. The group was undertaking a three-month cruise in the West Indies on a square-rigged sailboat that Hartford had recently purchased. Heyward was invited to go along, and he accepted. Heyward had a lifelong fascination with the sea and sailing, like many other Charlestonians, and he had always had the Charlestonians' armchair interest in West Indian culture, from which so many of the city's early settlers had hailed. It occurred to him that on such a cruise he might find the most original of Negro material: the Caribbean islands as the last enclaves of untouched primitivism in the modern world.

Hartford's boat, the *Joseph Conrad,* was one of the few full square-rigged vessels then in commission. Built in Copenhagen fifty-three years earlier, the boat served as a training ship for the Danish navy before being purchased by Alan Villiers, a famous writer of sea stories, who took it on a world cruise. The craft was later wrecked, and Hartford purchased it at auction. The *Conrad* was the smallest full-rigged craft afloat at the time, a mere 150 feet overall, including bowsprit. It carried a crew of twenty-three.

The purposes of the cruise were varied. With funding from the Smithsonian Institution, Hartford took along Dr. Waldo Schmitt, a marine biologist, and G. Robert Lunz, curator of crustacea at the Charleston Museum. These men were to collect marine specimens and bring them back to the Smithsonian for identification and study. Heyward was to write; Hartford intended to gather pirate lore. Other passengers included Virginia W. French, sister of John Jacob Astor III. The ship set sail from Charleston the evening of 2 March 1937. During the trip, Heyward kept a journal in which he recorded his observations about the ship and company, the flora and fauna of the islands, and the culture and governance of the cities and towns where the craft dropped anchor. Some of the entries were written as letters to Dorothy; others were less formal diary jottings.

It is a sign of Heyward's unsettled state of mind that he worried almost obsessively during the early stages of the trip. En route to Palm Beach, his fears were touched off by a nightmare in which he dreamed that his sister, Jeannie, had been injured in an automobile accident: "I was driving on the rear seat of a station wagon and she was sitting in front on [the] small seat. The door fell open and her left leg fell out, being caught against a tree and tearing it frightfully at the hip." The nightmare gave him a feeling of apprehension that he could not shake, and he hurriedly wrote to Dorothy to confirm that Jeannie was "well and happy and [his] hunch was all wrong." His fears redoubled when he learned that two close friends of Dorothy's had died while he was at sea and that one of them had experienced an accident superficially similar enough to the one he had dreamed about Jeannie. He explained to Dorothy that the omen was sadly correct: the "transposition" from Dorothy's friend to Jeannie, he said, "was quite easily accounted for psychically." Later still Heyward learned of a wave of influenza that was moving through Charleston during his absence; he wrote to Dorothy expressing the same types of paralyzing fears that Janie expressed about her family when Heyward was a young boy. Relieved to learn that his wife and daughter were well, he wrote, "We must thank God that . . . our little circle is still unbroken. . . . I shall try to keep from being depressed."

His spirits began to improve at West Palm Beach when he helped lay in supplies before the ship moved out for the islands: oilskins, pith helmets, and silk shirts, as well as tropical-weight pants and socks, in preparation for what he correctly predicted would be a heavy round of social obligations in certain ports.

In Nassau the group was entertained at the Governor's Mansion with rounds of tennis, followed by cocktails, then diving, followed by more cocktails. From the Bahamas, the ship took a leisurely route to San Salvador, where Heyward found some local color to interest him. He thought the island was a "self-sufficient little community" equitably governed both by locals and their British counterparts: the commissioner, a "lighter-colored man than the others," was "well educated, intelligent and human." He served as local magistrate and had "very little trouble with people. He showed me his police blotter. A man had just been let out of the immaculate little 'cooler' after one month servitude for stealing a stalk of cane and ten oranges. He had also been fined ten shillings. No wonder they behave." The beauty of the place was "indescribable" and evoked associations of a paradise to Heyward: "the natives happy, and the village immaculately clean—a little steamer stops in every fortnight with mail. It would be a fine place to dream away the rest of your life."

Tortuga, the next stop, was rich in lore: "we could almost visualize the pirates of a couple of centuries ago staggering up to [the cliffs] with their treasure chests." On a "small white beach," the passengers were "instantly surrounded by a deafening jabbering from the hundred or so black natives. They spoke a patois that sounded part French, part Spanish, and some African. We found one who could speak and understand a little English and he offered to conduct us on a tour. The place is wonderfully picturesque. The women in very bright dresses with scarlet or green headkerchiefs. The men in rags—shirts or undershirts and tattered pants, the children pretty much as God made them."

Heyward began to adjust to life at sea—oddly for someone who was so prone to sickliness. His hardier shipmates, in contrast, spent much of their time in the bunks, sometimes not even able to come to supper. When the company put in at San Juan a few days later, Heyward, however, was soon complaining of the tedious and sedentary social schedule: "I am beginning to long to get away from dinner and cocktails and out to sea again," he wrote to Dorothy.

In the U.S. Virgin Islands, the *Conrad*'s next ports of call, Heyward found the most interesting material, and he began to develop it into a novel. He was intrigued first by the islands' colonial administrators. He saw in such men an unsettling blend of benevolent paternalism, indifference to human needs, and ruthless efficiency. Heyward began to think about the wisdom of American intervention in such "unspoiled" cultures. Moreover, on St. Croix, Heyward found the most interesting mix of all: "a large group of Danes who were the old landed gentry, and a large group of officials of our government. Like most insular societies, these two do not seem to mingle, but both tried to outdo each other in our entertainment." In addition to the usual rounds of parties (at one dinner, places were set for eighty-five people), visits were arranged to a leper colony and to a hospital for indigents: "I even attended a dressing in the operating room and was rather pleased that I could 'take it' without giving any outward sign of weakness." (49).

Heyward began to tire of the journey, however, and was eager to get to work on his book. He felt that he had seen about all there was to see of the West Indies: "Proceeding slowly . . . we never dropped one island astern until we picked up the next"—St. Kitts, Nevis, Montserrat, Guadeloupe, and onward. "Hunt's idea of time," Heyward wrote to Dorothy, was "so vague that it [did not] register" how long they'd been at sea.

They continued to Martinique, then moved on to Barbados, but in both spots Heyward saw nothing as interesting as what he had seen on St. Croix. He persuaded Hartford to drop Trinidad from their itinerary and swing back up to the Virgin Islands. On St. Thomas Heyward met a staffer in the press office of the Department of the Interior, Daisy Reck. She was writing publicity material on the islands, and the two cooperated in sharing information "and putting each other on to good leads." When Heyward arrived back in San Juan several days later, he put together his notes from the Virgin Islands, and with help from Reck, who had taken a neighboring cottage, began "working to beat hell."

With his new novel in mind, Heyward wanted to get back to Charleston now more than ever. He was so homesick, he wrote to Dorothy, that he wished he could "fly home right now and see you." He began counting the days until journey's end. "Jamaica?" he wrote at their penultimate stop, "To hell with it!!!" The ship reached Charleston in early May.

Heyward returned from his cruise with a notebook full of new material and a clear idea of how he was going to use it. In January, before he had left on his trip, Heyward had heard from George Gershwin, who had proposed that they plan another opera: "I am sure you could turn out a grand book and I am very anxious to start thinking about a serious musicale," the composer wrote. "So, put your mind to it, old boy, and I know you can evolve something interesting." Indeed, Heyward could and did, for his early sketches on *Star Spangled Virgin* indicate that he was casting the story either as a short novel to be a prelude to another opera or as an opera by itself.

Heyward began work on the story and apparently kept at it until July, when his progress was shattered by news of Gershwin's tragic death. In the late spring the musician had begun to feel poorly, incurring dizzy spells and unsettling sensations, such as the curious smell of burning rubber. These spells became more frequent until his family forced him to see a physician. X-rays and psychoanalysis found little that was conclusive. Then, on the afternoon of 9 July, Gershwin took a nap that deepened into a coma. He was rushed to the hospital; a spinal tap revealed the existence of a brain tumor. He was operated on immediately, but to no avail. He died two days later, without regaining consciousness.

Along with the rest of the world, Heyward mourned Gershwin's death. Their close collaboration on *Porgy and Bess* and regard for each other's talents had created a deep and abiding friendship. After his brother's death, Ira Gershwin sent Heyward a silver tankard of George's that Heyward had once admired. "To the end of my days," Ira wrote, "I shall never forget the exciting and thrilling period of *Porgy and Bess*. George had, not only a great respect for you, but also a deep affection, and I assure you, though I believe you must have known, I felt the same way about you and considered it a great honor to be associated with you, however small my contribution."

Star Spangled Virgin thus became a novel rather than an opera and did not at all meet the high standards set by *Porgy* and *Mamba's Daughters.* It is a disappointing work, not just in the thinness of its treatment of Caribbean culture or in its title, which is more provocative than appropriate, but mostly in the surprisingly nonprogressive view of African Americans that Heyward displays. He seems at times to be laughing at their comic simplicity, more in the manner of Thomas Nelson Page or Octavus Roy Cohen than in the manner of the author of *Porgy and Bess.*

The story is set in the Virgin Islands just after the United States took over their governance from the Danish in 1917. Heyward applies his sympathetic treatment of Charleston Gullahs to the West Indian Negroes and shows them suddenly brought into contact with civilized nations. The plot revolves around Rhoda Berg and her common-law husband, Adam Work, a happy man and an earthy, genuine woman depicted as the eternal mother. Rhoda finds the shiftless Adam work and forces him to do it; she bears children joyfully, with the fertility of the tropical earth. Rhoda thus belongs with the characters of *Porgy and Bess.*

But halfway through the book, the tone shifts. The New Deal reaches the islands, and Heyward begins to satirize the natives' "worship" of the deity "Noodeal," which hands them "relief" by doling out food and finery and requiring no work in exchange. Heyward seems to have intended to ridicule the government, but he instead ends up ridiculing the people and their lack of understanding of politics, human relationships, and ethics. In this attempt to reach out and bring freshness to his tested material of Negro culture, Heyward's aim seems to have been unsteady, and reviewers were not kind. Most critics took Heyward to task for his thin and inappropriate portrayal of the "colorful natives."

Star Spangled Virgin illustrates as much a change in Heyward's attitude toward his profession as in his attitude toward blacks. After the disappointment of *Porgy and Bess,* Heyward became less sensitive to the quality of his treatment of Negro material and became more frankly a commercially oriented writer. Such was certainly the case with another, smaller undertaking in 1938 when his friend the naturalist and fiction writer Herbert Ravenel Sass approached him with a commercial publishing idea targeted at Charleston's growing tourist population. Both men had written separate fictional accounts of the two bombardments of Fort Sumter during the Civil War— Heyward of the firing on the fort in 1861 in *Peter Ashley* and Sass of the attempts by the Federals to retake the ironclad fleet there in 1863 in *Look Back on Glory*, a best-seller of 1933. Why not put the two dramatic episodes together, Sass asked Heyward, and "make a little book out of it, attractively arrayed, which would have undoubtedly a good and continuous local sale among the tourists . . . and which might even, with a little ballyhoo, have something of a sale outside?" Very little effort would be required, Sass explained. "You could write the short explanatory prologue in a couple of hours; I could write the short epilogue—or vice versa if you prefer. Then, sacrificing a couple of copies of the novels to the scissors, we could clip out the pages needed, paste them on letter-size sheets and bind the whole thing in a neat ms cover."

Heyward did not particularly enjoy selling the same story twice, but he felt he was running out of original material, so he justified his decision to do the book by saying that the two incidents had never really received much attention in fiction. The book was to be entitled *Fort Sumter*. Both men expected to reap large profits from the enterprise, but sales were disappointing, even with copies available in Charleston during the peak tourist season, between mid-March and mid-April. The book received no critical attention to speak of. As one reviewer noted, "it is a little hard to get interested in a set of fictional characters you are going to see for one moment and never see again."

Heyward then tried to sell the book to the movies but gave up by the following June with no takers. In spite of "the new Confederate-war-out-of-Margaret-Mitchell-enthusiasm," he wrote to Sass, "there is nothing doing. If Gone With etc. is not too utterly stale by the time it comes out to make a success, probably other War stories will be done, but when they are (if I know Hollywood) they . . . will stink, but they will probably make money. Truth, my dear fellow, may prevail, but it butters no bread in the fillum universe." Curiously, Heyward had earlier professed disdain for the memorialist trend in recent fiction, but in trying to exploit some more of his previously written material, he pitched *Peter Ashley* to film producers, also to no avail. Moreover, he had been importuning Margaret Mitchell to introduce him to David Selznick, the producer of *Gone with the Wind*, but Mitchell told him she had little creative control over the movie.

Heyward's determination to generate additional income from earlier work can also be seen in a stage dramatization of *Lost Morning* that he and Dorothy wrote. They stuck with the project through its gestation, writing, and rewriting over a nearly two-year period, even as prospects for its sale grew dimmer and ultimately came to nought. The idea was presented to them in September 1936 by George Waller, an editor at *Cosmopolitan* magazine who had a modicum of experience acting and directing amateur theater. With his collaborator, Nat Snyderman, Waller pitched the idea for a treatment to Heyward, who readily accepted Waller's terms. Although Waller was relatively untested as a playwright, Heyward seemed eager nonetheless, hotly pursuing any possible resale of the story. As an enticement, Waller mentioned to Heyward that even if the play did not get produced, the treatment could still be submitted to movie studios for possible filming.

With the author's go-ahead, Waller worked up an outline in March 1937. Heyward, having left on the *Conrad* cruise, turned the project over to Dorothy, the more able playwright, he always thought. Dorothy then corresponded with Waller for the next three months, exchanging notes and critiquing Waller's efforts. The correspondence confirms Dorothy's astuteness as a playwright, especially in knowing what an audience desired and in mastering the technical details of how to present dramatic material in a spoken rather than written format. She was also convinced of the advantages of not hewing too closely to the original novel when doing a dramatization. (She greatly doubted the stage value of the lewd painting scene, for example.) Heyward proposed a tryout that winter in Charleston with the newly formed Footlight Players, an amateur repertory working in the Dock Street Theatre. But even that possibility did not pan out, and when Heyward turned the script over to his agent, Audrey Wood, she could not sell it on Broadway.

Heyward's one success in this last phase of his career was the New York stage run of his and Dorothy's dramatization of *Mamba's Daughters*. As she had with the play version of *Porgy*, Dorothy produced the initial draft of this work, then Heyward helped her refine the much-compressed script, radically different from the book. Together the Heywards eliminated the white subplot almost entirely, deleted the novel's social criticism, and made Hagar the central focus.

They focused on Hagar at the request of Ethel Waters, whose life history was peculiarly suited to her playing that role. Moreover, the story of her career adds a chapter to the Heywards' ongoing involvement with African American theater. Waters, a singer and comedienne who had grown up in the slums of Philadelphia at the turn of the century, was an unwanted child in a broken family characterized mostly by indifference, abusiveness, and alcoholism. She had no formal music training but broke into the Harlem vaudeville circuit in the 1910s, eventually singing in such Harlem clubs as Edmond's Cellar in the early 1920s. She recorded some titles on the Negro Black Swan Label, gained some attention, then switched to a major label, Columbia, a few years later. By the time the Heywards met her in 1933, she was among the best black female vocalists: noted composers, such as Irving Berlin, Dorothy Fields, and Harold Arlen, wrote songs especially for her, and Carl Van Vechten became her close friend and informal publicist.

Waters's rise in the black entertainment industry had taken an unusual course. She specialized in a blues style that was quite different from the great "shouters" like Ma Rainey and Bessie Smith, who were popular with black audiences. Waters sang in a sophisticated style in which words were clearly enunciated, not slurred or strung out. Her sound was more northern than Deep South. She also disported herself in a playfully sensuous manner, somewhat like Josephine Baker, but with less overt clowning and more seriousness of purpose. And when Waters wanted, she could sing in a white or a black manner—sometimes within the confines of a single song. On a recording of Fields and Jimmy McHugh's "I Can't Give You Anything But Love," for example, she sang the first stanza in an elegant manner, then in the second stanza downshifted to a masculine growl reminiscent of Louis Armstrong.

Waters's manner of performing made her an ideal draw for white audiences, but she consistently refused to go into white show business. Until the mid-1920s, she performed exclusively for blacks, staying away from white audiences until, in her view, they were ready for her. Deliberately limiting her exposure meant that Waters developed her art to a fine degree—more varied, more black and white, than white audiences of the day would have permitted. Not only an inventive vocalist, Waters was also savvy to the cultural politics of the time. She sang exactly as she chose, to whom she chose. Staying away from white audiences was an announcement of her cultural independence as an African American, and she became, in fact, a fierce advocate of her race: "Our survival," she declared, "is proof of our strength, our courage, and our immunity to adversity." It is little wonder that when she read Heyward's story of Mamba and her daughters, she was drawn to it; it read much like her own life.

The Heywards had first heard Waters sing in 1933 at a society to-do at Katherine Brush's Long Island home. The Heywards were in the area because DuBose had just wrapped up work on *The Emperor Jones*. They were impressed by Waters and for some time thereafter closely followed her career. Then, at another party in 1935, soon after the opening of *Porgy and Bess*, the Heywards met Waters. Waters happened to be sitting on a couch next to Dorothy, chatting with her about *Porgy and Bess* without knowing who Dorothy was. Waters mentioned that she preferred the operatic version to the play, because in the opera the performers seemed to let themselves go emotionally. In the play, she explained, the actors were quite obviously acting, almost apologizing for what they were doing. In her characteristically frank manner, Waters told Dorothy, "I've known a great many bitches and whores in real life. They never apologize for what they are."

The redoubtable Dorothy could generally hold her own with most theatrical people, but she felt compelled in this case to tell Waters who she was. Waters then diplomatically changed the subject to *Mamba's Daughters*— again not knowing of Dorothy's connection to that novel. Waters spoke of how close the story was to that of her own family, but of the three generations in the book, it was Hagar who impressed her as the most tragic character. She thought of Hagar much as she had of her own mother, like "all Negro women lost and lonely in the white man's antagonistic world." The astute Dorothy then mentioned that her husband had written the novel and that they had wanted to dramatize it as soon as the novel had been published, but they could not think of a performer who could carry the role. Waters then made Dorothy promise that if they ever did do a stage version of the book, Waters would have the role. The deal was struck.

When the Heywards finished the draft of the play in the summer of 1938, they shopped it around to several producers. The Theatre Guild turned it down, unconvinced that Waters had the requisite acting talent to carry the show. When the guild suggested that a tested actress be hired instead of Waters, the Heywards rejected the idea: they had written the play for Waters as their Hagar. They would take the show elsewhere. Other producers also doubted Waters's abilities, until the script landed in the hands of Guthrie McClintic, an old friend of the Heywards who in 1930 had taken an option on *Brass Ankle* but did not stage it.

McClintic took the script out to the Martha's Vineyard home that he shared with his wife, actress Katherine Cornell, and read it aloud to her on the beach. Cornell wept when she heard it, and McClintic decided then and there to do the play. He liked the story, but according to Dorothy he too was uncertain about whether Waters was up to the role. Still, he trusted his wife's opinion, and so rehearsals began just after Thanksgiving. McClintic also approved of Heyward's plan to include spirituals, as he had in *Porgy*. In addition, Heyward wrote the lyrics to an original song for Waters to sing in the play, "Lonesome Walls," with music by Jerome Kern. "There must be music in an all-negro play," Heyward said.

For pure melodrama, the *Mamba* rehearsals rivaled those for *Porgy*. Cornell attended the rehearsals, assisting her husband. She wept at virtually every moment of sadness in the play and thought every line was perfect. The Heywards regarded the rehearsals as a workshop in which to shore up the weaker parts of the script and eliminate scenes that did not go over well. But Cornell kept interposing herself between the authors and her director husband, gushing, "It's magnificent; don't change a word." She liked the play too much, Dorothy concluded, and McClintic would not let them revise it. McClintic was also every bit as moody and volatile a director as Rouben Mamoulian had been, so rehearsals could be chaotic. He threw spectacular tantrums—as well as objects. Dorothy recalled one time when she tried to persuade McClintic to let her change a particularly maudlin scene, when Hagar carries Gilly Bluton's body through the swamp. Guthrie exploded, accusing Dorothy of calling his wife a nitwit because Dorothy could not see that everything she had written was excellent. McClintic picked up a chair threateningly but was careful to miss Dorothy when he threw it.

When *Mamba* premiered on 3 January 1939, it made a star out of Waters. She limned the determination and passion of the character with great skill. The critics and audiences loved her performance but took the play's authors to task for several defects. In addition to an overemphasis on melodrama, the play had technical problems: scenes took too long to change, the transitions were not very smooth, coincidence was relied on too much as a plot unifier, and some elements that were treated subtly in the novel were amplified to an exaggerated degree in the play. Marion MacDowell (of the MacDowell Colony) attended the second performance and concurred in the newspapers' opinion about the play's technical faults. She talked to Heyward afterwards and thought he looked "tired and sort of discouraged." Heyward had to take consolation in the fact that "people will go to hear the players, if not to hear the play." Dorothy took her lumps, too. According to MacDowell, she "looked a wreck," terribly stung by the papers' overemphasizing certain flaws in the production and continuing to "rub it in," even several days later.

As with the play version of *Porgy,* singing was key to the successful dramatization of *Mamba's Daughters.* Hagar insists that the Negro's one advantage over whites is the comfort afforded by singing: "Dere ain't no trouble so big we can't sing about um." Instead of singing at the Metropolitan Opera House, Lissa sings on the radio and shapes the music into a tribute to her mother, who has spent years in prison for her daughter's sake. Both mother and daughter, then, find comfort and identity in music, and music is the medium through which Lissa communicates her love for her mother. Hagar subsequently joins a church choir; later still, when she is banished from the city to a plantation for beating a man, she assuages her longing for her daughter's company by singing and "shouting" to the triumphal rhythms of Negro spirituals. The songs, which recall the most exuberant moments in the play *Porgy,* are more thematically integrated here than in the earlier play.

Yet *Mamba's Daughters* is also a sop that Heyward seems to have thrown to his New York audience, a recognition that such audiences were not interested in the innovation and polish of craft evident in *Porgy and Bess.* The play version of *Mamba* is mostly melodrama, lacking the powerful social criticism of the novel. Hagar's fate is the sole focus, and thus the theme of white injustice is greatly attenuated. The corrupt white mine owner, for example, is reduced to a stereotype, and Lissa's musical achievement is diminished.

Since Heyward had grown ambivalent toward the rewards of the New York theater, it is not surprising that he spent much of his energy on the project with which he had begun his career, regional art. In 1937 Heyward had accepted a seat on the board of the Carolina Art Association, which managed the Dock Street Theatre, a historic site that was renovated with the assistance of the Federal Arts Project. The structure was originally an elegant hotel, but like many other buildings in Charleston, it had deteriorated over the years and had become a tenement occupied by poor blacks. With the federal money, the city's preservation advocates turned the building into a reproduction of an eighteenth-century theater, similar in almost every detail to the original Dock Street Theatre on that site. When the theater reopened in November 1937, its resident acting company, the Footlight Players, presented George Farquhar's *The Recruiting Officer*, the same play that had opened the theater 201 years earlier. Heyward wrote a new prologue to the play and on opening night stepped through the curtain and into the stage lights to present it to his hometown audience.

With funds from a Rockefeller grant, Heyward was later appointed the theater's resident dramatist, and he set about forming a local playwrights' group to create native dramas that would then be staged at the new theater. The group was similar to the Carolina Playmakers in Chapel Hill, North Carolina, with whom Paul Green had been associated. Both programs sought to elevate the stuff of drama in the lives of primitive folk outside urban centers and to shape it into simple but moving plays as well as to take folk drama to the people. Both the Charleston and Chapel Hill plays thus featured Carolina scenes—fishermen, mountaineers, tenant farmers, and the exotica of Negro and Croatan people.

Both groups also emphasized the development of local talent. The ten writers that Heyward gathered around him met twice weekly with him and Dorothy to read what they had written, argue over it, and then go home to rewrite it. Sometimes the group would meet in the theater's spacious drawing room; others times the members would convene in the upstairs sitting room at 24 South Battery, looking out on White Point Gardens and the water. It must have seemed to Heyward like old times, when he and Hervey Allen were tutored by John Bennett. Heyward seems to have found his ultimate fulfillment in this endeavor.

On 10 June 1939 in Tryon, Heyward's mother, Janie, died of a heart ailment. She was seventy-four years old, but her age had not slowed the pace of her work. She had continued to live with the Heywards and to give her Gullah readings in South Carolina, Georgia, and points north. Her death was a "great shock" to her son. "Coming at the end of a long and exhausting spring," he wrote to Allen, his mother's passing had left him feeling "too shot . . . to work." Heyward felt tired, old for his years, and distinctly uncreative. He had previously written, "Every great capital is full of men whose genius died with their first success." Yet they went on "pottering among old tools." He clung even more closely to Allen these days, writing to him regularly, as if doing so could reenergize Heyward creatively, rekindle the spark that had ignited his imagination in the Poetry Society days. "I find myself thinking of you and what a hell of a lot of good it would do me to see you," he wrote on one occasion, "a good old-fashioned talk with you might start the wheels running over again."

He did publish a children's book, *The Country Bunny and the Little Gold Shoes*, a story he had invented for Jenifer about a little cottontail rabbit from the country whose ambition was to be selected one of five bunnies to deliver eggs on Easter eve. Today the book, with illustrations by Marjorie Flack, is still in print, a perennial best-seller, and has taken on something of the quality of a folktale. Heyward also found time to write a moving descriptive piece for *National Geographic*, "Charleston: Where Mellow Past and Present Meet," and to coauthor an article with Daisy Reck for the same periodical on "The American Virgins."

Heyward had ideas but did not know what to do with them. He, Dorothy, and Jenifer spent Christmas 1939 with the Allens in Florida and had a "perfectly grand time"—a visit with Robert Frost, in town for a series of readings, cheered him immensely—but when the Heywards returned home, DuBose remained melancholy. He wrote to Allen, "Much water has gone under the bridge since the Carolina Chansons days, and a gathering like this of the two patriarchs with wives and children in attendance does give one the feeling that it's all been pretty much worth while, and that the old bond of friendship still holds fast."

A few months later, Heyward accepted an offer from the University of Miami to give a series of talks there the following winter. He had pretty much given up lecturing, but he took the Miami engagement nonetheless, probably as an excuse to winter again in Florida, near the Allens. Money may also have been a factor. After the disposition of Janie's estate, Heyward was chagrined to learn that very little was left—mostly bonds that had decreased in value. Upkeep on Dawn Hill was also expensive, which gave

Heyward an excuse to sell the property. He wanted to reestablish himself fully in Charleston.

Unable to focus on writing and to find new material, Heyward began to pull in the boundaries of his life closer to home. He began to concentrate on doing what he started out doing nearly twenty years earlier: elevating the state of the arts in Charleston. With the limited energy he could summon, he flung himself into the work of the Dock Street group.

In the summer of 1940, with Dawn Hill sold, the Heywards stayed in North Carolina with friends, the Matthews. Heyward spent much of the time in Hendersonville pondering how to develop further the playwriting group. On 8 June he wrote to Green for his advice. Heyward thought he had done well: there was a solid feeling of esprit de corps within the group; more than $1,000 had been raised for expenses associated with the operation; the group's plays were finding producers and audiences; and even some royalties were being returned to the foundation through the work. Still, Heyward said he was "quite at sea" about what to do next. Could Green help?

Little more than one week later, on 16 June, Green sat down to reply to his friend's letter, but by great coincidence was interrupted by a visitor, who brought the news that Heyward had died of a heart attack. Heyward had been feeling poorly for some months—sluggish, unmotivated, unable to concentrate. Dorothy thought he was a "little below par" but did not make much of it; she had seen "so many periods" in their seventeen years together when Heyward "was tired and discouraged about his work." He had thought that the mountains might reanimate him, but each day he would come in from the tent he had set up to work in on the grounds of the Matthews' house "very blue, saying he had written nothing worth keeping." Dorothy kept urging him to go down to Tryon for a checkup before they went to the Mac-Dowell Colony for the rest of the season, but Heyward would not do so.

On Sunday, 16 June, almost one year and one week since his mother's death, Heyward died. Their friend Margaret Matthew had driven him down to Tryon to be examined by a physician-cousin, Allen Jervey, who suspected some heart impairment but detected no immediate danger. Five miles into the return trip, Heyward complained of intense pain, and they returned to the hospital. Jervey told Matthew to drive back to Hendersonville and fetch Dorothy, but when she arrived, her husband had died. On Tuesday, 18 June, DuBose Heyward was interred in the west churchyard of St. Philip's cemetery, "beneath the venerable oaks," at Dorothy's request. Approximately 150 people attended the ceremony, members of Charleston's original literary colony and other artists from the North and the South. No hymns were sung, as Heyward was not a churchgoer; instead, Heyward's poem, "Epitaph for a Poet," was read:

> Here lies a spendthrift who believed
> That only those who spend may keep;
> Who scattered seeds, yet never grieved
> Because a stranger came to reap;
> A failure who might well have risen;
> Yet, ragged sang exultantly,
> That all success is but a prison,
> And only those who fail are free.

DuBose Heyward's career belied a number of characteristics of the American author. He started life as something other than a writer but matured quickly into a gifted, unique type of artist: a poet who saw simple beauty in mountain vistas and the play of sunshine on white-capped waves as well as an uncompromising realist whose vital black characters fully engaged in the affairs of humanity told stories then virtually unknown to American literature. Heyward wrote with honesty and sympathy, unconcerned with promoting whatever literary theory was then in fashion. He shunned the spotlight, even when it shone on him without contrivance. He produced relatively slim books, elegant in their conciseness, at a time when much American writing tended toward thick, full-panoplied narratives. And as one newspaper editorial commented after his death, he adopted the always suspect and unpopular position of advocating that writers should write about the world they knew best rather than rushing off to Europe to sweat and starve in service to absorbing romantic locales and being "writerly."

Heyward should be remembered for a varied array of contributions to southern literature. His was the first major southern voice to write realistically about African Americans as human beings rather than as comic or sordid stereotypes. DuBose and Dorothy Heyward also worked hard to increase the opportunities for African Americans in theater and to elevate and recognize the state of African American art. Heyward's evolution into a social critic should also not escape notice, for his social attitudes matured and his views became more trenchant as he immersed himself deeper and deeper into the world of the African American. Such works as *Mamba's Daughters* and *Peter Ashley*, in particular, are—for the 1920s and 1930s—quite courageous critiques of southern class and culture.

Heyward's greatest contribution to southern art, of course, was his creation of the tragicomic characters of Porgy, Bess, and the other denizens of Charleston's Catfish Row. They are immortal. Who can think of Charleston today without imagining Porgy rolling his dice, invoking the gods of chance to lift him up, liberate his spirit, and enable him to go find his lost Bess? Heyward's story continues to act as a conduit that conveys cultural perceptions of the American South to international audiences. As long as issues of color continue to blight the American psyche, *Porgy and Bess* will survive. Like its creator, the work offers no facile answers to the persistent questions of racial attitudes. The story instead does what all great art should do: it bypasses categories, labels, and distinctions and celebrates the ability of the human spirit to triumph over seemingly insurmountable odds.

Although Heyward was never quite sure how the African American race, which in his view was unformed and still evolving, could accomplish this feat, much of what he wrote suggests his strong hope that it would. Heyward spent the greater part of his career trying in his own way to further that goal.

Sources

The major collection of DuBose Heyward's papers is at the South Carolina Historical Society in Charleston, South Carolina. These papers are the primary source for this book. Much information about Heyward has also been gleaned from related collections at SCHS, in particular the papers of John Bennett, Laura Bragg, Josephine Pinckney, the Poetry Society, Herbert Ravenel Sass, the Spirituals Society, and Elizabeth O'Neill Verner. The Bennett Papers have been particularly valuable both for establishing Heyward's whereabouts and for discerning the Charleston reaction to his writings: Bennett would frequently—often every day—write omnibus letters to his wife and children that were the equivalent of newsletters chronicling the life of Charleston and its residents.

Two other important collections are the papers of Heyward's mother, Jane Screven Heyward, and his wife, Dorothy Kuhns Heyward. The latter collection contains her unpublished autobiography, which has been a gold mine of information, especially about the history of *Porgy and Bess;* the autobiography contains much previously unknown material. All of these collections are well cataloged, and I have consequently listed items only by date and source: I have not given box and folder numbers, with the exception of several caches of letters from Heyward to Jane and to Dorothy that came to the society in 1985. When this book went to press, the collection had not yet been accessioned. References to these papers below are thus identified as "unprocessed collection, box 11." However, the material has since been cataloged and is now available for examination. Collections of Heyward papers at other libraries are identified in the notes. Where necessary for ease of reading, I have silently corrected spelling and typographical errors in Heyward's letters.

The scholarship on Heyward is minimal; all important books and articles are listed in the bibliography, following the essay. A primary bibliography of Heyward's writings also follows.

The following abbreviations are used in the notes:

DBH   DuBose Heyward
DKH   Dorothy Kuhns Heyward
GG   George Gershwin
HA   Hervey Allen
JB   John Bennett
JMH   James M. Hutchisson

JSH   Jane Screven Heyward
LC   Library of Congress
OHS   Jerome Lawrence and Robert Lee Theatre Research Institute, Ohio State
        University
UP   Hervey Allen Papers, University of Pittsburgh Library
SCHS   South Carolina Historical Society, Charleston
UNC   Southern Historical Collection, University of North Carolina, Chapel Hill
USC   Caroliniana Library, University of South Carolina, Columbia
YCAL   Yale Collection of American Literature, Beinecke Rare Book and
        Manuscript Library, Yale University, New Haven, Connecticut

Introduction

Allen Tate's view of southern literature is drawn from his "Remarks on the Southern Religion," in *I'll Take My Stand*, 174–75, and from "The Profession of Letters in the South" and "The New Provincialism," both in *Essays*, 517–34, 535–46. Tate's view has been most famously supported by Rubin in "Southern Literature" and in "The Southern Muse." A convincing counterview, on which I draw here, is O'Brien, "The South Considers Her Most Peculiar."

Quotation

"Imagine a Negro": Todd Duncan, "Reminiscence," Armitage 63.

Chapter 1: History and Story

Three books provide biographical information on Heyward: Durham, *DuBose Heyward;* Slavick, *DuBose Heyward;* and Alpert, *Life and Times.* Because none of these is a full-dress biography and because many primary materials have come to light since their publication, I have relied on the Heyward Papers and related collections at SCHS. Other details of Heyward's early life are taken from Creighton, "DuBose Heyward" (which contains one of the few surviving interviews that Heyward granted), and from DKH's unpublished autobiography at SCHS. DBH's unpublished stories, articles, and speeches are at SCHS, as is a large collection of press clippings about his career.

Further discussion of JSH's early life may be found in Greene, "Charleston Childhood." This article, like my commentary on JSH's early life, is based on her journals and other papers at SCHS. JSH's stories were collected in *Brown Jackets.* Her poetry collections are *Wild Roses, Songs of the Charleston Darkey,* and *Daffodils and Other Lyrics.* Information on JSH's career as dialect recitalist and her association with Georgia Ray Macmillan is drawn from publicity materials in the JSH Papers, SCHS.

Fraser relates the comprehensive history of Charleston in *Charleston! Charleston!* Robert Rosen, *Short History,* provides a concise overview. For details of the 1886 earthquake, see Whitelaw, *Charleston.* On the growth of Charleston's black population, see Powers, *Black Charlestonians.*

The best general study of African American history is Franklin and Moss, *From Slavery to Freedom.* Surprisingly little has been written about the sea island Gullah communities, but Joyner's *Down by the Riverside* and Crum's *Gullah* are useful. See also Bennett's "Negro Patois."

Quotations

"a city of ruins": qtd. in Rosen 111.

"Ned used to do everything for me": JSH journal, SCHS. Subsequent quotations about the Heyward family's early life are likewise drawn from this journal.

"never parted . . . by faith": publicity material for *Brown Jackets,* SCHS.

"this life which was going on within our own, yet was apart from it": DBH, introduction to *Porgy: A Play,* x.

"Give the boy": Anna Wells Rutledge, interview with JMH, 9 Aug. 1995, Charleston, South Carolina.

"crooned [him] to sleep": Phifer 6.

"almost nightly balls": Clark 554.

"something of the gay life": DBH, "Describes Paris" 8.

" 'heartrending narratives' of Dickens": DBH to Nannie Creighton, 6 Nov. 1931, DBH Papers, SCHS.

"large connection here": DBH to "Mr. Milberry," 25 Dec. 1917, DBH Papers, SCHS.

Chapter 2: The Poetry Society and the Charleston Renaissance

John Bennett's life is amply documented in the Bennett Collection at SCHS, as is the early history of the Poetry Society. Information about the Poetry Society's activities is taken from these collections and from the Poetry Society's yearbooks, also at SCHS. More discussion is available in Cox, "Charleston Poetic Renascence." Hervey Allen's career is treated at length in Knee, *Hervey Allen.*

On "clubbishness" in colonial and federal America, see Shields, *Civil Tongues.* On the Richmond literary revival, see Clark, *Innocence Abroad,* and Hobson, *Serpent;* for materials relating to literary New Orleans, I have relied on the essays in Kennedy, ed., *Literary New Orleans.* Cowan chronicles the history of the Fugitives in *Fugitive Group.*

For more on Amy Lowell, see Gould, *Amy.* On Harriet Monroe and *Poetry* magazine, see E. Williams, *Harriet Monroe.*

I am indebted to the following works for some details about the Charleston Renaissance and the figures associated with it: Severens, "Charleston" and "South Carolina"; and Patterson, *Alfred Hutty*. Donaldson treats Beatrice Ravenel's work in "Songs," as does Rubin in his introduction to *Yemassee Lands*.

DBH described the MacDowell Colony in "MacDowell Colony." DBH's dealings with Macmillan are documented in the Macmillan Publishing Archives, New York. Elinor Wylie's life is treated unsympathetically but perceptively in Olson, *Elinor Wylie*; for Maxwell Bodenheim, see Moore, *Maxwell Bodenheim*. On Jean Toomer see Kerman, *Lives*.

Details about DKH are drawn from her unpublished autobiography at SCHS.

Quotations

"Scratching gravel for subsistence": JB reminiscence, JB Papers, SCHS.
"to find some safe vent for their emotions": ibid.
"I cannot say that I am sorry to learn": DBH to JB, 30 July 1920, JB Papers, SCHS.
"acid opinions": JB to Susan Bennett, July 1921, JB Papers, SCHS.
"honest, man-talk": JB to DBH, 23 Aug. 1920, JB Papers, SCHS.
"strenuous labor": ibid.
"lay a blessing": DBH to JB, 30 July 1920, JB Papers, SCHS.
"a vast plain of mediocrity": Mencken 137 ff.
"literary General Sherman": "Worm" 14.
"stimulate an interest in the reading": ibid.
"keep abreast of the revolutionary movement": DBH, foreword, *Year Book of the Poetry Society of South Carolina for 1921* 7.
"no art has yet expressed adequately": Monroe, "Notes" 233.
"The town is beautiful with the past": Amy Lowell, letter, *Year Book of the Poetry Society of South Carolina for 1921* 17.
"found heaven": qtd. in Patterson 13.
"long silence was broken": DBH, rev. of *Arrow of Lightning*.
"proclamation": unidentified print in JB Papers, SCHS.
"heavy sledding": DBH to JB, May 1921, JB Papers, SCHS.
"some of the best stuff": DBH to HA, 18 July 1921, UP.
"loose ends": DBH to Laura Bragg, 29 July 1921, Bragg Papers, SCHS.
"hours and days of uninterrupted work": DBH to HA, 18 July 1921, UP.
Descriptions of the MacDowell Colony: DBH to JSH, "Tuesday" [summer 1921], unprocessed collection, box 11, SCHS.
"poet of the real old bard type": ibid.
"poetic vamp": Josephine Pinckney to Laura Bragg, 12 Aug. 1922, Bragg Papers, SCHS.
"psycho-neurotic Elinor Wylie": JB to Susan Bennett, 1 Sept. 1922, JB Papers, SCHS.
"one sees negation": ibid.

"Hansel and Gretel lost in a wood": Nina Purdy, "Love at Dawn Hill," [*True Love Magazine?*] ca. 1930, 66 (clipping in Yates Snowden Papers, USC)

"My memory does not go back far enough": DKH, unpublished autobiography, SCHS. Subsequent statements by DKH are also from this document.

"No more 'Mountain Graveyards' for DuBose": JB to Susan Bennett, 5 Sept. 1922, JB Papers, SCHS.

"a single Charleston shopkeeper": DBH to DKH, "Saturday" [Sept. 1922], unprocessed collection, box 11, SCHS.

"other side of my life": DBH to DKH, 6 Oct. 1922, unprocessed collection, box 11, SCHS.

"tons lighter": ibid.

"an educated northerner": G. Johnson, "Call" 28.

"a cullid gentleman": [editor] to DBH, 16 Dec. 1922, DBH Papers, SCHS.

"determined to make a favorable impression": DBH to DKH, [Jan. 1923], unprocessed collection, box 11, SCHS.

"no one else in America": DBH to H. S. Latham, 18 Feb. 1923, Macmillan Publishing Archives, New York.

"in [the] hands of artists": DBH to HA, [summer 1923], UP.

"no less than blasphemy": JB to DBH, 13 June 1923, DBH Papers, SCHS.

"the society is a society": DBH to HA, "Thursday," [summer 1923], UP.

"In this way we could present": ibid.

"'Armageddon' mess": DB to HA, 29 June 1923, UP.

"must omit the item": JB to DBH, 5 July 1923, DBH Papers, SCHS.

"quite proud to be elevated": DBH to HA, 13 July 1923, UP.

"Now, what is to be done?": JB to DBH, 19 Aug. 1923, DBH Papers, SCHS.

"I did . . . what appeared to me": JB to DBH, [Aug. 1923], JB Papers, SCHS.

"usual attack of cholera morbus": DBH to HA, "Tuesday," [summer 1923], UP.

"a fine black-and-white decorated mediaeval initial": JB to DBH, 13 June 1923, DBH Papers, SCHS.

Chapter 3: *Porgy:* The Negro in the New South

DBH's correspondence with Gerald Johnson is at SCHS. DBH's correspondence with Hervey Allen is in UP. For DBH's relationship with Pinckney and Bragg, see their correspondence with DBH at SCHS. The Spirituals Society archives are also at SCHS.

The story of the origins of *Porgy* has been told anecdotally in numerous articles and notes. Durham, *DuBose Heyward,* gives a full authoritative account, but Greene's addendum on the source of the name Porgy is also important ("Little Shining Word"), as is Bokinsky's note, "DuBose Heyward's Porgy." There are only a handful of critical assessments of the novel. The most comprehensive treatment is in Slavick, *DuBose Heyward.* See also Rhodes, "Writing Up." For Julia Peterkin, Susan

Millar Williams's *A Devil and a Good Woman Too* is indispensable. For some alternate interpretations of Peterkin, see Robeson, "Ambiguity."

Epstein, *Sinful Tunes,* is the standard work on black music as folk art. For spiritualism as practiced by whites, see Meyer, *Positive Thinkers.* And on the American popular culture, see Rourke, *American Humor,* and Seldes, *Great Audience.*

For insights into Zora Neale Hurston, her autobiography, *Dust Tracks,* is indispensable. See also Porter, *Jump.*

On mixed-race Manhattan in the 1920s, see Douglas, *Terrible Honesty.* On primitivism and modernism, see Togovnick, *Gone Primitive;* Levin, "Primitivism"; and Foster, " 'Primitive' Consciousness."

Quotations

"indistinguishable from an insurance agent": [G. Johnson], "Missionary," clipping in DBH Papers, SCHS.

"a pauperized section": Johnson to DBH, [Dec. 1923], Poetry Society Papers, SCHS.

"to *civilize*": DBH to Johnson, 10 Dec. 1923, Poetry Society Papers, SCHS.

"Not a breath of this to a soul": DBH to HA, 13 May 1924, UP.

"Am I left holding the bag?". . . "La renaissance est fini": JB to family, 28 May 1924, and HA to JB, 6 June 1924, JB Papers, SCHS.

"flung Charleston overboard": DBH to HA, 16 June 1924, UP.

"I know too little about anywhere else": DBH to Yates Snowden, 16 Oct. 1924, Snowden Papers, USC.

"I grew to see the primitive Negro": DBH to Nannie E. Creighton, qtd. in Creighton 24.

"obsessed with the material": DBH to HA, 15 July 1924, UP.

"so experimental": JB to family, 3 Aug. 1924, JB Papers, SCHS.

"the undiluted, unchanged point of view": JB to HA, 3 Aug. 1924, JB Papers, SCHS.

"instantly struck": JB to family, 22 May 1924, JB Papers, SCHS.

"their own Beloved Poet": JB to HA, 30 Nov. 1924, JB Papers, SCHS.

"I do guess it will really be a go": DBH to HA, 13 May 1924, UP.

"author's fund": DBH to HA, 8 Dec. 1924, UP.

"a contemporary story of white and black": DBH to HA, [Dec. 1924], UP.

"clean up enough to keep the wolf": ibid.

"the sound of his own voice": DBH to HA, [early 1925], UP.

"trying to talk Poetry Society plans": JB to DBH, 9 Apr. 1925, JB Papers, SCHS.

"sacrificial lamb": DBH to JB, [early Apr.] 1925, JB Papers, SCHS.

"you may think I do not mean it": JB to DBH, 9 Apr. 1925, JB Papers, SCHS.

"go forth with in the night": DBH to JB, [early Apr.] 1925, JB Papers, SCHS.

"earn a living out of literature": DBH to JB, 11 Apr. 1925, JB Papers, SCHS.

"What will become of the poor old Poetry Society?": DBH to Laura Bragg, 30 June 1925, Bragg Papers, SCHS.

"bitterly indignant": JB to his daughter, 17 Jan. 1925, JB Papers, SCHS.

"seem to live": qtd. in Rubin, "Southern Muse" 219.

"double function": Pinckney, "Charleston's Poetry Society" 50.

"breaking the ice": JB reminiscence, JB Papers, SCHS.

"No more beautiful": Wilson, "Perennial Rooster" 153.

"sympathetic and convincing": "Romance" 10–11.

"another of those condescending books": Broun, clipping in DBH Papers, SCHS.

"range of reactions": JB to DBH, 26 Oct. 1925, JB Papers, SCHS.

"their 'dearest concern' ": DKH, unpublished autobiography, SCHS.

"Pinopolis folk . . . WHITE": JB to DBH, 26 Oct. 1925, JB Papers, SCHS.

"psychologically true . . . picture": DBH, "New Note" 154, 156.

Chapter 4: *Porgy* on Stage

Biographical information about George Gershwin is drawn from Armitage, ed., *George Gershwin;* Schwartz, *Gershwin;* and Jablonski, *Gershwin.* The Heyward-Gershwin correspondence cited here and in chapter 7 is in the Music Division of the LC.

On Charleston and early American theater, see Jane H. Pease and William H. Pease, "Intellectual Life in the 1830s: The Institutional Framework and the Charleston Style," *Intellectual Life in Antebellum Charleston*, ed. O'Brien and Moltke-Hansen, 233–54. There is no biography of Paul Green, but Watson's chapter in *History* is useful, as is Green's memoir, *Home to My Valley.*

Information about the Heywards' work on the Theatre Guild production of *Porgy* is drawn from the Theatre Guild files, YCAL, and from DKH's unpublished autobiography, SCHS. DBH himself tells the story in the introduction to *Porgy: A Play.* Also see Alpert, *Life and Times.*

Overviews of the Harlem Renaissance appear in D. Lewis, *When Harlem Was in Vogue,* and Cruse, *Crisis.* W. E. B. DuBois gives a valuable sketch of early Negro migrants in "Black North." For contemporary accounts of Harlem life in the 1920s, see J. Johnson, *Black Manhattan,* and Hughes, *Big Sea.* Also useful is Locke, "New Negro," and Davis, *Nella Larsen.*

The Jenkins Orphanage is discussed in passing in books on jazz musicians, e.g., Lomax, *Mister Jelly Roll,* and Collier, *Duke Ellington.*

On the development of New York theater, see Poggi, *Theatre in America.* For the development of black musical theater, see Anderson, *This Was Harlem,* and H. Baker, *Modernism.* On African Americans on stage, see Hamm, *Yesterdays,* and Haskins, *Black Theatre.* The definitive biography of Josephine Baker is J.-C. Baker and Chase, *Josephine.*

Quotations

"My hat is off to you": DBH to Paul Green, 2 Feb. 1927, Green Papers, UNC.

"There are so many things to sap strength": DBH to JSH, "Tuesday," [26 Oct. 1926], unprocessed collection, box 11, SCHS.

"We were all outlanders": Brickell 18.

"a railroad ticket and a suitcase": Locke 49.

"Isn't Mr. Heyward interesting to meet?" qtd. in Davis 77.

"more satisfaction than any of the reviews": DBH to James Weldon Johnson, 29 Oct. 1925, Johnson Papers, YCAL.

"in a huge office": DBH to JSH, [Oct. 26, 1926], unprocessed collection, box 11, SCHS.

"a southern Negro of the old school": undated clipping, SCHS.

"Everywhere one looks": DBH to JSH, 12 Apr. 1927, unprocessed collection, box 11, SCHS.

"little Norman church": DBH to JSH, 18 Apr. 1927, unprocessed collection, box 11, SCHS.

"colony of retired families": DBH to JSH, 5 June 1927, unprocessed collection, box 11, SCHS.

"obvious fakes": DBH to JSH, 7 Mar. 1929, unprocessed collection, box 11, SCHS.

"a shade more self-respecting": DBH to Laura Bragg, 9 Mar. 1929, Laura Bragg Papers, SCHS.

"not changed for centuries": DBH to JSH, 10 Mar. 1929, unprocessed collection, box 11, SCHS.

"Negroes were magnificent": DBH to JSH, 17 Mar. 1929, unprocessed collection, box 11, SCHS.

"collection of Negro types and scenes": JB to family, 14 Aug. 1927, JB Papers, SCHS. (JB often wrote omnibus letters to his wife and children in multiple carbon copies. For ease of reference I have identified the recipients of these letters as "family.") Subsequent statements about Mamoulian's trip to Charleston are also from this letter.

"young, slender": DBH, introduction to *Porgy* xvi.

"I wonder what my friends in Charleston would have said": DBH to JSH, 21 Sept. 1927, unprocessed collection, box 11, SCHS.

"they had no conception": Rouben Mamoulian, reminiscence, in Armitage 51.

"everything was going too well": DBH to JSH, 21 Sept. 1927, unprocessed collection, box 11, SCHS.

"actually breathes Charleston": DBH to JSH, 18 Sept. 1927, unprocessed collection, box 11, SCHS.

"worked like galley slaves": DBH to JSH, 6 Oct. 1927, unprocessed collection, box 11, SCHS.

"Not again!": DKH, unpublished autobiography, SCHS.

"would be most unusual": DBH to JSH, 11 Oct. 1927, unprocessed collection, box 11, SCHS.

"forty feet tall": DBH in Armitage 36.

"only spasmodically vivid": Atkinson, "Play" 26.

"writing ourselves blind": DBH to JSH, 13 Oct. 1927, unprocessed collection, box 11, SCHS.

"You're crazy to change it. We're a hit": DKH, unpublished autobiography, SCHS.

"an illuminating chronicle of American folklore": Atkinson, "Negro" 1.

"more resourceful and more outstanding": Woolcott, clipping in DBH Papers, SCHS.

"Why did they get a nigger for that part?": qtd. in Haskins 61.

"About us . . . By us": W. E. B. DuBois, "Criteria for Negro Art," qtd. in D. Lewis, ed., *Portable*, 101.

"What a final wreath of romance": JB to family, 2 June 1929, JB Papers, SCHS; "Literary Lions," *London Evening News* [late] Apr. 1929, clipping in DBH Papers, SCHS.

"the young will talk like New York's East Side": JB to family, 19 May 1929, JB Papers, SCHS.

"exotic . . . pixie radiant": James Weldon Johnson, qtd. in Douglas 353.

"so well informed . . . about us and our records": ibid.

"coal-black Negro Jew": Clipping from the *Liverpool Post*, 5 June 1929, DBH Papers, SCHS.

Chapter 5: Evolution of a Social Critic

DBH's uncompleted novel about the Gastonia strike (entitled "Merryvale") is at SCHS. His correspondence with Walter White and Oliver Lafarge is in the Frank Durham Papers, USC. A perceptive overview of *Mamba* appears in Doyle, introduction.

For Donald Davidson's comments on Charleston, see "Meeting."

There is no substantial commentary on *Angel*, *Brass Ankle*, or *Lost Morning* except that in Durham, *DuBose Heyward*, and Slavick, *DuBose Heyward*. On *Peter Ashley*, see those works and Brown, "DuBose Heyward's *Peter Ashley*"; and O'Brien, "The South Considers Her Most Peculiar."

DBH's comments on the historical novel may be found in "New Theory." The Pinckney essay is "Bulwarks."

Quotations

"It was simply out of my depth": DBH to JSH, 29 Mar. 1929, DBH Papers, unprocessed collection, box 11, SCHS.

"would be possible in the Heyward family": JB to family, 15 Jan. 1928, JB Papers, SCHS.

"It has all been terrible": DBH to Josephine Pinckney, 2 June 1928, Pinckney Papers, SCHS.

"the publication would not pay much": DBH to Elizabeth O'Neill Verner, [Apr. 1929], Verner Papers, SCHS.

"fly-by-night millionaire novelist": Davidson, *Spyglass* 31–32.

"pointless and untrue to the Southern Negro": Cash 190.

Writer's League against Lynching: see Oliver Lafarge to DBH, 17 June 1931, DBH Papers, SCHS; Walter White to DBH, 8 Dec. 1933, Frank Durham Papers, USC.

"some fairly intense stuff": DBH to JB, 4 Oct. 1929, JB Papers, SCHS.

"isn't an awful lot to report": DBH to JB, 29 July 1930, JB Papers, SCHS.

"the month that has elapsed": DBH to Theresa Helbrun, 9 Feb. 1930, Barrett Clark Papers, YCAL.

"felt that it would never run": DBH to HA, 6 June 1930, UP.

"history 'in a post-mortem sense' ": DBH, "New Theory" 511.

"ironic hero of the book": C[hamberlain] 7.

"Charlestonians . . . were 'puzzled' by the novel": JB to DBH, 23 Aug. 1932, DBH Papers, SCHS.

"local divergences": Pinckney, "Bulwarks" 47.

"subtle balance of persistence": Davidson, "Some Day" 222.

Chapter 6: Man of Letters

Information on DBH's journalistic work and his contacts with Doubleday is drawn from the Ken McCormick Papers, Doubleday Collection, LC.

The best discussion of the Virginia conference is in Blotner, *Faulkner.* DBH's comments are from "Southern Writers' Conference." Davidson's comments on the 1932 Charleston "house party" are in Fain and Young, *Literary Correspondence* 272.

On Gertrude Stein's visit to Charleston, see T. Johnson, "Charleston" 12–13. Stein's correspondence with DBH is in the Stein Papers, YCAL. See also Hobhouse, *Everybody.*

DBH's comments on *The Emperor Jones* are from correspondence in the James Southall Wilson Papers, Alderman Library, University of Virginia, and in the Green Papers, UNC, and from W. Lewis and Herzberg, *Emperor Jones.* See also DBH, "Porgy and Bess Return on Wings of Song," in Armitage, ed., *George Gershwin.*

The most useful history of the movie industry is Sklar, *Movie-Made America.* Nathanael West's comment is quoted in Martin 205. DBH's comments on Hollywood are from "DuBose Heyward." The Tyler proposal is in the JB Papers, SCHS.

On the genesis of Vesey play, see DKH, "Denmark Vesey," and DKH's unpublished autobiography, SCHS. On Paul Robeson's involvement in Vesey play, see the DKH-Robeson correspondence, Theatre Guild Papers, YCAL.

Quotations

"I agree, I agree": qtd. in Blotner 711.

"there was an almost militant spirit present": DBH, "Southern Writers' Conference" 10.

"Southern Literary Houseparty": "Invites" 16; DBH to Sherwood Anderson, 15 July 1932, Anderson Papers, Newberry Library; DBH to Thomas Wolfe, Wolfe Papers, Houghton Library, Harvard University.

"I need to see something of my own kind": DBH to JB, [Oct. 1932], JB Papers, SCHS.

"dipping deeper into the well": DBH to James Southall Wilson, 8 Sept. 1932, DBH Papers, SCHS.

"I trust the 'glorified house party' ": Archibald Henderson to DBH, [Aug. 1932], DBH Papers, SCHS.

"stir up all the sleeping dogs": Donald Davidson to Josephine Pinckney, 5 Nov. 1932, Pinckney Papers, SCHS.

"There was no fighting at all": Fain and Young 272.

"utter futility and waste": DBH to JB, [Oct. 1932], JB papers, SCHS.

Gertrude Stein visit: T. Johnson 12–13.

Accounts: Robert Lathan to "Bab," 3 Mar. 1935, USC; Glenn Allan to JB, 31 Oct. 1935, JB Papers, SCHS.

"a gentle man . . . like his Porgy": qtd. in Sprigge 194.

Stein-Heyward correspondence: Gertrude Stein to DBH, n.d., DBH Papers, SCHS; DBH to Stein, 6 Apr. 1935, Stein Papers, YCAL.

"good, bad, or indifferent": DBH to James Southall Wilson, 4 May 1933, Wilson Papers, UVA; DBH to Hervey Allen, 25 June 1933, UP; and DBH to Paul Green, 21 July 1933, Green Papers, UNC. These and the statements following come from a series of undated letters from DBH to DKH, unprocessed collection, box 11, SCHS.

"slow moving novelist": DBH to Paul Green, 21 July 1933, Green Papers, UNC.

"the usual hecticness of movie companies": DKH to James Southall Wilson, 4 May 1938, Wilson Papers, UVA.

"about a years [sic] work": DBH to HA, 25 June 1933, UP.

"straight piece of creative writing": DBH comments in W. Lewis and Herzberg 59–61.

"black Horatio Alger": Slavick, *DuBose Heyward* 96–97.

"before my engagement closed": DBH, reminiscence, in Armitage 38 (reprint of DBH, "Porgy and Bess Return on Wings of Song").

"settling down, though in solitary": These and the statements following come from a series of undated letters, summer 1934, from DBH to DKH, unprocessed collection, box 11, SCHS.

"There's no fooling here": qtd. in Martin 205.

"and if they go": DBH to DKH, "Thursday afternoon" [summer 1934], unprocessed collection, box 11, SCHS.

Dwight Franklin in Hollywood: See DBH to DKH, n.d., unprocessed collection, box 11, SCHS. See also Robert N. S. Whitelaw to Laura Bragg, 7 Oct. 1934, Bragg Papers, SCHS.

"not a satisfying medium for a literary artist": "DuBose Heyward," clipping in DBH Papers, SCHS.

Tyler proposal: JB to DBH, 25 Apr. 1932; DBH to Tyler, 20 Apr., 11 May, and 18 Apr. 1932, SCHS; DBH to JB, unprocessed collection, box 11, SCHS.

"That is going to be our next play": DKH, unpublished autobiography, SCHS.

Chapter 7: Porgy and Bess Return on Wings of Song

I have reconstructed the history of *Porgy and Bess* primarily from letters between GG and DBH in the GG Collection, LC, and the Theatre Guild Collection, YCAL. A more comprehensive history of the opera (including its revivals) than I offer here is that by Alpert, *Life and Times*. See also Standifer (producer of the excellent 1998 public television documentary on *Porgy and Bess*), "Tumultuous Life." For more specific information on the musical score, see Hamm, "Theatre Guild," and Shirley, "Reconciliation."

On John Bubbles and other *Porgy and Bess* principals, see Stearns and Stearns, *Jazz Dance*, and Peretti, *Creation*.

On the rise of popular culture see Kammen, *Lively Arts* 199 ff. Also useful is Levine, *Highbrow/Lowbrow*. The standard work on the development of radio is Barnouw, *Tower*.

For Berlin, Bergreen's *As Thousands Cheer* is exhaustive. For specific details on the development of ragtime, see Blesh and Janis, *They All Played Ragtime*.

Quotations

"I am off on a new course": DBH to HA, [before 2 June 1934], UP.

"The peculiar jumps in the music": GG, qtd. in Jablonski 163.

"in thinking of ideas": GG to DBH, 29 Mar. 1932, GG Collection, LC.

"no possibility": GG to DBH, 20 May 1932, GG Collection, LC.

"Madison Avenue letter": DKH, unpublished autobiography, SCHS.

"these trying times": DBH to GG, 3 Sept. 1932, GG Collection, LC.

"very interesting that Jolson": GG to DBH, 14 Oct. 1932, GG Collection, LC.

"like to be able to afford": DBH to GG, 17 Oct. 1932, GG Collection, LC.

Contracts signed: "To Present" 23.

"It had to be arranged": DBH, in Armitage 38.

"I have cut everything": DBH to GG, 12 Nov. 1933, GG Collection, LC.

"there may be too much talk": GG to DBH, 25 Nov. 1933, GG Collection, LC.

"give the opera speed and tempo": DBH to GG, 12 Nov. 1933, GG Collection, LC.

"riot of noise": ibid.

"creative ability . . . paralyzed": DBH to GG, 6 Feb. 1934, GG Collection, LC.

"hear some spirituals": qtd. in Alpert 77.

"smallish place": DBH to Laura Bragg, 19 Feb. 1933, Bragg Papers, SCHS.

"You are doubtless discovering": DBH to HA, 22 Aug. 1933, Allen Papers, UP.

"type of secular dance": DBH to GG, 6 Feb. 1934, GG Collection, LC.

"I think I have managed": DBH to GG, 2 Mar. 1934, GG Collection, LC.

"Swell, show, George": ibid.

"letting everything else go": qtd. in DKH, unpublished autobiography, SCHS.

"Out of [twenty-five million radios]": DBH, in Armitage 38.

"When Bing Crosby spoke the name of Marcel Proust": qtd. in Kammen 199.

"all of one piece": GG, in Armitage 72.

"In *Porgy and Bess*": ibid. 74.

"almost a collection": ibid. 75.

"Act 2, scene 1": DBH to GG, 6 Feb. 1934, GG Collection, LC.

"There are many places where we can cut": DBH to GG, 27 Mar. 1934, GG Collection, LC.

"very interesting and touching": qtd. in Alpert 77.

"storm scene": DBH to GG, 27 Mar. 1934, GG Collection, LC.

"magnificent job": qtd. in Alpert 77.

"imagine [himself] at an oar": DBH to GG, 19 Mar. 1934, GG Collection, LC.

"sort of African chant": DBH, in Armitage 39.

"the quality in him": ibid.

"only white man": ibid.

"in Stein's manner": ibid. 79.

"In all honesty": Ira Gershwin to Frank Durham, 18 June 1951, Durham Papers (unprocessed collection), USC.

"George felt there was a spot": DKH, unpublished autobiography, SCHS.

"achieved a fine synchronization": GG, reminiscence, in Armitage 75.

"Heyward would never claim too much of the credit": Gerald Johnson to Josephine Pinckney, 21 July 1935, Pinckney Papers, SCHS.

"enjoyed his playing": Rouben Mamoulian, in Armitage 50.

"Imagine, there's not one telephone": qtd. in Alpert 88.

"Dumas drove Gershwin": Abe Dumas, interview with JMH, 17 June 1996, Charleston, South Carolina.

"with its large population": DBH, in Armitage 39.

"the quality in him": ibid.

"a complicated rhythmic pattern": ibid.

Mamoulian's role: Hamm, "Theatre Guild" 513

"I really believe": Warren Munsell to DBH, 18 Dec. 1934, DBH Papers, SCHS.

"I felt the play": Mamoulian, in Armitage 48.

"nearly every day": Steinert, ibid. 43.

"a superb actor": Corley.

Duncan recollections: Armitage 58–64.

"The first day of rehearsing a play": Mamoulian, in Armitage 51.

"presently there rose": Duncan, in Armitage 60.

"a tale of work-day-Negroes": *Boston American,* clipping in the Theatre Guild Collection, YCAL.

"George, you've done it": J. Rosamund Johnson, in Armitage 65.

"This is my thank you": Mamoulian, in Armitage 52.

"at one moment of opera": Downes 7.

"lies in Mr. Downes's bailiwick": Atkinson, "When" 7.

Chotzinoff, Swain, Thomson reviews: rpt. in Alpert 115–18.

Mamoulian comment: ibid. 322.

"admiring it": K[rutch] 518–19.

"sheer acting": Downes 7.

Brown comment: qtd. in Alpert 116.

"The times are here to debunk": Ellington, qtd. in Alpert 121.

Matthews comment: qtd. in Alpert 122.

"requisite knowledge": Hall Johnson, qtd. in Thompson 52.

"Gershwin managed to ruin": Glenn Allan to JB, 31 Oct. 1935, JB Papers, SCHS.

Brown, Jessye, Breen, Rosenfeld comments: Oral History Archives, Breen Collection, OHS.

Baltimore Afro-American: qtd. in Alpert 181–82.

Warfield, Ellington comments: qtd. in Alpert 183.

McCurry, McDaniel, Eisenhower comments: qtd. in Standifer 52–53.

"huge cast of blacks": Angelou 225.

"words that I wrote": Bill Banks, interview with JMH, 5 Nov. 1995, Newnan, Georgia.

"not material complimentary": qtd. in Alpert 261. For more information on the Goldwyn production, see Wainwright.

"most American opera": qtd. in Alpert 118.

Chapter 8: Return to Charleston

DBH's Caribbean journal is in the Frank Durham Papers, USC. DKH spoke several times to Durham about the existence of the notebook, but she apparently could not locate it until after Durham's book was published. The notebook then came into Durham's possession, where it remained, unknown, until after Durham's death. The notebook surfaced when Durham's papers were bequeathed to the library in 1995.

Quotations

"I was driving": DBH, Caribbean journal, Durham Papers, USC. Subsequent statements by DBH are from this document.

"I am sure": GG to DBH, qtd. in Alpert 131.

"To the end of my days": Ira Gershwin to DBH, 2 Aug. 1937, DBH Papers, SCHS.

"You could write the . . . prologue": Sass to DBH, 10 Dec. 1937, Sass Papers, SCHS.

"hard to get interested in . . . characters": S. V. B., *Saturday Review of Literature* 11
    June 1938: 21.
"the new Confederate-war-out-of-Margaret-Mitchell-enthusiasm": DBH to Sass, 24
    June 1939, Sass Papers, SCHS.
Heyward wrote Mitchell: DBH to Mitchell, 21 Oct. 1936, DBH Papers, SCHS.
Lost Morning dramatization: DBH and DKH letters to George Waller, 1936–37,
    Waller Papers, Harry Ransom Humanities Research Center, University of Texas,
    Austin.
Ethel Waters: for information on Waters, see Waters and Samuels, *His Eye*, and
    McCorkle, "Mother."
Mamba's Daughters rehearsals: Heyward, "Ethel Waters" 16, 66.
"Our survival": DKH, unpublished autobiography, SCHS.
"all Negro women": ibid.
"a great many bitches": qtd. in Alpert 132.
"There must be music": DKH, unpublished autobiography, SCHS.
"It's magnificent": ibid.
"tired and sort of discouraged": Marion MacDowell to Nina Maud Richardson, 7 Jan.
    1939, MacDowell Papers, LC.
Reception of *Mamba's Daughters:* Marion MacDowell to Nina Maud Richardson, 2,
    4, 7, 15 Jan. 1939, MacDowell Papers, LC.
Death of JSH: "Dialect Recitalist," *Charleston Evening Post* 16 Apr. 1938: 11; "Death
    Claims Mrs. Heyward," *Charleston Evening Post* 12 June 1939: 2.
"great shock": DBH to HA, 29 June 1939, UP.
"much water": DBH to HA, 8 Jan. 1940, UP.
"Every great capital": ms fragment, ca. 1935, DBH Papers, SCHS.
Disposition of Janie's estate: Charles Sinkler to DBH, 3 Feb. 1940, DBH Papers,
    SCHS.
"quite at sea": DBH to Paul Green, 8 June 1940, Green Papers, UNC.
"a little below par": DKH to Hervey and Anne Allen, [Aug. 1940], UP.
Death and burial: "Novelist of Negro Life," *New York Herald-Tribune* 17 June 1940:
    22; "DuBose Heyward, Author and Poet," *New York Times* 17 June 1940: 15;
    "Press Mourns Death of DuBose Heyward," *Charleston News and Courier* 20
    June 1940: 10.
"beneath the venerable oaks": "Funeral Rites Held for DuBose Heyward," *Charleston News and Courier* 19 June 1940: 2.

Heyward's Writings

Books

Angel. New York: George H. Doran, 1926.
Brass Ankle. New York: Farrar and Rinehart, 1931.

(with Hervey Allen). *Carolina Chansons: Legends of the Low Country.* New York: Macmillan, 1922.

The Country Bunny and the Little Gold Shoes, as told to Jenifer. Boston and New York: Houghton, Mifflin, 1939.

(with Herbert Ravenel Sass) *Fort Sumter.* New York: Farrar and Rinehart, 1938.

Jasbo Brown and Selected Poems. New York: Farrar and Rinehart, 1931.

Lost Morning. New York: Farrar and Rinehart, 1936.

Mamba's Daughters. New York: Doubleday, Doran, 1929. Serialized in *Woman's Home Companion* June 1928: 13–17; July 1928: 18–22; Aug. 1928: 27–30; Sept. 1928: 24–27; Oct. 1928: 31–32; Nov. 1928: 20–21.

(with Dorothy Heyward) *Mamba's Daughters: A Play.* New York: Farrar and Rinehart, 1939.

Peter Ashley. New York: Farrar and Rinehart, 1932. Serialized in *Woman's Home Companion* Aug. 1932: 7–10; Sept. 1932: 17–20; Oct. 1932: 22; Nov. 1932: 25–26; Dec. 1932: 25–26.

Porgy. New York: George H. Doran, 1925. Portions excerpted in *Bookman* Aug. 1925: 629–35; Sept. 1925: 13–20; Oct. 1925: 165–71.

(with Dorothy Heyward). *Porgy: A Play* (Theatre Guild acting version). New York: Doubleday, Page, 1927.

Porgy and Bess (libretto). New York: Gershwin Publishing, [1935].

Skylines and Horizons. New York: Macmillan, 1924.

Star Spangled Virgin. New York: Farrar and Rinehart, 1939.

Unpublished Plays

1773: An Historical Interlude. Sketch performed in Charleston, ca. 4 Apr. 1923.

An Artistic Triumph. Performed at the South Carolina Society Hall, Charleston, 10 Apr. 1913.

Short Fiction

"The Brute." *Pagan* Nov. 1918: 19–26.

"Crown's Bess." *Forum* Aug. 1925: 246–57.

The Half Pint Flask (novella). New York: Farrar and Rinehart, 1929. Originally in *Bookman* May 1927: 261–72. Reprinted in *Golden Book* Feb. 1934: 211–21; *Scholastic* 25 Oct. 1943: 25–26, 1 Nov. 1943: 21–22; Edward J. O'Brien, ed., *Fifty Best American Short Stories* (Boston: Houghton, Mifflin, 1939), 269–87.

"A Tragic Fable." *Cordially Yours.* Boston: Fuller, 1939. 44–47.

"The Winning Loser." *Ainslee's* Jan. 1920: 140–46.

Articles

"American Race Prejudice." *London Leader,* ca. 1927 [undated clipping, DBH Papers, SCHS].

(with Daisy Reck) "The American Virgins." *National Geographic* Sept. 1940: 273–308.

"And Once Again—The Negro." *Reviewer* Oct. 1923: 39–42.

"Beatrice Ravenel." *Library of Southern Literature,* supplement 1. Ed. Edwin Anderson Alderman and Charles Alphonso Smith. Atlanta: Martin and Hoyt, 1923. 473–75.

"Charleston: Where Mellow Past and Present Meet." *National Geographic* Mar. 1939: 273–312.

"Contemporary Southern Poetry." *Bookman* Jan. 1926: 561–64; Mar. 1926: 52–55.

"Describes Paris Since War Broke." *Charleston News and Courier* 7 Sept. 1914: 8.

"Dock Street Theatre." *Magazine of Art* Jan. 1938: 10–15.

"Ethel Waters—Collaborator." [unidentified clipping, DBH Papers, SCHS]: 16, 66.

(with Hervey Allen and John Bennett) Foreword. *Year Book of the Poetry Society of South Carolina for 1921.* Charleston: n.p., Oct. 1921. 5–7.

Foreword. *Year Book of the Poetry Society of South Carolina for 1923.* Columbia: State Company, Oct. 1923. 9–13.

Foreword. *Year Book of the Poetry Society of South Carolina for 1924.* Columbia: State Company, Oct. 1924. 9–12.

Introduction [on the American Negro in Art]. *Porgy: A Play in Four Acts* (Theatre Guild acting edition). By Dorothy Heyward and DuBose Heyward. New York: Doubleday, Doran, 1928. ix–xxi.

"The MacDowell Colony." *Southwest Review* Jan. 1926: 162–68.

"The Negro in the Low-Country." *The Carolina Low-Country.* Ed. Augustine T. Smythe, Herbert Ravenel Sass, Alfred Huger, Beatrice Ravenel, Thomas Waring, Archibald Rutledge, Josephine Pinckney, Caroline Pinckney Rutledge, DuBose Heyward, Katharine C. Hutson, and Robert W. Gordon. New York. Macmillan, 1932. 171–87.

"The New Note in Southern Literature." *Bookman* Apr. 1925: 153–56.

"A New Theory of Historical Fiction." *Publishers' Weekly* 13 Aug. 1932: 511–12.

(with Hervey Allen) "Poetry South." *Poetry* Apr. 1922: 35–48.

"Porgy and Bess Return on Wings of Song." *Stage* Oct. 1935: 25–28.

"Southern Writers' Conference." *Chicago Tribune* 4 Nov. 1931; rpt. *The State* 5 Nov. 1931: 10 [clipping in DBH Papers, SCHS].

Reviews

Rev. of *Arrow of Lightning,* by Beatrice Ravenel. *Charleston News and Courier,* 12 Dec. 1926: 4.

Rev. of *The New Poetry: Revised and Enlarged Edition,* ed. Harriet Monroe. *The State,* 8 July 1923: 6.

Uncollected Poems

"The Autumn." *Everybody's* Nov. 1921: 137.

"Love and Passion." *Snappy Stories* n.d. [c. 1916].

Prologue to "The Recruiting Officer" (recited at the rededication of the Dock Street Theatre, 1937). *Come to Charleston and the Low Country*, 2d annual ed. Charleston: Schindler's Antique Shop, 1950. 54.

"Respite." *Southwest Review* Jan. 1926: 168.

Forewords

Black Genesis: A Chronicle. By Samuel Gaillard Stoney and Gertrude Mathews Shelby. New York: Macmillan, 1930. N.p.

Carolina Gardens: The History, Romance, and Tradition of Many Gardens of Two States through More Than Two Centuries. By Edward Terry Hendrie Schaffer. New York: Huntington Press, 1937. ix–xi.

Bibliography

Allen, Hervey. *DuBose Heyward: A Critical and Biographical Sketch, Including Contemporary Estimates of his Work.* New York: George H. Doran, [1926].

Alpert, Hollis. *The Life and Times of Porgy and Bess: The Story of an American Classic.* New York: Knopf, 1990.

Anderson, Jervis. *This Was Harlem: A Cultural Portrait 1900–1950.* New York: Farrar, Straus, Giroux, 1982.

Angelou, Maya. *Singin' and Swingin' and Gettin' Merry Like Christmas.* New York: Random House, 1976. Rpt. New York: Bantam, 1977.

Armitage, Merle, ed. *George Gershwin.* London: Longmans, Green, 1938.

Atkinson, Brooks. "Negro Mystery." *New York Times* 16 Oct. 1927: sect. 9, p. 1.

———. "The Play, Negro Lithography." *New York Times* 11 Oct. 1927: sect. 1, p. 26.

———. "When Critics Disagree." *New York Times* 20 Oct. 1935: sect. 10, p. 7.

Bailey, Rosalie Vincent. "DuBose Heyward: Poet, Novelist, and Playwright." Master's thesis, Duke U, 1941.

Baker, Houston A. *Modernism and the Harlem Renaissance.* Chicago: U of Chicago P, 1987.

Baker, Jean-Claude, and Chris Chase. *Josephine: The Hungry Heart.* New York: Random House, 1993.

Barnouw, Eric. *A Tower in Babel: A History of Broadcasting in the United States.* 2 vols. New York: Oxford UP, 1966.

Bennett, John. *The Doctor to the Dead: Grotesque Legends and Folk Tales of Old Charleston.* New York: Rinehart, 1946.

———. *Madame Margot: A Grotesque Legend of Old Charleston.* New York: Century, 1921.

———. "A Negro Patois." *South Atlantic Quarterly* 7 (Oct. 1908): 332–47; 8 (June 1909): 39–52.

————. *The Treasure of Peyre Gaillard.* New York: Century, 1906.

Bergreen, Laurence. *As Thousands Cheer: The Life of Irving Berlin.* New York: Viking, 1990.

Blesh, Rudi, and Harriet Janis. *They All Played Ragtime.* 1950. 4th ed. New York: Oak Publications, 1971.

Blotner, Joseph. *Faulkner: A Biography.* Vol. 1. New York: Random House, 1984.

Bokinsky, Caroline. "DuBose Heyward's Porgy." *Names in South Carolina* 29 (1982): 23–25.

Brickell, Herschel. "Creator of Catfish Row." *New York Herald-Tribune Books* 10 Mar. 1929: 16–18. Clipping in DBH Papers, SCHS.

Brooks, Cleanth, Jr. "The Modern Southern Poet and Tradition." *Virginia Quarterly Review* 11 (Apr. 1935): 305–20.

Broun, Heywood. "It Seems to Me." *New York World* 14 Oct. 1925. Clipping in DBH Papers, SCHS.

Brown, Rosellen. "DuBose Heyward's *Peter Ashley.*" *Classics of Civil War Fiction.* Ed. David Madden and Peggy Bach. Jackson: U of Mississippi P, 1991. 117–30.

Capote, Truman. *The Muses Are Heard.* New York: Random House, 1956.

Cash, W. J. "The Mind of the South." *American Mercury* Oct. 1929: 185–92.

C[hamberlain], J[ohn]. "DuBose Heyward's Civil War Novel." *New York Times Book Review* 23 Oct. 1932: 7.

Clark, Emily. "DuBose Heyward." *Virginia Quarterly Review* 6 (Oct. 1930): 546–56. Reprinted in *Innocence Abroad.* New York: Knopf, 1931.

————. *Innocence Abroad.* New York: Knopf, 1931.

Coles, Robert A., and Diane Isaacs. "Primitivism as a Therapeutic Pursuit: Notes toward a Reassessment of Harlem Renaissance Literature." *The Harlem Renaissance: Revaluations.* Ed. Amritjit Singh, William S. Shiver, and Stanley Brodwin. New York: Garland, 1989. 3–12.

Collier, James Lincoln. *Duke Ellington.* New York: Oxford UP, 1987.

Cooley, John. "White Writers and the Harlem Renaissance." *The Harlem Renaissance: Revaluations.* Ed. Amritjit Singh, William S. Shiver, and Stanley Brodwin. New York: Garland, 1989. 13–22.

Cooper, Anice Page. *DuBose Heyward: An Appreciation.* New York: Farrar and Rinehart, 1930.

Cooper, John Webb. "A Comparative Study of *Porgy,* the Novel; *Porgy,* the Play; and *Porgy and Bess,* the Opera." Master's thesis, Columbia University, 1950.

Corley, Pauline. "Noted Southern Author Works on Final Chapters of Novel in 'Hide-a-Way' in South Area of County." *New York Herald* Dec. 1935?: n.p.

Cowan, Louise. *The Fugitive Group: A Literary History.* Baton Rouge: Louisiana State UP, 1959.

Cox, Headley Morris, Jr. "The Charleston Poetic Renascence, 1920–1930." Diss., U of Pennsylvania, 1958.

Creighton, Nannie Elizabeth. "DuBose Heyward and His Contribution to Literature." Master's thesis, U of South Carolina, 1933.

Crum, Mason. *Gullah: Negro Life in the Carolina Sea Islands.* Durham: Duke UP, 1940.

Cruse, Harold. *The Crisis of the Negro Intellectual: A Historical Analysis of the Failure of Black Leadership.* 1967. New York: Quill, 1984.

Dale, Corinne. "William Gilmore Simms's Porgy as Domestic Hero." *Southern Literary Journal* 13:1 (1980): 55–71.

Davidson, Donald. "The Artist as Southerner." *Saturday Review of Literature* 15 May 1926: 781–83.

———. "A Meeting of Southern Writers." *Bookman* Jan.–Feb. 1932: 494–96.

———. "Merely Prose." *The Fugitive* June–July 1923: 66–67.

———. "Some Day, in Old Charleston." *Still Rebels, Still Yankees and Other Essays.* Baton Rouge: Louisiana State UP, 1957. 213–27.

———. *The Spyglass: Views and Reviews, 1924–1930.* Ed. John Tyree Fain. Nashville: Vanderbilt UP, 1963.

———. "The Trend of Literature, a Partisan View." *Culture in the South*, ed. W. T. Couch. Chapel Hill: U of North Carolina P, 1935. 183–210.

Davis, Thadious. *Nella Larsen: Writer of the Harlem Renaissance.* Baton Rouge: Louisiana State UP, 1994.

Donaldson, Susan. "Songs with a Difference: Beatrice Ravenel and the Detritus of Southern History." *The Female Tradition in Southern Literature.* Ed. Carol Manning. Urbana: U of Illinois P, 1993. 176–92.

Douglas, Ann. *Terrible Honesty: Mongrel Manhattan in the 1920s.* New York: Farrar, Strauss, Giroux, 1995.

Downes, Olin. "Roots of Native Opera." *New York Times* 20 Oct. 1935: sect. 10, p. 7.

Doyle, Don H. Introduction. *Mamba's Daughters.* Columbia: U of South Carolina P, 1995. vii–xxiii.

DuBois, W. E. B. "The Black North." *New York Times Magazine Supplement* 17 Nov. 1901:10.

———. *The Souls of Black Folk.* Chicago: McClurg, 1903.

"DuBose Heyward Here for Summer." *Asheville Citizen Times* 7 June 1936. Clipping in DBH Papers, SCHS.

Durham, Frank. *DuBose Heyward: The Man Who Wrote Porgy.* Columbia: U of South Carolina P, 1954.

———. "DuBose Heyward's 'Lost' Stories." *Short Fiction Studies* 2 (winter 1965): 157–63.

———. *DuBose Heyward's Use of Folklore in His Negro Fiction.* Citadel Monograph Series 2. Charleston: The Citadel, 1961.

———. "The Rise of DuBose Heyward and the Rise and Fall of the Poetry Society of South Carolina." *Mississippi Quarterly* 19 (1966): 66–78.

———. "South Carolina Poetry Society." *South Atlantic Quarterly* 52 (1953): 277–85.

Engel, Lehman. *The American Musical Theater.* New York: Macmillan, 1975.

Epstein, Dana J. *Sinful Tunes and Spirituals: Black Folk Music to the Civil War.* Urbana: U of Illinois P, 1977.

Fain, John Tyree, and Thomas Daniel Young, eds. *The Literary Correspondence of Donald Davidson and Allen Tate.* Athens: U of Georgia P, 1974.

Farrar, John. "The Gossip Shop." *Bookman* June 1925: 506.

———. "The Gossip Shop." *Bookman* Aug. 1927: 729.

Foster, Hal. "The 'Primitive' Consciousness of Modern Art." *October* 34 (fall 1985): 47–50.

Franklin, John Hope, and Alfred A. Moss Jr. *From Slavery to Freedom: A History of Negro Americans.* New York: McGraw-Hill, 1988.

Fraser, Walter J., Jr. *Charleston! Charleston!: The History of a Southern City.* Columbia: U of South Carolina P, 1989.

Geraty, Virginia Mixson. *Porgy, a Gullah Version: From the Original Play by Dorothy Heyward and DuBose Heyward.* Charleston: Wyrick, 1990.

Glasgow, Ellen. "The Novel in the South." *Harper's* Dec. 1928: 93–100.

Gould, Jean. *Amy: The World of Amy Lowell and the Imagist Movement.* New York: Dodd, Mead, 1975.

Green, Paul. *Home to My Valley.* Chapel Hill: U of North Carolina P, 1970.

Greene, Harlan. "Charleston Childhood: The First Years of DuBose Heyward." *South Carolina Historical Magazine* 83 (1982): 154–67.

———. " 'The Little Shining Word': From Porgo to Porgy." *South Carolina Historical Magazine* 87 (1986): 75–81.

Hamm, Charles. "The Theatre Guild Production of *Porgy and Bess.*" *Journal of the American Musicological Society* (1987): 495–532.

———. *Yesterdays: Popular Song in America.* New York: Norton, 1983.

Harrigan, Anthony. "DuBose Heyward: Memorialist and Realist." *Georgia Review* 5 (fall 1951): 335–44.

Harrison, James G. "South Carolina's Poetry Society: After Thirty Years." *Georgia Review* 7 (summer 1953): 204–9.

Hart, Eleanor P. "Lo: His Name Led All the Rest." *Preservation Progress* 10.2 (Mar. 1965): 8–11.

Haskins, James. *Black Theatre in America.* New York: Crowell, 1982.

Hatcher, Harlan. *Creating the Modern American Novel.* London: Williams and Norgate, 1936.

Heyward, Dorothy. "Denmark Vesey—Whose Life Was a 'True Thriller.' " *New York Herald- Tribune* 4 Nov. 1948: 3–4.

———. "Porgy's Goat." *Harper's* Dec. 1957: 38–43.

———. "Porgy's Native Tongue: A Dissertation on Gullah, the Negro Language of the Play." *New York Times* 4 Dec. 1927: 2.

Heyward, Jane Screven. *Brown Jackets*. Columbia: State Publishing, 1923.

———. *Daffodils and Other Lyrics*. Charleston: Southern Printing and Publishing, 1921.

———. *Songs of the Charleston Darkey*. Charleston: n.p., 1912.

———. *Wild Roses*. New York: Neale, 1905.

Hibbard, Addison. "Literature South—1924." *Reviewer* Jan. 1925: 52–58.

———, ed. *The Lyric South*. New York: Macmillan, 1929.

Hobhouse, Janet. *Everybody Who Was Anybody: A Biography of Gertrude Stein*. New York: Putnam, 1975.

Hobson, Fred. *Serpent in Eden: H. L. Mencken and the South*. Chapel Hill: U of North Carolina P, 1974.

Hoffman, Frederick J. *The Art of Southern Fiction: A Study of Some Modern Novelists*. Preface by Harry T. Moore. Carbondale and Edwardsville: Southern Illinois UP, 1967.

Hughes, Langston. *The Big Sea: An Autobiography*. New York: Knopf, 1940.

———. "Writers: Black and White." *The American Negro Writer and His Roots: Selected Papers from the First Conference of Negro Writers, March 1959.* Ed. John O. Killens. New York: American Society of African Culture, 1960.

Hurston, Zora Neale. *Dust Tracks on a Road*. Foreword by Maya Angelou. New York: HarperPerennial, 1996.

I'll Take My Stand: The South and the Agrarian Tradition, by Twelve Southerners. Intro. Louis D. Rubin Jr. 1930. New York: Harper and Brothers, 1962.

"Invites Southern Writers." *New York Times* 26 Sept. 1932: 16.

Jablonski, Edward. *Gershwin: A Biography*. New York: Doubleday, 1987.

Jablonski, Edward, and Lawrence D. Stewart. *The Gershwin Years*. New York: Doubleday, 1958.

Jackson, Bruce. *"Get Your Ass in the Water and Swim Like Me": Narrative Poetry from the Black Oral Tradition*. Cambridge: Harvard UP, 1974.

Johnson, Gerald W. "Call for a Custom-Built Poet." *Southwest Review* Apr. 1925: 26, 28–30.

———. "The Horrible South." *Virginia Quarterly Review* 11 (Apr. 1935): 201–17.

[———.] "A Missionary to the Philistines." *Greensboro Daily News* 20 Jan. 1924. Clipping in DBH Papers, SCHS.

Johnson, James Weldon. *Black Manhattan*. New York: Knopf, 1930.

Johnson, Thomas L. "Charleston Was Charleston." *The State* 17 Feb. 1985: 12–13.

Joyner, Charles W. *Down by the Riverside: A South Carolina Slave Community*. Urbana: U of Illinois P, 1984.

Kammen, Michael. *The Lively Arts: Gilbert Seldes and the Transformation of Cultural Criticism in America*. New York: Oxford UP, 1996.

Kennedy, Richard S., ed. *Literary New Orleans*. Baton Rouge: Louisiana State UP, 1993.

Kerman, Cynthia. *The Lives of Jean Toomer: A Hunger for Wholeness.* Baton Rouge: Louisiana State UP, 1987.

Kimball, Robert, and Alfred Simon. *The Gershwins.* New York: Atheneum, 1973.

King, Edward. "The Great South." *Scribner's Monthly* 7–8 (Dec. 1873–June 1874). Rpt. *The Great South.* Ed. W. Magruder Drake and Robert R. Jones. Baton Rouge: Louisiana State UP, 1972. 438–53.

Knee, Stuart E. *Hervey Allen: A Literary Historian in America.* Lewiston, N.Y.: E. Mellen Press, 1988.

K[rutch], J[oseph] W[ood]. "Drama Dissenting Opinion." *Nation* 30 Oct. 1935: 518–19.

Levin, Gail. " 'Primitivism' in American Art: Some Literary Parallels of the 1920s and 1930s." *Art Magazine* (Nov. 1984): 101–5.

Levine, Lawrence. *Highbrow/Lowbrow: The Emergence of Cultural Hierarchy in America.* Cambridge: Harvard UP, 1988.

Lewis, David Levering, ed. *The Portable Harlem Renaissance Reader.* New York: Viking, 1994.

————. *When Harlem Was in Vogue.* New York: Oxford UP, 1989.

Lewis, William, and Max J. Herzberg. *The Emperor Jones, with a Study Guide for the Screen Version of the Play.* Student ed. New York: Appleton, 1949.

Locke, Alain. "The New Negro." Lewis, *Portable* 46–51.

Lomax, Alan. *Mister Jelly Roll: The Fortunes of Jelly Roll Morton, New Orleans Creole and "Inventor of Jazz."* 1950. New York: Pantheon, 1993.

Long, Richard A. "The Outer Reaches: The White Writer and Blacks in the Twenties." *The Harlem Renaissance Re-Examined.* Ed. Victor A. Kramer. New York: AMS, 1987. 43–50.

Martin, Jay. *Nathanael West: The Art of His Life.* New York: Farrar, Strauss, Giroux, 1970.

McCorkle, Susannah. "The Mother of Us All." *American Heritage* Feb.–Mar. 1994: 60–73.

McKay, Ian. *The Quest of the Folk: Antimodernism and Cultural Selection in Twentieth Century Nova Scotia.* Montreal: McGill-Queen's UP, 1994.

Mencken, H. L. "The Sahara of the Bozart." *Prejudices: Second Series.* New York: Knopf, 1920. 136–54.

Meyer, Donald. *The Positive Thinkers.* Garden City: Doubleday, 1965.

Milnes, Rodney. " 'Grimes' Moves on, Straight On." *Opera* 42.6 (1 June 1991): 521.

Monroe, Harriet. "Notes." *Poetry* July 1920: 233.

————. "Southern Shrines." *Poetry* May 1921: 91–96.

[————]. "This Southern Number." *Poetry* Apr. 1922: 31–34.

Moore, Jack B. *Maxwell Bodenheim.* New York: Twayne, 1970.

Morley, Harold P. "The Negro in Recent Southern Literature." *South Atlantic Quarterly* 27 (Jan. 1928): 29–41.

O'Brien, Michael. " 'The South Considers Her Most Peculiar': Charleston and Modern Southern Thought." *South Carolina Historical Magazine* 94.2 (Apr. 1993): 119–33.

O'Brien, Michael, and David Moltke-Hansen, eds. *Intellectual Life in Antebellum Charleston*. Knoxville: U of Tennessee P, 1986.

Olson, Stanley. *Elinor Wylie: A Life Apart*. New York: Dial, 1979.

Patterson, Boyd. *Alfred Hutty and the Charleston Renaissance*. Orangeburg, S.C.: Sandlapper, 1990.

Peale, Marjorie Elizabeth. "Charleston as a Literary Center, 1920–1933." Master's thesis, Duke U, 1941.

Peretti, Burton W. *The Creation of Jazz: Music, Race, and Culture in Urban America*. Urbana: U of Illinois P, 1992.

Phifer, Mary H. "DuBose Heyward." *Holland's Magazine* Dec. 1929: 6, 37.

Pinckney, Josephine. "Bulwarks against Change." *Culture in the South*. Ed. W. T. Couch. Chapel Hill: U of North Carolina P, 1935. 40–51.

———. "Charleston's Poetry Society." *Sewanee Review* 38 (Jan. 1930): 50–56.

———. "Southern Writers Congress." *Saturday Review of Literature* 7 Nov. 1931: 266.

———. *Three O'Clock Dinner*. New York: Viking, 1945.

Poggi, Jack. *Theatre in America: The Impact of Economic Forces, 1870–1967*. Ithaca: Cornell UP, 1968.

Porter, A. P. *Jump at de Sun: The Story of Zora Neale Hurston*. Foreword by Lucy Ann Hurston. Minneapolis: Carolrhoda Books, 1992.

Powers, Bernard E., Jr. *Black Charlestonians: A Social History, 1822–1885*. Fayetteville: U of Arkansas P, 1994.

Ransom, John Crowe. "Modern with the Southern Accent." *Virginia Quarterly Review* 11 (Apr. 1935): 184–200.

Ravenel, Beatrice. *Arrow of Lightning*. New York: Vinal, 1926.

Rhodes, Chip. "Writing up the New Negro: The Construction of Consumer Desire in the Twenties." *Journal of American Studies* 28.2 (Aug. 1994): 191–207.

Richardson, Eudora Ramsey. "The South Grows Up." *Bookman* Jan. 1930: 545–50.

Rittenhouse, Jessie. *My House of Life: An Autobiography*. Boston and New York: Houghton Mifflin, 1934.

Robeson, Elizabeth. "The Ambiguity of Julia Peterkin." *Journal of Southern History* 61.4 (Nov. 1995): 761–86.

Robinson, Selma. "The Newly Articulate South: An Interview with DuBose Heyward." *Wings* Dec. 1931: 11–12, 23.

"Romance of Negro Life." *New York Times Book Review* 27 Sept. 1925: 10–11.

Rosen, Robert. *A Short History of Charleston*. San Francisco: Lexicos, 1982.

Rourke, Constance. *American Humor: A Study of the National Character*. New York: Harcourt, Brace, 1931.

Rubin, Louis D., Jr. Introduction. *The Yemassee Lands: Poems of Beatrice Ravenel*. Chapel Hill: U of North Carolina P, 1969.

————. "Southern Literature: A Piedmont Art." *William Elliott Shoots a Bear: Essays on the Southern Literary Imagination*. Baton Rouge: Louisiana State UP, 1975. 195–212.

————. "The Southern Muse: Two Poetry Societies." *American Quarterly* 13 (1961): 365–75. Reprinted in *The Curious Death of the Novel: Essays in American Literature*. Baton Rouge: Louisiana State UP, 1967. 207–21.

————. *Southern Renascence: The Literature of the Modern South*. Baltimore: Johns Hopkins UP, 1953.

Rubin, Louis D., Jr., and Robert D. Jacobs, eds. *South: Modern Literature in Its Cultural Setting*. Garden City: Doubleday, 1961.

Sass, Charles W. *Old Charleston*. Richmond: Dale Press, 1933.

Sass, Herbert Ravenel. *Look Back to Glory*. Indianapolis: Bobbs-Merrill, 1933.

Schwartz, Charles. *Gershwin: His Life and Music*. Indianapolis: Bobbs-Merrill, 1973.

Seldes, Gilbert. *The Great Audience*. New York: Viking, 1950.

————. *The Seven Lively Arts*. New York: Harper and Brothers, 1924.

Severens, Martha. "Charleston in the Age of *Porgy and Bess*." *Southern Quarterly* 38.1 (fall 1989): 5–23.

————. "South Carolina and the American Scene." *The American Scene and the South: Paintings and Works on Paper, 1930–1946*. Athens: Georgia Museum of Art, 1996.

Shields, David S. *Civil Tongues and Polite Letters*. Chapel Hill: U of North Carolina P, 1997.

Shirley, Wayne D. "Reconciliation on Catfish Row: Bess, Serena, and the Short Score of *Porgy and Bess*." *Quarterly Journal of the Library of Congress* 38.3 (summer 1981): 145–65.

Sklar, Robert. *Movie-Made America: A Social History of American Movies*. New York: Random House, 1975.

Slavick, William H. *DuBose Heyward*. Boston: Twayne, 1981.

————. "Going to School to DuBose Heyward." *The Harlem Renaissance Re-Examined*. Ed. Victor A. Kramer. New York: AMS, 1987. 65–92.

Sprigge, Elizabeth. *Gertrude Stein: Her Life and Work*. New York: Harper, 1957.

Standifer, James A. "The Tumultuous Life of *Porgy and Bess*." *Humanities* Nov.–Dec. 1997: 8–19.

Stearns, Marshall, and Jean Stearns. *Jazz Dance: The Story of American Vernacular Dance*. New York: Macmillan, 1968.

Tate, Allen. *Essays of Four Decades*. Chicago: Swallow Press, 1968.

Thompson, Era Bell. "Why Negroes Don't Like 'Porgy and Bess.'" *Ebony* Oct. 1959: 50–54.

Tischler, Nancy M. *Black Masks: Negro Characters in Modern Southern Fiction*. University Park and London: Pennsylvania State UP, 1969.

Togovnick, Marianna. *Gone Primitive: Savage Intellects, Modern Lives*. Chicago: U of Chicago P, 1990.

"To Present 'Porgy' as a Musical Show." *New York Times* 3 Nov. 1933: 23.

Van Doren, Carl. "The Roving Critic: The Negro Renaissance." *Century* Mar. 1926: 635–37.

Wainwright, Loudon. "The One Man Gang Is in Action Again—At 76 Sam Goldwyn Conquers Crisis after Crisis to Produce *Porgy and Bess*." *Life* 16 Feb. 1959: 102–16.

Warren, Robert Penn. "A Note on Three Southern Poets." *Poetry* May 1932: 41–49.

Waters, Ethel, with Charles Samuels. *His Eye Is on the Sparrow*. 1951. New York: Da Capo, 1992.

Watkins, Wren. "DuBose Heyward." *Southern Literary Messenger* 2 (July 1940): 423–25.

Watson, Charles S. *The History of Southern Drama*. Lexington: UP of Kentucky, 1997.

Wauchope, G. A. *Literary South Carolina*. U of South Carolina Bulletin 133. Columbia: U of South Carolina, 1926.

Whitelaw, Robert N. S. *Charleston: Come Hell or High Water*. Columbia: R. L. Bryan, 1976.

Williams, Ellen. *Harriet Monroe and the Poetry Renaissance: The First Ten Years of Poetry, 1912–1922*. Urbana: U of Illinois P, 1977.

Williams, George. "Peregrinations of a Goat Cart." *Sandlapper* 6 (Oct. 1973): 41–49.

Williams, Susan Millar. *A Devil and a Good Woman Too: The Lives of Julia Peterkin*. Athens: U of Georgia P, 1996.

Wilson, James Southall. "Back-Country Novels." *Virginia Quarterly Review* 8 (July 1932): 466–71.

———. "The Perennial Rooster." *Virginia Quarterly Review* 2 (Jan. 1926): 152–55.

Woolcott, Alexander. "The Stage." *New York World* 11 Oct. 1927. Clipping in DBH Papers, SCHS.

"The Worm Turns, Being in Some Sort a Reply to Mr. H. L. Mencken." *Year Book of the Poetry Society of South Carolina for 1921*. Charleston: n.p., Oct. 1921. 14–16.

Young, Stark. "Opera Blues." *New Republic* 84 (30 Oct. 1935): 338.

Index

African Americans: actors, 82–84, 87–88; and jazz, 81; literary depiction of, 49–50, 53–55, 60–68, 75, 134; and theatre, 73–77; writers, 88–90, 106. *See also* Gullahs; Harlem Renaissance

Agrarian poets. *See* Fugitive-Agrarian poets

Alger, Horatio, 130

Allen, Hervey, xiv, 27, 34, 35, 36, 38–39, 40, 43, 46, 47, 52–53, 55, 56, 57, 59, 108, 128, 184, 185; meets Heyward, 22; teaches at Vassar, 102

Works

—*Anthony Adverse,* 109, 144

—*Ballads of the Border,* 22

Alpert, Hollis, *Life and Times of Porgy and Bess,* xviii

American Negro Theater group, 76

American Opera Company, 81

Anderson, Maxwell, *Eneas Africanus* (with Kurt Weill), 136; *What Price Glory?* (with Laurence Stallings), 73

Anderson, Sherwood, xiv, 26–27, 123

Angelou, Maya, 166

Arlen, Harold, 180

Armstrong, Louis, 180

Association of Negro Writers, 102

Astor, John Jacob, 173

Atkinson, Brooks, 85, 86, 159, 166

Atlantic, 34

Austin, Mary, xvi

Baker, Josephine, 91, 180

Baltimore Afro-American, 161, 165

Banks, Bill, 168

Barnes, Maggie, 53

Basie, Count, 81

Bayly, William, 40

Belafonte, Harry, 168

Bellaman, Henry, 33, 44

Benet, Stephen Vincent, 33

Bennett, John, xiv, xvi, 15, 20, 27, 31, 35, 53, 59, 61, 103, 106, 113–14, 125, 134, 162, 184; background, 21–22; helps DBH with *Porgy,* 55, 57; helps with *Porgy: A Play,* 81; interest in Gullahs, 21–22, 58; literary tastes, 23–24, 37–38; mentors Heyward and Allen, 22–24, 35; work with Poetry Society, 33, 46–48, 56–57

Works

—*Doctor to the Dead, The,* 22

—*Madame Margot,* 22

—*Master Skylark,* 20

—*Treasure of Peyre Gaillard,* 22

Berlin, Irving, 180; "Alexander's Ragtime Band," 70

Bethune, Mary McLeod, 162

Blair, Mary, 106

Blake, Eubie, 70

Bodenheim, Max, 36

Bonnet, Stede, 172

Bookman, 60

Boston American, 158

Botkin, Henry, 151, 152

Harrisburg Area Community College
McCormick Library
One HACC Drive
Harrisburg, PA 17110-2999